HIGHER EDUCATION IN THE ASEAN REGION

SHAPING THE FUTURE

EDITORS
Glenda Crosling
Graeme Atherton
Siti Norbaya Azizan

Published by Sunway University Press
An imprint of Sunway University Sdn Bhd

No. 5, Jalan Universiti
Sunway City
47500 Selangor Darul Ehsan
Malaysia

sunwayuniversity.edu.my/press

ISBN 978-629-7646-00-8

Cataloguing-in-Publication Data

Perpustakaan Negara Malaysia

A catalogue record for this book is available from the National Library of Malaysia

ISBN 978-629-7646-00-8

Edited by Hani Hazman
Designed and typeset by Rachel Goh
Printed and bound by CPI Group (UK) Ltd, Croydon, CR0 4YY

Cover image: Tri Arianti/Shutterstock.com
Image used under licence from Shutterstock.com

CONTENTS

ACKNOWLEDGEMENTS

Higher Education in ASEAN: Shaping the Future would not have been possible without the focus of Sunway University's Centre for Higher Education Research since its inception in 2017 on pivotal and current higher education issues. Research projects, publications, international reports and annual seminars have paved the way, extending and solidifying our appreciation of higher education's key role in socioeconomic developments not only internationally, but in the dynamic and rapidly developing region of the Association of Southeast Asian Nations (ASEAN). This book thus reflects the organisational efforts of many people engaged in these initiatives prior to and during its development. To all involved, we express our sincere appreciation.

Significantly, our deep appreciation goes to Professor Graeme Wilkinson, former Vice-Chancellor of Sunway University, Malaysia who guided and trusted us as editors to deliver a publication of quality and value for the higher education community. We also acknowledge Professor Mahendhiran Nair, Pro Vice-Chancellor (Research Engagement and Impact), for his interest in the project.

This book would not have been possible without all the distinguished contributors of the chapters of the book from across the ASEAN region. Listed in alphabetical order, the book brings together the following experts: Dr Abdul Razak Ahmad, Dr Benedict Valentine Arulanandam, Professor Dr Melinda dela Peña Bandalaria, Professor Dato' Dr Morshidi Sirat, Dr Muhammad Muftahu, Associate Professor Dr Nicolas Hamelin, Mr Rafael Ibe Santos, Associate Professor Dr Razwana Begum Abdul Rahim, Dr Sally Anne Malar S Paramanathan, Dr Stephen J Hall, Dr Thiruchelvi K Murugiah and Ms Wendy Ong. We thank them for their insightful perspectives that add to the understanding of higher education in the region and thus the shaping of its future.

We also would like to extend our profound appreciation to the chapter reviewers: Professor Dr Shukran Abdul Rahman, Dr Mable Chan, Professor Ron Edwards, Associate Professor Christian Kahl and Associate Professor Dr Ooi Pei Boon. Their expertise and meticulous critical and constructive feedback have been valuable in ensuring the quality and relevance of the book content.

Importantly, this book would not have been possible without the wonderful staff of Sunway University Press, especially Carol Wong and Hani Hazman for their collegiality, expert guidance and input into this book.

Glenda Crosling, Graeme Atherton & Siti Norbaya Azizan
Editors

EDITORIAL BOARD AND REVIEWERS

LIST OF CONTRIBUTORS

ABDUL RAHIM, Razwana Begum
razwana@suss.edu.sg

Dr Razwana Begum Abdul Rahim is Head of the Public Safety and Security Programme and Military Studies Minor at the Singapore University of Social Sciences, Singapore. She joined the university in 2018 and worked closely with the Ministry of Home Affairs, Singapore in the conceptualisation and development of the programme. In 2022, she was promoted to Associate Professor. Abdul Rahim holds a PhD in education and restorative justice from Monash University, Australia, as well as postgraduate qualifications in social work, criminology and counselling. Prior to joining the university, Abdul Rahim spent 18 years working as a Probation Officer/Assistant Director with the Ministry of Social and Family Development, Singapore.

AHMAD, Abdul Razak
abdul@baitalamanah.com; delpiso2000@gmail.com

Dr Abdul Razak Ahmad is Founding Director of Bait Al Amanah, a political security and development think tank based in Kuala Lumpur, Malaysia. He served the Malaysian government in various advisory capacities and is formerly a faculty member at the National Defence University of Malaysia. He has done extensive work in the areas of higher education and human capital development. Besides public policy and development-related issues, his research interests include counter-terrorism, international affairs especially on the Association of Southeast Asian Nations (ASEAN), issues affecting Muslim minorities globally, and conflict resolution.

ARULANANDAM, Benedict Valentine
benedicta@sunway.edu.my

Dr Benedict Valentine Arulanandam is a Senior Lecturer at the Victoria University (Melbourne) Undergraduate Programme with Sunway College, Malaysia. He has been in the Malaysian corporate arena for more than two decades, encompassing manufacturing, education, biotechnology and banking. In the academic field, he has close to 14 years of experience conducting lectures and seminars. Apart from publications, Dr Arulanandam has also co-authored several manuals on financial planning and has conducted talks on financial management and taxation in several institutions of higher learning in Malaysia.

ATHERTON, Graeme

graeme.atherton@uwl.ac.uk

Professor Graeme Atherton is Head of Centre for Inequality and Levelling Up at the University of West London, United Kingdom (UK) and former Adjunct Professor of the Centre for Higher Education Research (CHER) at Sunway University, Malaysia. He founded and leads both AccessHE and the National Education Opportunities Network in the UK. He has extensive experience producing higher education policy reports in the international context. He has produced over 100 other publications and conference papers looking at higher education participation, research and policy.

AZIZAN, Siti Norbaya

norbayaa@sunway.edu.my; sitinorbaya49@gmail.com

Siti Norbaya Azizan is a Research Associate at the CHER, Sunway University, Malaysia with a first degree in Electronic Engineering and an MA in Educational Technology from Universiti Sains Malaysia. She has experience in a wide range of educational research areas, including software testing, distance education, mobile learning, online and blended learning, teaching and learning, higher education, and community engagement. Her international research experience includes a research assistantship in a global reach programme and an ASEAN-centric research project.

CROSLING, Glenda

glendac@sunway.edu.my; glendacrosling@gmail.com

Professor Glenda Crosling is Head of the CHER and was previously Dean of Academic Enhancement at Sunway University, Malaysia. As an internationally recognised scholar of higher education development, she has extensively published books, chapters, journal articles and research reports for international bodies and has been invited as keynote and plenary speaker at international conferences. Dr Crosling has worked with the Malaysian

Qualifications Agency in developing national educational policy and guidelines, and has been an invited reviewer for quality audits in universities in Australia, Malaysia and Oman. She has been a visiting academic in Singapore, Hong Kong, China, Thailand, the UK and at Harvard University in the United States (US).

DELA PEÑA BANDALARIA, Melinda
mbandalaria@upou.edu.ph

Professor Dr Melinda dela Peña Bandalaria, PhD is a full professor at the University of the Philippines Open University, the Philippines and its Chancellor for the 2016–2025 period. She has more than 25 years of experience in developing and teaching courses in the distance e-learning mode of instruction and doing research in the field of open, flexible and distance e-learning. Among her regional and international involvements include serving as President of the Asian Association of Open Universities (2017–2019), Ambassador for Open Educational Resources (2021–2022), and Board Member of the International Council on Open and Distance Education (2022–2025).

HALL, Stephen J
kiakaha88@gmail.com

Dr Stephen J Hall is former Head of the Centre for English Language Studies at Sunway University, Malaysia. He has managed Malaysian national education projects, been in business as a corporate trainer in Singapore, and trained teachers ASEAN-wide. Dr Hall has lived and worked in Southeast Asia since 1991. He has over 50 publications, including seven books, and recently co-authored *Manglish: Malaysian English at Its Wackiest* (2nd edition) with Lee Su Kim. He is passionate about teaching and learning in this time of great change. More about Dr Hall can be found at www.stephenjhall.com.

HAMELIN, Nicolas
nicolas.hamelin@aucegypt.edu

Dr Nicolas Hamelin is Associate Professor and Director of SPJAIN Neuroscience Lab in Sydney, Australia. His main research interests are in the fields of neuromarketing, social marketing, public relations and environmental communication. Hamelin holds a PhD in Physics from Sussex University, an MSc in Environmental Management from Ulster University, and a PhD in Business at the Royal Docks Business School from the University of East London, UK. He is also a qualified TV news reporter from INA in Paris, France. He is the founder of Mindbci, a neuroscience start-up based in Sydney and Singapore. In international business, he was a strategic marketing manager for STMicroelectronics, Nokia Business Unit for over 10 years, and a principal scientist at the Foundation for Fundamental Research on Matter and the Energy Centre, the Netherlands. He also worked as a country analyst for Euromonitor International. He routinely acts as a consultant for various companies such as Ogilvy, United Nations Development Programme, Gray Advertising and KAB International. As an academic, he was Research Fellow at the City University of Hong Kong, served as an Assistant Professor at the Al Akhawayn University School of Business Administration, Morocco and was Associate Professor at the American University in Cairo, Egypt and at the American University of Central Asia and at Franklin University, Switzerland.

IBE SANTOS, Rafael

rafael.santos@uap.asia

Rafael Ibe Santos is a print journalist/editor and broadcaster in the Philippines and US territories for more than two decades, and teaches full time at the University of Asia and the Pacific, the Philippines, handling English and media/technology courses. A published researcher and reviewer, Santos was one of the Emerging Scholar Awards recipients in 2020 and 2021 by Common Grounds Research Network based at the University of Illinois, US. He is a PhD candidate in English Studies (Language) from the University of the Philippines Diliman, the Philippines.

MUFTAHU, Muhammad

muftahu@usm.my

Dr Muhammad Muftahu is currently a Senior Lecturer, Acting Director, Deputy Director and Coordinator of the Global Higher Education Network at the National Higher Education Research Institute (IPPTN), Universiti Sains Malaysia. He is also the Coordinator of the Professional Programme in Higher Education Leadership and Management, Head of the Higher Education Access and Success research cluster, and Commission Member of the Academic Talent Management Review 2021, Universiti Sains Malaysia. His research interests and expertise include higher education sustainable leadership and management, comparative and international higher education, higher education and industry, and higher education as a field of study and qualitative methodology.

MURUGIAH, Thiruchelvi K
chelvim@sunway.edu.my

Dr Thiruchelvi K Murugiah currently works with Sunway University, Malaysia with the School of American Education in the Department of American Degree Transfer Program. Along with the team of Alibaba GDT-certified lecturers, she delivers remotely the Alibaba Global Digital Economy course, a free elective to all second-year and above degree students. She is a former Business School Programme Lead and Lecturer at Sunway College Ipoh, Malaysia. She holds a Doctorate in Education Majoring in Educational Management from Open University Malaysia, and MBA (Marketing) from Cardiff University, UK, and a Postgraduate Diploma in Marketing from the Chartered Institute of Marketing, UK.

ONG, Wendy
bringitong@gmail.com

Wendy Ong is a graduate student in the Department of Psychology at Brunel University, UK where she has an interest in disability psychology, trauma and post-traumatic growth. Previously, she worked in various engineering and consulting roles. She holds a BS and an MS in Mechanical Engineering from Stanford University, US.

PARAM, Sally Anne
sallyp@sunway.edu.my

Dr Sally Anne Param has been a lecturer with Sunway Education Group, Malaysia for more than seven years, and her research focus is the qualitative study of identity. Param's current work is with young people, as exemplified in the Future Cities research project with Sunway University and a book project with Universiti Malaya, Malaysia. Her most recent engagements concerning young people are a book chapter in *Aspirations of Young Adults in Urban Asia: Values, Family, and Identity* and a paper presentation with the Asian Research Institute, Singapore in 2021. When not working, Sally enjoys reading and a cup of *teh tarik*.

SIRAT, Morshidi
morshidi@usm.my

Professor Dato' Dr Morshidi Sirat is Emeritus Professor at the IPPTN, Universiti Sains Malaysia. He has served as Founding Director of the Commonwealth Tertiary Education Facility, Malaysia, as Director-General of Higher Education, as Vice-Chancellor of Universiti Malaysia Sarawak, and as Director of the IPPTN. Sirat continues to undertake consultancies, conduct training and provide advisory services on higher education policy and development. He is founding Chairman and now adviser of the Malaysian Society for Higher Education Policy and Research Development.

FOREWORD

Higher education has become an enormous global industry which is key to social and economic progress. Institutions of higher learning both public and private have themselves become collectively an essential element of the fabric of developing and newly industrialised nations, driving growth and the expansion of knowledge-based businesses. Higher education enables young people to construct the foundations of their future lives as aspirational professionals operating in a dynamic and rapidly changing world, replete with unprecedented challenges including potential existential threats to humanity. As the region of the Association of Southeast Asian Nations (ASEAN) emerges as one of the most dynamic economic powerhouses of the world, higher education will play a vital role in the region's future evolution. But many questions need to be answered about how higher education should be organised in the future, including what and how it should deliver in terms of its educational mission. The Coronavirus Disease 2019 or COVID-19 global pandemic exposed weaknesses in traditional forms of higher education delivery, but helpfully forced a rapid and necessary transformation to more innovative technology-based models, and the ASEAN region was overall relatively fast to adapt.

But at this juncture in history, it can be argued that higher education is at a crossroads without a clear direction for the future. Fundamental questions need to be answered, such as the following: how will learning and teaching evolve and what will the role of the physical campus be in the era of ubiquitous online delivery? How can institutions become more sustainable and contribute more effectively to global sustainability challenges? How can nations ensure equity and fair access to higher education to the benefit of their whole populations? How can institutions best take advantage of transnational and trans-regional educational opportunities? What business models should be used for higher education at a time of inflationary cost pressures on families and governments? What mechanisms can be used to better bridge the gap between educational institutions and commercial enterprises and employers? What kind of smart education do we need to optimise the quality of life in smart cities? How can institutions ensure that their graduates gain secure and well-remunerated employment and have the skills to succeed in the workplace and create new opportunities for growth when disruptive forces of automation, artificial intelligence and other advanced technologies are progressively eating out the core of longstanding jobs?

These and other issues underlie the discourses that are laid out in this thought-provoking book, which focuses specifically on future thinking for higher education in the ASEAN region. These are also the very issues that taxed me as the leader for a decade of an ASEAN-based higher education institution, and which formed the background to my discussions and debates with many colleagues about where we and our whole industry were heading. I cannot think of a time during my entire career when the uncertainty about the future of higher education has been so great, yet the opportunities for reinvention so tremendous. This is an exciting time to witness the development of the higher education industry and to contemplate where it will go, especially in the ASEAN region in the decade or two ahead.

I congratulate the editors and authors for producing this excellent volume which provides stimulating material for educational thought leaders to debate. Their efforts will surely benefit many higher education practitioners, managers and policymakers and may potentially enable ASEAN to lead the way globally in terms of revolutionising higher education as we head towards the middle of the 21st century.

Graeme G Wilkinson
Tan Sri Jeffrey Cheah Distinguished Professor & Former Vice-Chancellor
Sunway University
Malaysia

This page is intentionally left blank.

Chapter 1

Introducing Future Higher Education and the ASEAN Region

Glenda Crosling,* Graeme Atherton‡ & Siti Norbaya Azizan*

INTRODUCTION

This book of edited chapters is framed by two significant aspects of today's world. The key and overriding one is the development of higher education as we move forward to the future. The second of these aspects contextualises higher education development in the region of the Association of Southeast Asian Nations (ASEAN). Both of these themes are dynamic and evolving. In higher education worldwide where teaching, learning and research, along with associated community and outreach, are seen as the major activities, movement and development are inevitable as higher education interacts with, responds to, and indeed contributes to shaping the demands of an ever-changing external environment. The notion underpinning this book is thus the progress of higher education and the understanding that it has and continues to evolve. In looking to the future, this book contributes a small step further along this pathway.

In this chapter, the current setting and antecedents for an edited collection of views on the future of higher education in ASEAN are presented, followed by an overview of each chapter in the book.

* Sunway University, Malaysia
‡ University of West London, United Kingdom

HIGHER EDUCATION AND CHANGE

This book is concerned with change as higher education goes forward. However, higher education evolution and thus change is not a new concept. For example, earlier changes were seen in times such as the Industrial Revolution of the 18th and 19th centuries, when the need for factual or procedural models of knowledge ushered in changes to the approach to knowledge (Joynes et al., 2019). This time also reflected the dramatic global rise in democratic governments (Blessinger, 2022a), which impacted higher education. Reflecting a massive increase in the Gross Domestic Product (GDP) per capita, an increase in average life expectancy, advanced social systems, and high levels of scientific discoveries and technological inventions, these developments paved the way for contemporary higher education's directions, some of which we discuss below. In turn, the circumstances of contemporary higher education influence projections for the future of higher education, as seen in the chapters in this book.

Contemporary higher education worldwide is now facing a future where progress and resulting changes are even more rapid and all-encompassing than in previous eras. We need only to look at the recent worldwide experiences with the Coronavirus Disease 2019 (COVID-19) pandemic to realise the power and imminence of change and the huge impact of technological and scientific developments on people and societies globally. These developments are reflected in Information and Communication Technology (ICT), which was the mainstay of life during the pandemic, and scientific developments such as medical treatments and vaccinations which contributed to alleviating the effects of the pandemic.

Framed by the movements of globalisation and internationalisation, higher education is operating in a world of increased interconnection between nations, their activities and the economy (Altbach, 2016). This has impacted all levels of the value chain and the lives of citizens globally. However, on top of these is the massive and unrelenting impact of the developments in ICT, automation and digitalisation. Known as the Industrial Revolution 4.0 or IR 4.0 and the global knowledge society,[1] the accelerated rate of technical

[1] With its focus on the analysis and use of information to solve uprising problems, the knowledge society differs from the previous period of the information society, when the emphasis was on the accumulation and collating of data and information (Crosling et al., 2018).

and scientific developments simultaneously disrupt and continue to shape life across the world, including higher education (Altbach, 2016). This rapidly changing digital landscape that enables expansion in the reach of higher education socially also poses challenges for higher education in its mission to prepare students to survive, contribute positively, and prosper in an increasingly dynamic world.

Another significant factor in discussing the future of higher education is a concern for the Earth's environment. This impacts within and between countries, as sustainable practices are expected and demanded. However, in higher education, literature indicates that the focus has been on specific projects and their economic impact (Findler & Schonherr, 2017), and the need to embed sustainable development in higher education systems is yet to be fully addressed, including in curricula and teaching and learning approaches (Findler & Schonherr, 2017). Looking to the future, Blessinger and de Castro Soeiro (2022) envision the knowledge-based "Society 5.0", which will feature a combination of human imagination and creativity for a more sustainable life and planet.

One major aspect in higher education of the latter part of the 20th century that continues to impact the world today is its massification (Trow, 1973), seen in the unprecedented growth in student enrolment. Worldwide, student participation in higher education is expected to continue to increase and reach nearly 600 million by 2040 (Blessinger, 2022a). Allied with this to cater for the demand for higher education globally is the internationalisation of higher education, and the physical movement of students and academic programmes across national boundaries. Altbach (2016) refers to massification and the global knowledge economy as twin forces that have driven unprecedented transformations in higher education. The outcome is that higher education now needs to develop globally minded citizens, with expertise and knowledge that is universalistic and scientific (Schofer et al., 2020).

Accompanying the increase in the numbers of students in higher education are the calls continuing today and into the future for equity and thus access for all suitably qualified people, regardless of their life circumstances. As part of this development, student cohorts are now diverse, including in areas like language and cultural backgrounds, learning approaches prior to higher education participation, expectations of study experience, and the approach to knowledge development they bring to their studies. While the English language currently operates worldwide as the common language between speakers of different languages (the "lingua franca"), students may use alternative varieties of English in their studies as they adjust to the Standard English of higher education. Thus, to address such diversity, some commentators point out the need for diversification in the forms of institutions. In line with this, questions have even been raised about the nature of knowledge in ethnically diverse locations, and investigation of teaching, learning and pedagogical approaches can help to democratise knowledge (Chankseliani, 2022).

The positive impact of higher education on the economies of countries is relevant to this discussion, especially in terms of ASEAN and its socioeconomic development. Research has highlighted that the increase in the number of universities in a region is linked to that region's higher GDP per capita through the supply of human capital and increased innovation (Valero & Van Reenen, 2019). A specific example is the case of China, where Xia and Qiu (2021) report in their study that regional economic development has been positively correlated with the quality of teaching and research activities of higher education institutions (HEIs). As ASEAN countries continue to seek socioeconomic development, higher education via teaching and especially via research activities is set to contribute to the development of the region and its countries.

To sum up, higher education does not evolve and develop in a vacuum and is impacted by external factors, some of which we have outlined above. Importantly and reciprocally, though, higher education in itself is a catalyst for change (Blessinger, 2022b). Seen as having a pivotal role in society (Siemens & Matheos, 2010) since its inception centuries ago, HEIs, in their mission to improve society, are active players in societal developments and will continue to do so in ways that cannot yet be conceived. Higher education intersects, interacts, influences and, in turn, is influenced by societies (Siemens & Matheos, 2010). For example, via its intermediatory role between schools and the workplace, higher education crucially impacts the lives of citizens (Dhirathiti, 2022). Graduates of higher education are imbued with many of the features from which modern society emanates through "the distinctive form of higher education that has become institutionalised worldwide" (Schofer et al., 2020). For instance, higher education helps to construct global citizens (Schofer et al., 2020) who can then participate effectively in their societies and the increasingly interlinked and dynamic world.

HIGHER EDUCATION AND THE ASEAN REGION

ASEAN is composed of 10 member states, namely Brunei, Cambodia, Indonesia, Laos, Malaysia, Myanmar, the Philippines, Singapore, Thailand and Vietnam. Established on 8 August 1967 in Bangkok, Thailand, ASEAN strives to achieve the aims and purposes towards promoting and enhancing the cooperation of regional peace and stability, where one of the key aspects is education, alongside economic, social, cultural, technical and other fields (ASEAN Secretariat, 2020a).

Education has long been regarded as a powerful force to transform the lives of ASEAN's communities. Evidently, the countries in this region have shown a strong commitment to socioeconomic and educational development at all levels (Atherton et al., 2018a). As part of ASEAN's commitment to education, lifelong learning is promoted throughout its member countries through three underpinning principles: equity, inclusion and quality (ASEAN Secretariat, 2020b). The ASEAN Economic Community (AEC) was realised at the end of 2015 when the AEC Blueprint 2025 was put forward to achieve economic integration impacting various economic sectors in the region. Higher education specifically plays a critical role in supporting this envisaged regional economic integration (Sa-ngiamwibool & Wisaeng, 2021). It is one of the key drivers towards achieving economic development in the region by producing a ready, skilled and educated workforce through universities, institutes, high schools and worker training academies.

The development of higher education in Southeast Asia was shaped by different historical backgrounds and driven by various challenges due to the diverse socioeconomic, cultural, political and environmental conditions in each country. Early case study analyses revealed that the countries' historical past, nation-building efforts and current global trends are the key factors influencing higher education development in this region (Asia-Pacific Programme of Educational Innovation for Development, 2006). According to Ratanawijitrasin (2015), there has been drastic development in the higher education sector in Southeast Asia over the past few decades, particularly in terms of governance and finance on both supply and demand sides. Generally, the changing landscape of higher education in this region was caused by four major trends: massification, diversification, marketisation and internationalisation (Ratanawijitrasin, 2015).

The massive changes due to the globalisation and regionalisation efforts of ASEAN nations have provided both opportunities and challenges to the development of higher education in this region. On the positive side, the internationalisation of higher education has paved the way for increasing intra-ASEAN and international academic mobility, international study programmes and collaborative research. The majority of ASEAN countries have the necessary strategic planning for the internationalisation of higher education, which is commonly embedded within the broader higher education planning framework through different drivers (Atherton et al., 2018a). Some countries also have made significant steps to further improve student mobility, while providing mutual efforts in developing a regional system for academic credit transfer and recognition (Ratanawijitrasin, 2015). Additionally, measures are also in place by the governments and HEIs in order to strengthen higher education performance based on various forms of indicators, including teaching, learning, research, and commercialisation through enterprise and innovation (Yan Zhang, 2021).

Market-wise, there is a growing demand for quality tertiary education in the Southeast Asian region. As Martinus (2022) states, there is an encouraging trend in the consumer market for tertiary education in the region, which has potential upsides for future regional development. Prior to the pandemic, ASEAN countries were increasing their significance in higher education participation through student enrolment, where statistical evidence by the United Nations Educational, Scientific and Cultural Organisation Institute for Statistics suggests increasing trends of outbound tertiary students in the region, particularly from Vietnam which was the highest contributor of outbound students in 2019 (Martinus, 2022). In terms of inbound, reportedly more than 324,000 international students enrolled in higher education study programmes in the region in 2018 (von Kameke, 2021).

Yet, at the same time, ASEAN countries are also facing intense pressure due to heightened demand and the need to maintain quality education. As stated by Nithyavathy (2022), concerns about higher education development in the ASEAN nations emerged due to the expansion and strengthening of the sector in which the challenges are related to student enrolment, economic restructuring, finance and funding, as well as the need for closer constructive and productive cooperation. Furthermore, since the emergence of the COVID-19 pandemic in 2019, HEIs in the region have been challenged by massive economic disruptions and pedagogical issues due to travel restrictions and campus lockdowns. The pandemic brought crises upon higher education in three key areas, namely student enrolment, teaching, as well as staffing and operation (PwC, 2022).

At the institutional level, HEIs throughout the region are challenged by greater competition and, at the same time, are constrained by limited capacity and pressured by the push towards self-reliance (Ratanawijitrasin, 2015). In the era of the free market in ASEAN, where opportunities for various types of products, services and technologies are widely available, competition is no longer limited to the world of business but also covers the educational sector. The private higher education sector in developing countries, particularly, is now confronted with significant declines in student enrolment and higher drop-out rates due to prolonged pandemic-related crises, campus closures, financial constraints and disruptions to existing face-to-face modes of teaching (Bustos-Orosa, 2022).

At the national level, there are significant and crucial higher education policy issues in the ASEAN region. Changes due to conflicting imperatives, spiralling demand and limited resources have impacted the balance between public and private sectors throughout this region (Welch, 2011). In most cases, the higher education sector is heavily maintained and regulated by governments, while privatisation may be regarded as a threat that questions the role of universities in contributing to the people (Nithyavathy, 2022).

Regionally, existing gaps between low-income and high-income countries in the region have also become more significant than before. The report by Asia Development Bank (ADB, 2022) on critical themes associated with economic recovery from the pandemic in Southeast Asia revealed that inequality and income gaps have increased throughout the region due to the impact of mobility restrictions and lockdowns. Investments in education were also hampered for those with severely impacted income (ADB, 2022). While urbanisation has quickened, the gaps in educational standards between rural and urban areas in Southeast Asian countries have widened (Nithyavathy, 2022).

In the aftermath of the COVID-19 pandemic, Southeast Asian countries, like other nations, are slowly gaining momentum; the region is now expected to increase their economic growth through various sectors significantly, while overcoming pandemic challenges. While moving towards the endemic stage, the lifting of mobility restrictions in many countries in the region has brought a brighter hope for the higher education sector to recover. Yet, the fact remains that the future of higher education is also shaped by other forces, like technological progress and the new world of work. Thus, it remains to be seen how the ASEAN region is progressing in the recovery of the higher education sector in the post-pandemic setting.

TRENDS IN HIGHER EDUCATION: TOWARDS THE FUTURE IN THE ASEAN REGION

Building on its earlier development, higher education in more recent decades is charged with preparing students for the highly interconnected and interdependent world of digitalisation, which operates on an increasingly fragile planet where its sustainability is a vital issue. Thus, in a world characterised by change, disruption and uncertainty (Blessinger, 2022a), citizens must constantly learn to manage and function effectively. Indeed, Scott (2022) comments that higher education studies are concerned with intellectual formation and growth involving imagination and criticality, and that universities should include in their teaching and research democratic agendas such as social justice, human rights and a rebalancing of the environment. Other commentators also perceive that lifelong learners underpin an "equalising learning democracy" (Blessinger et al., 2020); with the explosion of new knowledge and ways of operating in a changing world, citizens must be able to update themselves continually. For higher education, the need is to embed sustainable development in higher education curricula as an inherent responsibility for societies to be more sustainable (Crosling et al., 2020; Findler et al., 2019).

Equally important, emerging trends in higher education curriculum, teaching and learning approaches, and the assessment of student learning put forward by commentators are that, without undermining academic standards, curricula should reflect and foster inclusive approaches that address the learning backgrounds, circumstances surrounding their study and thus the needs of students from diverse backgrounds.

Studies should cross industries and disciplinary boundaries. Such multi- and interdisciplinary approaches support the development of solutions to new and arising problems. Real-world skills gained through authentic and experiential learning and the increasing use of competency-based micro-credentials in academic programmes (McGreal & Olcott, 2022), as well as the capacity for creative, problem solving and entrepreneurial thinking (Crosling et al., 2014; Wilkinson, 2017). Underpinned by critical and analytical thinking, these attributes support post-study employment. Also implicated is the capacity to think and operate at the global level rather than solely the local level. These attributes are furthered by programmes that enable student mobility to other regions or countries, and exposure and interaction with larger global issues (Atherton et al., 2018b).

To cater for the scenarios outlined above, further developments of curriculum, learning, teaching and assessment approaches will support students so that regardless of their location, they can access higher education through online or hybrid modes (Azizan et al., 2022). The interactive and participatory nature of these modes can assist students' development as active, independent learners, not only comfortable with but effective in collaborative, possibly international and multidisciplinary teamwork (Wilkinson, 2017). Assessments that are formative support the development of students' independence in learning and critical consciousnes (El-Azar, 2022).

Overall, however, it seems that in the knowledge economy, higher education in the coming times will need to adjust to shifting values, with emphasis on outcomes, learning rather than teaching, and student- rather than a teacher-focused teaching approach (Levine & Van Pelt, 2021).

THE BOOK

The chapters in this book reflect the investigations and views of authors from some ASEAN countries on various aspects of the future of higher education. In this first chapter, we place the focus of the chapters in the book into the context of higher education's evolution and change, moving from the past to the present time and, as occurs in the ensuing chapters, projecting to the future.

We also discuss some of the issues that have shaped higher education for the current times and those reflected in the book. In the final Chapter 12, the book chapters under their themes are summarised, with the authors' key points presented as suggestions for higher education in ASEAN as it goes forward.

The chapters and their reviews may be thematised as outlined below. These themes are not exclusive, and the individual chapters may address more than one of these themes.

Theme 1 Higher Education Sustainability

Chapter 2: Malaysia's Higher Education: Getting Out of the Doldrums and Implication for ASEAN *by Abdul Razak Ahmad and Morshidi Sirat*

In recognising the current vulnerability in ASEAN countries in the aftermath of the COVID-19 pandemic, Abdul Razak Ahmad and Morshidi Sirat discuss how the COVID-19 experience exposed structural weaknesses in Malaysia's higher education system and those of other regional countries. They posit that the weaknesses identified provide an opportunity for Malaysia, and indeed the ASEAN region, to refocus for an enhanced future. In the case of Malaysia, this would move the country out of what they term the "post-COVID-19 doldrums". Linked in with the future of ASEAN, they argue that higher education leaders, in their influential roles, can take charge in integrating regional higher education systems. Specific directions for this include accelerating the digital revolution; encouraging the mobility of students, researchers and academic programmes; and collaborating and cooperating on academic matters. Underpinning all these, they point out, is the need to prioritise higher education on the ASEAN agenda. These strategies will support the ongoing development and future sustainability of the region.

Chapter 3: Bridging the Higher Education Divide in Southeast Asia Through Open, Flexible and Distance eLearning (OFDeL): Now and Beyond 2030 *by Melinda dela Peña Bandalaria*

In Chapter 3, Melinda dela Peña Bandalaria highlights equitable access to higher education as a major means for enhancing the region's competitiveness globally and, by implication, its sustainability. Bandalaria draws on the 2015 Kuala Lumpur Declaration signed by ASEAN country leaders and, in overviewing the region's tertiary education enrolment statistics, notes that regional enrolment rates are relatively low on a global scale, even though they did increase overall from 2000 to 2018. The author identifies that access has not yet penetrated across the socioeconomic levels in the region. To address and bridge this gap in the under-enrolment and barriers to the participation of lower socioeconomic group citizens, she advocates for open, flexible and distance e-learning. For students, this would reduce educational costs, increase their capacity to work and be mobile while studying, and decrease possible discrimination.

Chapter 4: To Get Cracking: Discussing the Sustainability of Malaysia's Role as a Provider of Global Higher Education Through a Case Study of International Students *by Sally Anne Param*

In this chapter, Sally Anne Param explores from a more specific focus the sustainability of Malaysia's role as a global higher education provider. In the context of the high influx of students to Southeast Asia for study purposes, Param's qualitative and in-depth study explores the satisfaction of seven international students from different countries enrolled in higher education in Malaysia. The author notes these students' positive comments on the digital infrastructure and facilities provided by their institutions during the pandemic. More importantly, however, Param reports that their institutional experiences were not as positive from the sociocultural perspective; they felt "othered" in the university setting due to cross-cultural issues. Param argues that the inclusion of international students needs to be addressed for Malaysia to maintain its current position as an academic destination of choice for international students. As such, the author argues that to sustain their current competitive position in the international student field, international students need to feel welcomed, valued and included.

Theme 2 Access and Equity

Chapter 5: English Language Legacies, Policy and Practice in Malaysian Educational Systems: Reverberations in Higher Education *by Stephen J Hall*

In any country, enhancing access and equity in higher education is intimately related to the structure of the schooling system. Hall's chapter is a rich, detailed analysis of how there have been differing approaches to the use of English as the primary medium for teaching in different subjects within the Malaysian schooling system over recent years. As political views and parties have changed, so has the importance placed on teaching in English, particularly in the key subjects of mathematics and science. Hall argues that to effectively support learners from all backgrounds to succeed in schooling and then make effective transitions into higher education, both the national language and English in Malaysia need to be seen as not competing with each other. An inclusive approach is needed that recognises both these major languages and the other 137 languages in Malaysia, that different languages are appropriate for particular contexts and students especially may commonly code-switch between languages as circumstances across their lives dictate. He concludes by describing how the multilingual nature of students in Malaysia is an asset to be nurtured in the pedagogy of the local higher education.

Chapter 6: Attaining Equity and Diversity in the Massified System of Higher Education: A Qualitative Study of the Malaysian Context *by Muhammad Muftahu*

Muhammad Muftahu attempts to tackle the broad issue of massification of higher education and its implications for equitable access and success in higher education via an in-depth, qualitative study examining the views of senior and middle managers in Malaysian public universities. As in many other higher education systems in the world, Malaysia has experienced significant increases in student enrolment in recent decades. However, Muftahu's chapter points to the ongoing challenges that exist in terms of ensuring that these increases include opportunities for those from all socioeconomic and ethnic groups, as well as enabling all students to achieve their full potential when they enter higher education. The participants in the study highlight the barriers to entry that still exist in terms of admission arrangements, costs, the use of English as the dominant language in teaching, and limitations in the number of students that can be recruited to particular courses. However, work is underway to address these barriers, such as lower-cost opportunities for entry, and it is reassuring to read of the belief in the principles regarding higher education access and entry that the participants from different universities in Malaysia hold.

Theme 3 Curriculum Development

Chapter 7: Resilient Southeast Asian Education Through Humane and Compassionate Pedagogical Framework: An Autoethnography in Online Teaching and Learning Amid COVID-19 Health Crisis *by Rafael Ibe Santos*

In this chapter, Rafael Ibe Santos advocates the need for empathy and compassion for students to be a feature of the curricula in higher education studies. Santos points out that this approach will support higher education as a pivotal player in the socioeconomic recovery from COVID-19 in Southeast Asian countries. Using an interpretist-constructivist approach in the traditions of educational theorists Jean Piaget and Lev Vygotsky and through autoethnographic narratives, Santos highlights the importance of pedagogy grounded in empathy and caring for students, particularly during the pandemic. Humane pedagogy is captured, he states, in a curriculum that is mindful of learners' circumstances, flexible and adaptive but without sacrificing academic standards. Examples provided in the chapter of humane curriculum include flexible deadlines for work submission, manageable requirements and scaffolding learning to achieve curriculum goals.

Chapter 8: Rethinking Malaysian Universities' Business Models: Building Sustainable Business School Graduates *by Benedict Valentine Arulanandam, Glenda Crosling, Siti Norbaya Azizan and Graeme Atherton*

This chapter considers the sustainability of higher education business studies in the light of United Nations Sustainable Development Goal 4 of quality education, the changing landscape of the business world and its inclusion of technically based inputs. In auditing the websites and syllabi of business programmes in a representative sample of Malaysian private universities, supported by comments from academic staff members, the study identifies a low level of information technology and meta-dimensional analysis skills in the curricula of these universities. For the benefit of Malaysian businesses and, consequently, national development, the authors conclude in this chapter that curricula require quality and frequent review to ensure they are aligned with the changing demands of the business world, thus supporting the curricula not only in continuing to attract students, but in the sustainability of business activities in Malaysia in their contribution to increased global competitiveness.

Theme 4: Learning and Teaching Innovation

Innovation in learning and teaching reflects a myriad of approaches, including online and hybrid programmes that are multidisciplinary, student-centred, problem-solving and research-based, as we have outlined in the earlier section of this book. Under this theme, the following chapter presents one student-centred approach that lays the groundwork through scientific means for an effective teaching and learning programme that responds to the identified needs of the students.

Chapter 9: Smart Education for Smart Cities: Cloud-Based EEG Solution for Mental Health and Cognitive Skills Assessment for Higher Education in the ASEAN Region *by Nicolas Hamelin and Wendy Ong*

As Nicolas Hamelin and Wendy Ong emphasise in Chapter 9, while the prevalence of mental health issues among higher education students in this region is high, there are currently limited resources and costly support for assessing students' mental health at universities. Therefore, the authors propose using a cloud-based portable electroencephalogram or EEG system for the early detection of mental health issues among higher education students. This novel, affordable and practical technological solution can also be used to assess the cognitive and emotional skills students need as the future workforce of ASEAN's smart cities. The reported experimental design involved Master of Business Administration students in selected universities, where they were given emotional stimuli from the database and their cognitive capacity was assessed using a Stroop test. Based on their results, the authors then put forward the proposed system's potential for mental health detection among the student population and personality and cognitive traits assessment for society at large.

Theme 5: Post-Graduation Employment

Chapter 10: Future-Ready Graduates: Work-Study Programme in Singapore *by Razwana Begum Abdul Rahim*

Producing employable graduates is part of the educational outcomes of HEIs. In this chapter, Razwana Begum Abdul Rahim shares Singapore's experience in developing and implementing the work-study degree (WSDeg) programmes to produce future-ready graduates as resilient workforce. Initiated by Singapore's Ministry of Education and SkillsFuture, the programme initiative was developed upon the government's realisation of the challenges and needs for equipping the country's future cohorts with the necessary core skills for their employability. The author begins the discussion by presenting the educational background of higher education in Singapore, which has led to the development of the WSDeg in HEIs. After discussing the implementation of Singapore's work-study programme in detail, the author then reviews related work-study policies in other countries, i.e. Germany and Thailand. This discussion finally contributes to identifying areas for improvement and successful practices which can be further incorporated into the existing framework towards developing future-ready graduates in Singapore.

Chapter 11: Improving Employability of Future Business Graduates Through Sustainable Private College-Industry Partnership: A Phenomenological Study *by Thiruchelvi K Murugiah*

Employability issues are at the very core of higher education. Chapter 11 reports the phenomenological study by Thiruchelvi K Murugiah that looks into unemployment factors among future business graduates in Malaysia, from a broader view of the job market and the mechanisms to improve gradutes' employability through sustainable partnerships of private colleges with industry. The author identifies the needed values for establishing such a connection to enhance graduate employability vis-à-vis industry. Multiple data resources are gathered, representing academic staff members and students from a private college as well as the industry. Emerging from the study's findings are five themes explaining factors of graduate unemployment: (1) skills mismatch regarding 21st-century skills, (2) for business: transformation required, (3) for education: development required of sustainable shared value partnerships, (4) for graduates: stakeholder gap issues existing, and (5) for learning: academic insights required. In addition, three themes suggest the needed values for building the partnership, which are business transformation, education (shared value partnerships) and learning (academic insights). The author concludes by highlighting the significant roles of HEIs, together with relevant stakeholders and policymakers, to facilitate the development of the future workforce through symbiotic relationships between educational institutions and the industry in the digital ecosystems.

CONCLUSION

In conclusion, the chapters in this book explore the varying aspects and diverse perspectives on the future development of higher education in the ASEAN nations. Generally, rigorous scholarly analysis of higher education systems from both local and global views is presented in this book to build a comprehensive cross-country understanding. Five main themes are addressed to reflect the variation of current and emerging practices shaping the future of higher education delivery in the region: (1) Higher Education Sustainability, (2) Access and Equity, (3) Curriculum Development, (4) Learning and Teaching Innovation, and (5) Post-Graduation Employment. The final conclusion in Chapter 12 integrates the key points that arise from the chapters in this book and presents a way forward for higher education development in the region.

REFERENCES

Altbach, P. (2016). *Global perspectives on higher education.* Johns Hopkins University Press.

ASEAN Secretariat (2020a). *The founding of ASEAN.* Association of Southeast Asian Nations. https://asean.org/about-asean/the-founding-of-asean

ASEAN Secretariat (2020b). *Education: Overview.* Association of Southeast Asian Nations. https://asean.org/our-communities/asean-socio-cultural-community/education

Asia Development Bank (ADB). (2022). *Southeast Asia rising from the pandemic.* https://www.adb.org/sites/default/files/publication/779416/southeast-asia-rising-pandemic.pdf

Asia-Pacific Programme of Educational Innovation for Development, United Nations Educational, Scientific and Cultural Organisation. (2006). *Higher Education in South-East Asia.* UNESDOC Digital Library. https://unesdoc.unesco.org/ark:/48223/pf0000146541

Atherton, G., Azizan, S. N., Munir Shuib, M., & Crosling, G. (2018a). The shape of global higher education: Understanding the ASEAN region (Volume 3). *British Council.* https://www.britishcouncil.org/sites/default/files/h233_the_shape_of_asean_higher_education_report_final_v2_web_1.pdf

Atherton, G., Crosling, G., Shuib, M., & Azizan, S. N. (2018b). Internationalisation and transformation of higher education in ASEAN countries: A distinctive emerging approach (Special Issue). *The Journal of Social Sciences Research,* 540–553.

Atherton, G., Crosling, G., Shuib, M., & Azizan, S. N. (2020). International student mobility in ASEAN: An overview and way forward. In C. Kahl (Ed.), *Higher Education challenges in South-East Asia.* IGI Global Publishers.

Azizan, S. N., Lee, A. S. H., Crosling, G., Atherton, G., Arulanandam, G. B., Lee, C. E., & Begum, R. (2022). Online learning and COVID-19 in higher education: The value of IT models in assessing students' satisfaction. *International Journal of Educational Technologies, 17*(3), 245–278. https://doi.org/10.3991/ijet.v17i03.24871

Blessinger, P. (2015). *Higher education for a hyper-connected world.* Higher Education Tomorrow, *3*(1). https://www.patrickblessinger.com/higher-education-for-a-hyper-connected-world

Blessinger, P. (2022a). *The shift towards hyper-learning.* Higher Education Tomorrow, *8*(3). https://www.patrickblessinger.com/the-shift-towards-hyper-learning

Blessinger, P. (2022b). *Rethinking higher education for the future.* Higher Education Tomorrow, *8*(1). https://www.patrickblessinger.com/rethinking-higher-education-for-the-future

Blessinger, P., & de Castro Soeiro, F. (2022). *Shaping learning futures with lifelong learning.* Higher Education Tomorrow, *8*(2). https://www.patrickblessinger.com/shaping-learning-futures-with-lifelong-learning

Blessinger, P., Sengupta, E., & Makhanya, M. (2020, March 7). Mapping higher education's literacies of the future. *University World News.* https://www.universityworldnews.com/post.php?story=20200303131923730

Bustos-Orosa, M. A. (2022). Private higher education in developing economies in Southeast Asia: Challenges to and prospects for its sustainability in a post-pandemic world. In S. Gopinathan & P. G. Altbach (Eds.), *Higher education in Southeast Asia and beyond.* HEAD Foundation.

Chankseliani, M. (2022). International development higher education: Looking from the past, looking to the future. *Oxford Review of Education, 48(*4), 457–473.

Crosling, G., Atherton, G., Shuib, M., Rahim, A. A., Azizan, S. N., & Nasir, M. I. M. (2020). The teaching of sustainability in higher education: Improving environmental resilience in Malaysia. In E. Sengupta, P. Blessinger, & T. S. Yamin (Eds.), *Introduction to sustainable development leadership and strategies in higher education.* Emerald Publishing Limited.

Crosling, G., Nair, M. S., & Vaithilingam, S. (2014). A creative learning ecosystem, quality of education and innovative capacity: A perspective from higher education. *Studies in Higher Education, 40*(7), 1–17.

Crosling, G., Shuib, M., & Rahman, S. (2019). Introduction. In S. Abdul Rahman, M. Shuib, & G. Crosling (Eds.), *Creativity in education.* Penerbit Universiti Sains Malaysia.

Dhirathiti, C. (2022, May 31). Asean universities must focus on quality to catch up with the West. *Times Higher Education.* https://www.timeshighereducation.com/opinion/asean-universities-must-focus-quality-catch-west

El-Azar, D. (2022). 4 trends that will shape the future of higher education. *World Economic Forum.* https://www.weforum.org/agenda/2022/02/four-trends-that-will-shape-the-future-of-higher-education

Findler, F., Schönherr, N., Lozano, R., Reider, D., & Martinuzzi, A. (2019).The impacts of higher education institutions on sustainable development: A review and conceptualization. *International Journal of Sustainability in Higher Education, 20*(1), 23–38.

Joynes, C., Rossignoli, S., & Fenyiwa Amonoo-Kuofi, E. (2019). *21st-century skills: Evidence of issues in definition, demand and delivery for development contexts (K4D Helpdesk Report).* Department for International Development.

Levine, A., & Van Pelt, S. (2021). The future of higher ed is occurring at the margins. *Inside Higher Ed.* https://www.insidehighered.com/views/2021/10/04/higher-education-should-prepare-five-new-realities-opinion

Martinus, M. (2022, April 26). ASEAN's consumers on the move: Tertiary education. *FULCRUM Analysis on Southeast Asia.* https://fulcrum.sg/aseans-consumers-on-the-move-tertiary-education

McGreal, R., & Olcott, D. (2022). A strategic reset: Micro-credentials for higher education leaders. *Smart Learning Environments, 9*(1), 1–23.

Nithyavathy, N. (2022). Higher education in Southeast Asian countries: A review. *Higher Education Review.* https://www.thehighereducationreview.com/magazine/higher-education-in-southeast-asian-countries-a-review-NHRH388478344.html

PwC. (2022). Impact on the higher education sector. *PwC.* https://www.pwc.com/sg/en/publications/a-resilient-tomorrow-covid-19-response-and-transformation/higher-education.html

Ratanawijitrasin, S. (2015). The evolving landscape of South-East Asian higher education and the challenges of governance. In A. Curaj, L. Matei, R. Pricopie, J. Salmi, & P. Scott (Eds.), *The European higher education area.* Springer. https://doi.org/10.1007/978-3-319-20877-0_15

Sa-ngiamwibool, A., & Wisaeng, K. (2021). ASEAN economic community and its impacts: Opportunities, challenges, and implications for higher education. *Problems and Perspectives in Management, 19*(3), 247–260. http://doi.org/10.21511/ppm.19(3).2021.21

Schofer, E., Ramirez, F., & Meyer, J. (2020). The societal consequences of higher education. *Sociology of Education, 94*(1), 1–19.

Scott, P. (2022, May 25). The space for a new saga for higher education is emerging. *University World News.* https://www.universityworldnews.com/post.php?story=20220525141306100

Siemens, G., & Matheos, K. (2010). Systematic changes in higher education. *In Education, 16*(1), 3–18. https://www.researchgate.net/publication/48603969_Systemic_Changes_in_Higher_Education

Trow, M. (1973). *Problems in the transition from elite to mass higher education.* Carnegie Commission on Higher Education Berkeley.

Valero, A., & Van Reenen, J. (2019). The economic impact of universities: Evidence from across the globe. *Economics of Education Review, 68*, 53–67.

von Kameke, L. (2021). Number of international tertiary students studying in Southeast Asia from 2013 to 2018 (in 1,000s). *Statista.* https://www.statista.com/statistics/1093609/southeast-asia-number-of-international-tertiary-students

Welch, A. (2011). *Higher education in Southeast Asia: Blurring borders, changing balance (1st ed.).* Routledge.

Wilkinson, G. (2017). Access and new employability skills. In G. Crosling & G. Atherton (Eds.), *Current and emerging themes in global access to post-secondary education, 15–23.* Emerald Publishing Limited.

Xia, X, & Qiu, X. (2021). The impact of the quality of higher education on the development of regional economy: Empirical analysis based on provincial panel data. *Proceedings of the 7th international conference on social science and higher education (ICSSHE 2021).*

Yan Zhang, C.Y. (2021, March 3). The rise of glocal education: ASEAN countries. *QS Top Universities.* https://www.topuniversities.com/where-to-study/region/asia/rise-glocal-education-asean-countries

Chapter 2

Malaysia's Higher Education: Getting Out of the Doldrums and Implications for ASEAN

Abdul Razak Ahmad* & Morshidi Sirat‡

ABSTRACT

Malaysia's higher education sector is in the doldrums as a result of the Coronavirus Disease 2019 (COVID-19). The pandemic has laid bare the inherent and structural weaknesses in the higher education system from the perspectives of leadership, governance-autonomy and internationalisation. Several member countries within the Association of Southeast Asian Nations (ASEAN) have experienced a similar predicament. In Malaysia, during the pre-pandemic period, the success of several top-rated universities and the system as a whole in the international arena made policymakers oblivious to the structural weaknesses. To resolve the current predicament and for the post-pandemic future, Malaysia needs a recovery plan based on future prospects and resilience in the higher education system over reactionary lamentation of past limitations. The recovery plan should focus on six key strategic areas, namely an acceleration of the digital revolution, expansion of new revenue streams, cost leadership and optimisation, new synergies for long-term growth, modernisation of governance structure and practices, and a comprehensive internationalisation agenda supported by immigration reforms.

Keywords Cost leadership and optimisation, COVID-19 pandemic, digital revolution, governance, immigration reforms, internationalisation, recovery plan

* Bait Al Amanah, Malaysia

‡ Universiti Sains Malaysia, Malaysia

INTRODUCTION

The COVID-19 pandemic has presented Malaysia with an opportunity to revisit its current policies and practices and to act upon new possibilities by looking to Southeast Asia and beyond. This chapter explores these possibilities, focusing on governance and institutional leadership that are willing to apply new and "business-unusual" approaches. The contention is that Malaysia's recovery plan should be designed in line with ASEAN's future higher education trajectory. Arguably, the future of the envisioned "ASEAN higher education area" is highly dependent on the progressive moves of its constituent membership, with the more sophisticated higher education systems acting as catalytic agents for the regional system.

COVID-19 AND HIGHER EDUCATION: MALAYSIA AND THE PRELUDE TO IMPLICATIONS FOR ASEAN

According to Jensen et al. (2022), the higher education sector in the Asia-Pacific region during the COVID-19 pandemic has shown great resilience, but there are regional variations and diversity. In Malaysia, the disruption to the higher education sector was unprecedented. Azman and Abdullah (2021) find that it was particularly evident, with respect to teaching and learning, that academics and higher education institutions (HEIs) in general were not prepared for the shift of teaching and learning to remote or online delivery. According to Choong (2020), Sharma (2020) and the World Bank Group (2020), apart from the need for virtual interaction, other influencing factors that contributed to the ill-preparedness include reduced financial support from the government due to diverted resources to the healthcare sector, and the financial troubles of private institutions where tuition fee collection was affected. Abdullah and Fernandez-Chung (2021) and Imrie (2020) point out that international students' mobility was severely hit, affecting HEIs' financial sustainability and Malaysia's target for international student numbers. Inequality was also more apparent (Choong, 2020), coupled with increased difficulty in the transition to the labour market (World Bank Group, 2020; Department of Statistics Malaysia, 2021). Sirat and Ahmad (2021) argue that Malaysia's status in higher education was altered, making projecting a new higher education scenario based on past achievements increasingly difficult. While Jensen et al. (2022) report the impact on governance, there has been little study on the impact of COVID-19 on university leadership in Malaysia and ASEAN. Examples of studies on more developed higher education systems include Ahern and Loh (2020), who highlight the need for trust in leadership for transformative, collective action in uncertain times such as a pandemic, and Kaul et al. (2020) whose study in the United States (US) emphasises commitment to leadership training in medicine based on the pandemic experience.

According to Azman and Abdullah (2021), the pandemic demonstrated the structural weakness of Malaysia's current system in coping with the disruption, especially in relation to the delivery of services, teaching and learning. While a strategic focus on digitisation was introduced in the Malaysia Education Blueprint (Higher Education) in 2015, this has not been fully implemented. Choong (2020) and Azman and Abdullah (2021) note that the higher education system initially struggled to migrate to digital modes of teaching and learning. The exception was private universities, which were already conducting online distance learning (ODL). In realising HEI's predicament, Lau (2020) notes that Malaysian universities were given funds to weather the pandemic, demonstrating the government's commitment to education and improving information technology and teaching quality.

The pandemic also presented Malaysia with an opportunity to reinvent its higher education system. In fact, according to The Head Foundation (2021), it was an opportunity for other ASEAN member countries to reset their higher education trajectory as well. In the same spirit, the current disruption should be viewed positively, which is the focus and objective of this chapter. This chapter largely draws on the experience of the two authors over several years of top-level policy formulation and management in Malaysia's Ministry of Higher Education (MOHE) rather than empirical research, and focuses on two important strategies for other ASEAN countries in the context of the future of higher education in ASEAN.

The first strategy is for HEIs to enhance their national and regional engagement strategies surrounding government, industries, communities and networks, since institutional capacity is extremely limited. This is evidenced by the need for greater collaboration and engagement during the pandemic, brought about by factors such as the movement control order, border closures, lack of internal resources, and the need for growth and development. Sirat

(2017) posits that intra- and inter-regional collaborative initiatives must be invigorated with an effective implementing mechanism for the betterment of Malaysia and the region's future. He further mentions the tendency for university collaborations to focus outside ASEAN for reputation and image.

The second strategy is based on Malaysia's National Recovery Plan; HEIs are merely treated as locations for reopening. However, the government needs to realise that recovery in higher education is as essential as health for the country's economic and social progress in a post-pandemic scenario. If higher education issues continue to be considered secondary to health and security, Malaysia's human capital and development will be compromised in the long run. Hence, this pandemic is an opportunity for Malaysia to press the reset button for tertiary education. Based on the authors' involvement in policy directions concerning HEIs, the recovery plan should focus on six key strategic areas, namely an acceleration of the digital revolution, expansion of new revenue streams, cost leadership and optimisation, new synergies for long-term growth, modernisation of the governance arrangement/structure and practices, and a comprehensive internationalisation agenda supported by immigration reforms.

With these two strategies in place, it is hoped that Malaysia's HEIs can get out of the doldrums and be well-poised for a new development trajectory that accords with the development within ASEAN. Indeed, a recovered higher education sector is Malaysia's contribution to ASEAN's vision for higher education. To realise this objective, Malaysia must first re-examine its higher education system from the perspectives of leadership, governance-autonomy and internationalisation. Sirat et al. (2011), Wan et al. (2015) and Abdullah et al. (2022) all find these three areas to have inherent structural weaknesses.

THE PAST, THE FUTURE: EXTRAPOLATION OF TREND VS CLEAN BREAK POST-PANDEMIC

This chapter intends to critically analyse three focus areas: (1) university leadership, (2) governance and autonomy, and (3) internationalisation. Arguably, the future of a resilient higher education system in Malaysia will be underpinned by changes and reforms in these three areas as they reflect the key major spheres of higher education operations. In the contemporary internationalised higher education scenario, these are also areas of concern in other ASEAN countries.

University leadership

Malaysian university leadership was presented with a unique opportunity to be at the forefront of the national effort to fight against the COVID-19 pandemic. Unfortunately, despite the enormous resources, brains trust and expertise, the mitigation of the crisis was completely led by the civil service and not by the very best of Malaysia's experts in academia. This is evidenced by the fact that none of the Malaysian university Presidents or Vice Chancellors was made members of the National Recovery Committee, the National Security Council or the National Disaster Management Agency. At the onset of the pandemic, the Ministry of Health did not leverage the experts in public and private universities, where the best Malaysian public health experts were to be found. Epidemiologists and other experts in universities were not made key advisers or spokespeople for the government on health and pandemic-related matters. This lack of representation presented an image of serious trust issues with HEI leadership and university experts in Malaysia.[1]

When COVID-19 struck in 2020, many universities scrambled for months, sending students home to study, moving to virtual teaching and learning, managing work from home for administrative and faculty members, and using campuses as vaccination centres. Many simply complied with the instructions of federal agencies, especially the National Disaster Management Agency and the Malaysian Qualifications Agency (MQA, 2021) advisory notes on the conduct of teaching and learning. While the pandemic has put more pressure on issues of immediate concern such as financing and funding, student mobility, student demographic changes and budding technological

[1] Based on personal communication with the Vice Chancellor of Universiti Malaysia Sarawak (UNIMAS), experts from UNIMAS were involved in state-level committees handling the Coronavirus Disease 2019 pandemic. Communication with a professor from Universiti Malaya revealed that university experts were involved in the Ministry of Science, Technology and Innovation committees and the Greater Klang Valley Task Force. However, the Ministry of Health did not involve experts from universities except for services, such as laboratory testing and patient treatment.

capabilities for the long term should not be neglected. While it is understood that the crisis is a new challenge for most HEI leaders, university leadership quality is arguably best tested in trying times.

A university recovery plan is crucial to strengthen the HEIs' ability to move their agenda and plans. While it is incumbent on a university's Board of Directors to initiate conversations about strategies for recovery and accelerate the allocation of resources as needed, such conversations should be backed by rigorous data analytics. A data-driven strategy for weighing projected and long-term impacts of any policy decisions is critically important in a pandemic and post-pandemic scenario. Planning for pandemic-related infrastructure and development projects in universities should be prioritised, especially during crises such as the pandemic. Choong (2020) notes that the disruption caused by the pandemic requires extensive investment in digital infrastructures if the digitisation strategy is to succeed. However, these have not been made central to the COVID-19 response due to critical financial issues. At the core of the problem is prioritisation.

To sum up, the apparent absence of strong leadership by Malaysian HEI leaders during the national emergency is disconcerting. The root cause for this situation can be traced back to the relationship between federal agencies and universities in times of international and national crises. Universities are crucial since they have the research capacity and achievements from which solutions to national predicaments should come. However, central agencies may not view universities in such a favourable light. On the part of the universities, university leadership should have prioritised engagement with national constituents and provided cutting-edge solutions in health, economy and social security.

Governance and autonomy

Even before COVID-19, Malaysian public universities were supervised while private universities were regulated centrally. Wan et al. (2019) and Netto (2017) argue that public universities in particular have not had genuine financial autonomy. In fact, whatever limited autonomy they had was severely curtailed during the pandemic. For example, according to Menon and Rajaendram (2021), decisions on the opening and closure of campuses and university operations were wholly determined by federal agencies. In fact, the "one size fits all" health protocols were imposed on universities without regard for a university's unique character, mission and operational requirements. Notably, the MOHE periodically issued directives on when students could be on campus, the percentage of staff allowed to be on campus physically, and even who was allowed to undertake research work in university laboratories. Such unilateral direction undermined the autonomy of universities and interfered heavily with universities' core functions of teaching and research. Universities themselves should determine prescriptions of permissible actions during the movement control order, as they are in the best position to navigate concerns for health and security without compromising their functions. Interestingly, the MQA (2021) via its advisory note, had appropriately addressed issues relating to universities' academic autonomy, stating that the university senate decides on academic matters. This shows that the MQA, being headed by academics, understood well the role of the university senate during times of crisis.

Overall, HEIs have experienced severe financial deficits, depending on key features of their funding models. For instance, public universities are dependent on the government. Else (2016) notes that even before COVID-19, the government had reduced funding to public universities, with COVID-19 exacerbating resource constraints among public universities. Conversely, private universities are dependent on income from tuition fees, where low admission means low income. Although financial sustainability has been central to the Malaysia Education Blueprint (Higher Education), public universities continue to rely heavily on the government. This arguably leads to more control and bureaucratisation of public universities, less autonomy and quasi-independence. Resetting higher education post-COVID-19 requires massive investments; for instance, greater digitisation calls for huge investments in its infrastructure. With changes to working, learning and teaching modes, investment in the professionalisation of academic and non-academic staff would also be substantial.

In summary, for Malaysian universities, there were implications for governance arrangement and decision-making processes in times of crisis. While decision-making related to health is a national urgency, academic matters need to be left to the universities to decide.

Internationalisation

Jensen et al. (2022) note that the impact of COVID-19 is most apparent with the global decline in the internationalisation of higher education. While no intervention strategies were implemented to sustain global interests in Malaysia as a higher education destination, facilitation strategies could have supported international students stranded on campuses. More wide-ranging assistive initiatives for potential incoming and returning international students could have been implemented. A major constraint was the ever-changing central policies as the COVID-19 situation worsened. While initiatives to lessen the financial burden of international students were introduced, such as fee reductions and deferred fee payments or rebates, welfare support should also have been put in motion.

Malaysia is expected to face many challenges for higher education internationalisation to recover. For example, in finding new sources of potential international students, will China, Indonesia, Pakistan and Bangladesh continue to be the primary sources? What are the prospects of international students' mobility in view of Malaysia's border restrictions and unfavourable pandemic-induced global economic conditions? How will the higher education sector manage other internationalisation agenda items, such as academic mobility, research cooperation and other international university business? How can universities intensify their brand positioning globally? Also, how can higher education providers innovate to remain competitive in delivering higher education services?

In summary, the internationalisation of higher education, especially the mobility of students, involves many internal and external factors beyond the universities' control and influence during a crisis.

RECOVERY PLAN AND FUTURE HIGHER EDUCATION LANDSCAPE

From the discussion, the status quo of Malaysia's higher education achievements in governance and autonomy has been seriously altered, affecting other spheres of the system. In this respect, the Malaysia Education Blueprint (Higher Education) that was to be implemented until 2025 is somewhat off course because of the realignment of considerations by the government, industries, students and institutions to recover from the impacts of COVID-19. Key to recovery is mutually linked and coordinated policy realignment across ministries, governmental agencies and regulatory authorities. Resetting Malaysia's HEIs requires stronger and better coordination of policies in technology, economy, finance, health, social development and the environment. The policy and bureaucracy interface at every level of government and institutional operations is more crucial now than ever. Ensuring policy coherence is pertinent to minimise future disruptions and vulnerabilities, for without it, a balance between recovery, growth and long-term resilience strategy may not be achieved.

The issue now is how fast a recovery plan can be put into action and, assuming there is policy coherence, how effective it will be. The challenge is getting all players to collaborate to ensure greater policy coordination. The prevalent territorial and jurisdictional-centric mindset between ministries and government agencies needs to be overcome. The MOHE can no longer allow the compartmentalisation of state bureaucracy. It needs a new sequencing of actions based on the bureaucracy and society approach. To realise this, effective leadership is critical. However, are the figureheads of Malaysian HEIs equipped with such leadership sophistication, especially in managing the interplay between state, society and institutions? The authors have no answer to that question, but the following imperatives could be considered for a strong and sustainable recovery of the HEI sectors.

New governance model propelled by technology and collaborations

Malaysian HEIs must consider embracing the technological future. Mixed modalities, such as hybrid learning, will stay. Selingo et al. (2021) argue that hybrid campuses could make institutions and learning more accessible with better cost management, while simultaneously encouraging innovation and providing a valuable campus experience. Conceptually, this could also help institutional resilience and minimise future disruptions. However, such transitions are never easy for universities. According to Diamond (2006), ancient institutions are known to be conservative and resistant to significant changes. What HEIs need is a transition model that helps preserve their intellectual and academic tradition but is modernised to accommodate new and innovative approaches to learning, researching and administering—a model that provides the equilibrium brought about by the pressures of technological disruptions. Universities cannot continue to ignore how technology and innovation can propel their operational effectiveness, growth and relevance. Indeed, a new governance model will emerge post-pandemic, freeing Malaysian HEIs from being trapped in a closed, bureaucratic and archaic governing model. The new governance model will be less about new laws, refined charters or new structures of ministerial jurisdictions; instead, it will be driven by a rapid telecommunication revolution, big data and a global network. The new model will embrace interdependence, inclusiveness, the power of networks and community diversity. It will also allow Malaysian HEIs to have an international presence, irrespective of their relationship with the MOHE.

Malaysia's higher education scene has evolved from providing the nation with home-educated professional talents to enhancing the quality of education and intellectual prowess of the people while filling the gap in industrial needs. The higher education system was initiated as a national agenda with federal autonomy to catalyse progress and development of society in every aspect. While the system has served Malaysia well, we have seen its limits, and change is inevitable. With the emergence of private higher education providers and technological advancements on top of the ever-changing human needs, some regions in Malaysia can no longer expect to hold autonomy over the higher education system and its internationalisation. Malaysia needs a reset not only in terms of the current governing framework but also the role of the state, HEIs, private entities and society, and how they interact to provide a more sustainable and better quality higher education.

In summary, the catalyst for a radical transformation is the pandemic itself. We have seen how teaching, research and administration of universities have been conducted virtually since the first quarter of 2020. University leaders, scholars and students have engineered new ways to collaborate and communicate at a rate no one has ever imagined, going beyond campus, chancelleries and classes. It is global in every sense, propelled by technology and powered by a network of networks. Such a transformation will produce a flexible governance model, making governing more modern, seamless yet transparent, accountable and inclusive.

New synergies for long-term growth

According to Azman (2021), more than 60 private colleges closed in 2020. What Malaysian HEIs need now is a new strategy for long-term growth. Such growth can only happen with a fresh synergy between higher education and industrial, commercial and multinational players. Why is such synergy crucial? SaLemi (2018) finds at least three reasons. First, there are changes in the business and social world and workforce skills—85% of jobs in 2030 are yet to exist, and the best way for universities to understand this is to work in synergy with business enterprises. Second, the speed and scale of innovation and advancement of global technology are faster than the speed of adaptation by HEIs. Only through greater synergies may such deficits and gaps be overcome. Third, collaborations and synergies enable leveraging combined strength, resources and growth.

The Malaysian Education Blueprint 2015–2025 (Higher Education) hints at a greater blurring of boundaries between public and private higher education providers, with various hybrid institutions already established. In fact, the future will see the growth of diverse, non-traditional players delivering higher education services. The Education Malaysia Global Services (2022) also highlights that the current myriad of local and global alliances is driven by complex motivations and objectives. These result from adopting sophisticated management and business models propelled by advanced technology and data science. The new higher education enterprises may emerge and operate in the form of public-private, or private++, or social enterprises-private, public + private + non-governmental organisations, non-governmental individuals ++, or even philanthropy ++.

Fundamental to the new higher education business model will be more alliances and collaborations in a generally competitive environment, a more global outlook and orientation, and less state and more society engagement. The new synergy will be more of inclusion rather than prestige or elitism, focusing on unleashing the potential of each and everyone instead of a select few. Empowerment, diversity and sustainability, and debunking of exclusivity will be the key aspects emphasised by the new synergy to create the most impact and dismantle and reconstruct the higher education landscape. In short, such a synergy will introduce a flexible mode of learning, researching and governing, based on innovative models of alliances, collaborations and socially driven enterprise.

Internationalisation with immigration reform

Internationalisation was probably the most severely impacted aspect of higher education due to the pandemic. However, de Wit and Altbach (2022) argue it was a temporary disruption and would return to normal quickly. The current trend indicates that the crisis was effectively mitigated through the successful vaccination of a significant number of the population. The strategy to coexist with the virus means that the worst is over, and the internationalisation of higher education will eventually prevail. Despite the optimism, there are some real challenges on the road to recovery for the Malaysian higher education sector. In this regard, Wan and Abdullah (2021) argue that the disconnection with the United Nations Sustainable Development Goals, specifically Goal 4 of quality education, is a persistent issue. Additionally, many lingering uncertainties arise from the pandemic; for example, relaxing border closures to promote internationalisation may result in new COVID-19 variants spreading.

Optimistically, the global disruption of the internationalisation of higher education provides an impetus for rethinking Malaysia's future strategy. While international students will continue to be a source of revenue, other strategies such as acquiring institutions in foreign jurisdictions should be considered. Another strategy could be offshore campuses for Malaysian universities through the right collaboration and synergy. Offering online courses by Malaysian universities may also be intensified, with options to spend some semesters at Malaysian campuses. Services in higher education should now be a priority for the Ministry of International Trade and Industry.

However, a larger strategic interest for Malaysia must accompany those shifts, and the qualitative dimension of internationalisation must not be neglected. The globalisation of Malaysia's higher education sector should be pursued parallel with enhancing Malaysia's soft power, global influence and international visibility. The idea of making Malaysia a knowledge powerhouse should be intensified with multipronged approaches. A hub for international students is a thing of the past; the next stage is making Malaysia the knowledge and talent powerhouse.

Such strategic consideration is crucial because the current focus on international students' mobility is rather narrow. Malaysia's future growth depends on the interplay between talent, knowledge and globalisation. Malaysia can no longer be a transit country for educational experience and learning per se, but a place where people converge for ideas, innovations and knowledge enterprises. To realise this, universities cannot just be a conduit in the nation-building process. They must be the prime mover for quality education, talent nurturing, and start-up growth and flourishing. They must also have the power of network that can connect talents to the business and service sectors for the greater good of Malaysia and global competitiveness. Malaysia's tertiary education standard should be one that the developing world wishes to associate with. Thus, the expansion of Malaysia's brand of tertiary education must be a strategic initiative for export consideration.

Another dimension for qualitative reset of the internationalisation agenda is increased inclusivity. According to de Wit and Marinori (2020, as cited by Bergan et al., 2021), internationalisation inherently leads to inequality. It is also Western-biased, exclusive to the wealthy and the cause of brain drain. As international mobility is costly, the resulting low number of students from low-income backgrounds makes it intrinsically unequal. Thus, as de Wit and Marinori (2020) recommend, a more inclusive strategy in the form of curriculum and campus internationalisation through the creation of a more globalised environment for learning should be seriously enhanced.

Finally, a successful internationalisation agenda requires a progressive immigration regime. Immigrants and immigration benefit Malaysia, but the interplay between immigration and higher education has always been secondary to issues relating to national security. The federal authority's response to the aftermath of September 11, the rise of terror groups in the Middle East, and now COVID-19 are testimonies to this fact. Sulong (2021) describes how international students and even academics coming to Malaysia, and those already in Malaysia, have been forced to endure an extremely complex, obsolete visa regime. Immigration politics and policies have had huge impacts on students, academics and communities. For instance, Sarawak and Sabah have their own immigration powers separate from Peninsular Malaysia. It follows that a departure from the current regulatory regime is necessary if we are to welcome and support international students, talents and faculties in a more coordinated manner. Lessons may be drawn from the recent announcement made by the United Arab Emirates (UAE) government. Saseendran (2021) describes how the UAE introduced a green visa regime, which permits residency for pioneers, entrepreneurs, talented students and other professionals. The visa holder can sponsor their children's visas until they turn 25; formerly, the practice was 18 years. Green visa holders can also sponsor their parents. Another category is the country-wide freelance visa, which gives flexibility to freelancers and professionals to work and live in the UAE without being tied to one employer. This is a massive incentive for Millennials to make Dubai their preferred destination to study, work and live.

Digitisation in higher education

Digital disruptions have always been an expected phenomenon in tertiary education. Abd Rahim and Abd Rahim (2021) point out that digitisation in many spheres of life aligns with the Internet penetration rate projection from 70.75% in 2015 to 97.5% by 2025. In 2018, the MOHE published the *Framing Malaysian Higher Education 4.0: Future-Proof Talent* document as part of the Malaysia Education Blueprint 2015–2025 (Higher Education) (Figure 2.1). The framework document is referred to again in the Way Forward for Private Higher Education Institution: Education as an Industry 2020–2025 Blueprint. In these documents, there is an emphasis on improving pedagogical mechanisms in line with the latest technological developments to produce quality university graduates.

The Malaysian Investment Development Authority (2021) acknowledges that the unprecedented COVID-19 pandemic accelerated the process of digitisation because of the rising need for ODL. Therefore, the tertiary learning sector needs to adapt so HEIs can recover and maintain the sector's sustainability and relevance in the long run. For this reason, the Malaysia Digital Economy Blueprint (MDEB) announced in February 2021 the strategies to incorporate digital skills in HEIs (Economic Planning Unit, Prime Minister's Department, 2021). The MDEB also aims to drive large-scale digitisation in HEIs.

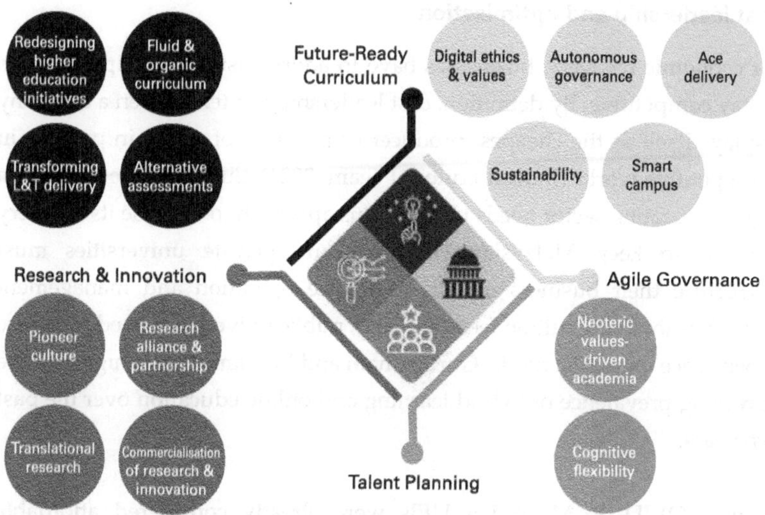

Figure 2.1 The direction of Malaysian higher education as outlined by the Ministry of Higher Education
Source: Ministry of Education (2020)

On the implementation side, evidence suggests that HEIs in Malaysia are going through digital development. Launched by MOHE and the Malaysia Digital Economy Corporation in 2005, the Malaysian Research and Education Network (MyREN) drives high-speed connectivity for the education sector. While MyREN has been underutilised since its establishment, Ahmad (2021) highlights that RM50 million was allocated for MyREN in Budget 2021 to provide 200,000 data plans and 4,000 devices for B40 students' ODL during COVID-19. There is much hope for the role of MyREN in future digitisation.

While the initiative to assist students from families with a gross monthly income of less than RM4,850 (B40 households) during the pandemic is welcome, this move is temporary and does not address the need for long-term digitalised tertiary education. More digitisation initiatives should be championed through MyREN because the organisation has domestic and international HEI networks, which can offer opportunities for digital collaboration and intellectual exchanges (Ministry of Higher Education, 2021). Aligned with internationalism, Malaysian HEIs can tap into global databases and research connections with a more comprehensive digital framework.

Cost leadership and optimisation

For economic recovery, businesses have to adopt cost leadership strategies to stay competitive. By definition, cost leadership is a term when a company displays itself as the cheapest producer or provider of a certain product in a competitive world (Indeed Editorial Team, 2021). Similarly, the Malaysian higher education sector needs to adopt this approach to catalyse its recovery process. To keep Malaysian HEIs relevant, private universities must restructure their business models to reduce operation and management costs, thus lowering tuition fees. Similarly, public universities need to reduce dependence on public funds. Gurubatham and Williams (2021) highlight the increasing prevalence of hybrid learning and online education over the past two years.

Before COVID-19, Malaysian HEIs were already considered affordable for high-quality tertiary education. For instance, a two-year tuition fee in Malaysia for the American Degree Transfer Program in 2018 ranged between USD7,500 and USD12,500 (RM30,000 and RM50,000), while the tuition fee in the US ranged between USD25,000 and USD35,000 annually (StudyMalaysia.com, 2020).

Malaysia was also listed as one of the most affordable places for international students in 2019. Specifically, in 2019, Kuala Lumpur ranked second out of 10 in the world for affordability for the second year running (Lane, 2021). Based on the QS Top Universities ranking of Best Student Cities 2022 that compared 115 cities worldwide, Kuala Lumpur was expected to be the most affordable for students in 2022 (Lane, 2021). The factors considered in measuring the affordability index were HEI tuition fees, costs of living and the Big Mac index.[2]

Gurubatham and Williams (2021) say that about 97% of private HEIs would experience losses in 2021, and 51% of those would face the risk of shutting down. Therefore, it is imperative for private HEIs in Malaysia to adopt the

[2] Invented by *The Economist* magazine, the Big Mac index is a measure of comparing the purchasing power parity between different countries. By converting the local price of a Big Mac to US dollars, one can informally compare the price levels of the same burger (goods) between different locations.

cost leadership strategy to remain viable. Drawing from Gurubatham and Williams (2021), conducting online education and hybrid learning may be the way forward, as many Malaysian HEIs have some experience in offering remote and online learning. Whether the marginal costs are almost zero with this new mechanism needs further study among these HEIs. Given the reputation of Malaysia as an attractive location for higher education, private HEIs can easily rebound and attract international enrolment if they adopt a low-cost business model.

POST-PANDEMIC HIGHER EDUCATION: MALAYSIA AND ASEAN

What does Malaysia's higher education sector recovery mean for the region, especially ASEAN? ASEAN cooperation in areas other than trade and political security is underdeveloped. Heng (2020) notes that the ASEAN Political, Economic and Social Community Blueprint envisioned a regional community by 2025, but this is progressing slowly because of old and new challenges. Lee and Fukunaga (2013) argue that ASEAN's idea of regional cooperation is in security matters, but competition in others was, and still is, a major item that needs serious attention.

When the pandemic began, the ASEAN secretariat issued a work plan called the ASEAN Comprehensive Recovery Framework (ACRF). According to ASEAN (2020), the framework was adopted at the 37th ASEAN Summit in November 2020. A review of this document revealed nothing specific to higher education and ASEAN's vision to accelerate its recovery. Enhancing digitisation is generally mentioned, but a concrete mechanism to undertake such an initiative is nowhere to be found. The Fifth ASEAN Plus Three Education Ministers Meeting held on 1 October 2021 reaffirmed ACRF, but again, no concrete programme was considered for stronger cooperation in higher education.

The ASEAN Work Plan on Education 2021–2025 was adopted at the ASEAN Education Ministers Meeting in May 2021. McDermott (2021) rightly observes that the higher education components in the communiqué touched on harmonisation of lifelong learning provision and strengthening ASEAN's capacity through strategies, mechanisms and scholarship provisions.

However, no concrete initiatives were introduced or mentioned to address the sector's recovery. In the post-pandemic period, ASEAN should leverage the European Union's experience in its higher education harmonisation and integration. The joint effort of ASEAN-SHARE should now be channelled towards member countries that need technical expertise in crafting and designing a post-pandemic future for higher education.

ASEAN, as a regional institution, needs rethinking, especially in the area of higher education development. One of the most effective strategies to accelerate greater connectivity and integration is the higher education sector. ASEAN has developed many strong HEIs, with Malaysia, Singapore, the Philippines, Thailand and Indonesia emerging as educational hubs. Each of these country hubs operates independently to attract international students. There are opportunities to coordinate efforts to create a much-expanded ASEAN education hub in line with the region's higher education space objective. ASEAN is presented with a unique opportunity to reset such an agenda. Leveraging on member states' experiences, a renewed focus should be on higher education recovery work. Member states' experiences in accelerating digitisation could be a focal point for immediate deliberation. Making ASEAN a cost-competitive educational hub with ease of regional mobility should be seriously explored. A platform for synergy-building should be set up for greater collaboration and cooperation. An ASEAN new model for shared governance propelled by technology and collaboration could pave the way for better governance systems of regional universities. On internationalisation of higher education, ASEAN could start with more commitment among member states towards the harmonisation of higher education initiatives, allowing hybrid programmes and greater mobility within ASEAN. The framework and mechanism for this harmonisation are already in place; implementation on a full scale will ultimately unveil strengths and limitations.

Are the recovery and resetting of higher education based on the propositions for Malaysia possible in the ASEAN context? The answer lies with ASEAN leadership. With the resources at their disposal, ASEAN leaders could have the potential to make integration central to ASEAN's identity, success and focus. Arguably, ASEAN's post-pandemic recovery is ideally manifested in all sectors, not just economics and trade. Therefore, the higher education sector's recovery should be ASEAN's top priority. The future of higher education in ASEAN is highly dependent on its constituent membership, comprising more sophisticated higher education systems as a catalytic agent for the regional system. In this respect, Malaysia's recovery plan should not be designed in isolation from ASEAN's future higher education trajectory. For now, it is more about the recovery plans of ASEAN's member states to provide the impetus for ASEAN's sectoral recovery.

CONCLUSION

The pandemic has laid bare the structural weaknesses of Malaysia's higher education system in coping with disruptive impacts. Malaysia has to recalibrate and chart a new higher education development trajectory in the post-COVID-19 era. However, this cannot be done in isolation. The future of Malaysia's higher education is inevitably linked to ASEAN's future, especially with respect to: (1) mobility of students, researchers and academic programmes, (2) collaboration and cooperation in academic matters, and (3) prioritisation of higher education in the ASEAN agenda. ASEAN member countries should prioritise the recalibration and resetting of higher education systems and institutions post-pandemic. The focus areas identified for the reset are also relevant and should be considered in developing higher education systems in ASEAN. For the recovery plan, a concrete programme and action plans are needed to build stronger cooperation. Admittedly, there are lessons learnt in the context of coexistence and collaboration post-pandemic. Above all, in the context of ASEAN's future higher education landscape, there must be an acceptable level of preparedness for future disruptions at the regional level.

REFERENCES

Abd Rahim, M. E., & Abd Rahim, E. M. (2021). Redefining digital divide in Malaysian higher education: The case of COVID-19. *E-Proceedings of International Conference on Language, Education, Humanities & Social Sciences (i-LEdHS2021)*, 369–373. https://ir.uitm.edu.my/id/eprint/44921

Abdullah, D., & Fernandez-Chung, R. M. (2021, June 16). Can the Malaysian higher education system survive without international students? *Astro Awani.* https://www.astroawani.com/berita-malaysia/can-malaysian-higher-education-system-survive-out-international-students-303509

Abdullah, D., Wan, C. D., & Morshidi, S. (2022). International students in Malaysian higher education. In H. de Wit, E. Minaeva, & L. Wang (Eds.), *International student recruitment and mobility in non-anglophone countries theories, themes, and patterns* (pp. 237–254). Routledge.

Ahern, S., & Loh, E. (2020). Leadership during the COVID-19 pandemic: Building and sustaining trust in times of uncertainty. *BMJ Leader, 5*(4), 266–269. https://bmjleader.bmj.com/content/5/4/266

Ahmad, N. (2021, October 4). Honouring higher education educators. *The Star.* https://www.thestar.com.my/news/nation/2021/10/04/a-heartfelt-thank-you-to-higher-education-educators-on-academia-day

Association of Southeast Asian Nations (ASEAN). (2020). *ASEAN comprehensive recovery framework.* Association of Southeast Asian Nations. https://asean.org/book/asean-comprehensive-recovery-framework

Azman, N. H. (2021, May 17). Private universities, colleges risk permanent closure. *The Malaysian Reserve.* https://themalaysianreserve.com/2021/05/17/private-universities-colleges-risk-permanent-closure

Azman, N., & Abdullah, D. (2021). A critical analysis of Malaysian higher education institutions' response towards COVID-19: Sustaining academic program delivery. *Journal of Sustainability Science and Management, 16*(1), 70–96.

Bergan, S., Gallagher, T., Harkavy, I., Munck, R., & van't Land, H. (Eds.). (2021). *Higher education's response to the COVID-19 pandemic: Building a more sustainable and democratic future* (pp. 233–240). Council of Europe. https://www.dcu.ie/sites/default/files/inline-files/prems-006821-eng-2508-higher-education-series-no-25.pdf

Choong, P. Y. (2020, May 8). COVID-19: Impact on the tertiary education sector in Malaysia. *Penang Institute.* https://penanginstitute.org/publications/covid-19-crisis-assessments/covid-19-impact-on-the-tertiary-education-sector-in-malaysia

deWit, H., &, Altbach, P. G. (2022). The impact of COVID-19 on the internationalisation of higher education, revolutionary or not? In C. R. Kumar, M. Mukherjee, T. Belousova, & N. Nair (Eds.), Global higher education during and beyond COVID-19 (pp. 219–231). Springer. https://doi.org/10.1007/978-981-16-9049-5_18

de Wit, H., & Marinori, G. (2020). Internationalisation of higher education in a post-COVID-19 world: Overcoming challenges and maximising opportunities. In S. Bergan, T. Gallagher, I. Harkavy, R. Munck, & H. van't Land (Eds.), *Higher education's response to the COVID-19 pandemic: Building a more sustainable and democratic future* (pp. 233–240). Council of Europe. https://www.dcu.ie/sites/default/files/inline-files/prems-006821-eng-2508-higher-education-series-no-25.pdf

Department of Statistics Malaysia. (2021, July 27). *Graduate statistics 2020* [Press release]. https://www.dosm.gov.my/v1/index.php?r=column/cthemeByCat&cat=476&bul_id=U1ltVWpwNXRNRUR2NlhRSHZmenRMUT09&menu_id=Tm8zcnRjdVRNWWlpWjRlbmtlaDk1UT09

Diamond, R. M. (2006, September 7). Why colleges are so hard to change. *Inside Higher Ed.* https://www.insidehighered.com/views/2006/09/08/why-colleges-are-so-hard-change

Economic Planning Unit, Prime Minister's Department. (2021). *Malaysia digital economy blueprint.* https://www.epu.gov.my/sites/default/files/2021-02/malaysia-digital-economy-blueprint.pdf

Education Malaysia Global Services. (2022). *Malaysia higher education in brief.* https://educationmalaysia.gov.my/malaysia-higher-education-in-brief

Else, H. (2016, November 7). Malaysia cuts public university funding: Academic says budgeting measures will hit research hardest. *Times Higher Education.* https://www.timeshighereducation.com/news/malaysia-cuts-public-university-funding

Gurubatham, M. R., & Williams, G. (2021, April 17). The future is hybrid learning focusing on value added. *University World News.* https://www.universityworldnews.com/post.php?story=20210416140633392

Heng, K. (2020). ASEAN's challenges and the way forward: As the grouping turns 53, it faces old and new challenges, both internal and external. *The Diplomat.* https://thediplomat.com/2020/08/aseans-challenges-and-the-way-forward

Imrie, B. (2020, June 21). Changing international student mobility patterns an advantage. *The Star.* https://www.thestar.com.my/news/education/2020/06/21/changing-international-student-mobility-patterns-an-advantage

Indeed Editorial Team. (2021, September 4). What is cost leadership strategy? *Indeed.* https://www.indeed.com/career-advice/career-development/create-cost-leadership-strategy

Jensen, T., Marinori, G., & van't Land, H. (2022). *Higher education one year into the COVID-19 pandemic: Second IAU global survey report.* International Association of Universities. https://www.iau-aiu.net/IMG/pdf/2022_iau_global_survey_report.pdf

Kaul, V., Shah, V. H., & El-Serag, H. (2020). Leadership during crisis: Lessons and applications from the COVID-19 pandemic. *Gastroenterology, 159*(3), 809–812. https://doi.org/10.1053/j.gastro.2020.04.076

Lane, C. (2021, March 30). 10 most affordable cities for students in 2019. *QS Top Universities.* https://www.topuniversities.com/university-rankings-articles/qs-best-student-cities/10-most-affordable-cities-students-2019

Lau, J. (2020, December 1). Malaysian universities given funds to 'weather the pandemic'. *Times Higher Education.* https://www.timeshighereducation.com/news/malaysian-universities-given-funds-weather-thepandemic

Lee, C., & Fukunaga, Y. (2013). ASEAN regional cooperation on competition policy. *Economic Research Institute for ASEAN and East Asia Discussion Paper Series.* https://www.eria.org/ERIA-DP-2013-03.pdf

Malaysian Investment Development Authority. (2021, February 8). Evolution of e-learning in the Malaysian higher education institutions. *Bernama.* https://www.bernama.com/en/thoughts/news.php?id=1928731

Malaysian Qualifications Agency (MQA). (2021). Advisory Note No. 2/2021: *Panduan pengendalian program pendidikan tinggi semasa perintah kawalan pergerakan.* https://www.mqa.gov.my/new/document/2021/publications/Advisory%20Note%20Panduan%20Pengendalian%20Program%20PKP2.0_8.2.2021.pdf

McDermott, D. J. (2021, August 28). Catalysing development of an ASEAN higher education space. *University World News.* https://www.universityworldnews.com/post.php?story=20210824155030216

Menon, S., & Rajaendram, R. (2021, September 19). Breathing life back into higher education. *The Star.* https://www.thestar.com.my/news/education/2021/09/19/breathing-life-back-into-higher-education

Ministry of Education. (2020). *Way forward for private higher education institutions: Education as an industry.* Department of Higher Education. https://jpt.mohe.gov.my/portal/index.php/ms/penerbitan/74-way-forward-for-private-higher-education-institution-education-as-an-industry-2020-2025

Ministry of Higher Education. (2021). *Malaysian Research and Education Network* (MyREN). https://www.mohe.gov.my/en/services/research/myren

Netto, A. (2017, July 14). Universities do not have genuine autonomy, report says. *University World News*. https://www.universityworldnews.com/post.php?story=2017071415573087

SaLemi, L. (2018, October 28). 85% of jobs that will exist in 2030 haven't been invented yet. *LinkedIn*. https://www.linkedin.com/pulse/85-jobs-exist-2030-havent-been-invented-yet-leo-salemi

Saseendran, S. (2021, September 11). UAE green visa, freelancer visa, golden visa: What we know about the new visa schemes so far. *Gulf News*. https://gulfnews.com/uae/uae-green-visa-freelancer-visa-golden-visa-what-we-know-about-the-new-visa-schemes-so-far-1.82137981

Selingo, J. J., Clark, C., Noone, D., & Wittmayer, A. (2021). The hybrid campus: Three major shifts for the post-COVID university. *The Deloitte Center for Higher Education Excellence*. https://www2.deloitte.com/us/en/insights/industry/public-sector/post-pandemic-hybrid-learning.html

Sharma, Y. (2020, December 2). Private universities at risk as foreign students stay away. *University World News*. https://www.universityworldnews.com/post.php?story=2020120216283461

Sirat, M. (2017). ASEAN's flagship universities and regional integration initiatives. *Higher Education Evaluation and Development, 11*(2), 68–80. https://www.emerald.com/insight/content/doi/10.1108/HEED-07-2017-0004/full/pdf?title=aseans-flagship-universities-and-regional-integration-initiativeshttps://doi: 10.1108/HEED-07-2017-0004

Sirat, M., & Ahmad, A. R. (2021). Malaysia's higher education: Tumbled out of its trajectory? *Higher Education in Southeast Asia and Beyond* (Issue 10). https://headfoundation.org/2021/04/06/hesb-issue-10

Sirat, M., Ahmad, A. R., & Azman, N. (2012). University leadership in crisis: The need for effective leadership positioning in Malaysia. *High Education Policy, 25*(4), 511–529. https://doi.org/10.1057/hep.2012.10

StudyMalaysia.com. (2020, July 3). The cost of higher education in Malaysia. *StudyMalaysia.com*. https://www.studymalaysia.com/education/top-stories/the-cost-of-higher-education-in-malaysia

Sulong, N. (2021). *A phenomenological study on international students' withdrawal from Malaysian higher education institutions to universities in the Turkish Republic of Northern Cyprus* [Doctoral thesis]. Universiti Teknologi Malaysia.

The Head Foundation (2021). State of the region: The commemorative 10th issue. *Higher Education in Southeast Asia and Beyond* (Issue 10).

Wan, C. D., & Abdullah, D. (2021). Internationalisation of Malaysian higher education: Policies, practices and the SDGs. *International Journal of Comparative Education and Development, 23*(3), 212–226. https://doi.org/10.1108/IJCED-08-2020-0052

Wan, C. D., Chapman, D. W., Md Zain, A. N., Hutcheson, S., Lee, M., & Austin, A. E. (2015). Academic culture in Malaysia: Sources of satisfaction and frustration. *Asia Pacific Education Review, 16*(4), 517–526. https://doi.org/10.1007/s12564-015-9398-1

Wan, C. D., Lee, M. N. N., & Loke, H. Y. (Eds.). (2019). *The governance and management of universities in Asia global influences and local responses.* Routledge.

World Bank Group. (2020). *COVID-19 impact on tertiary education in East Asia and Pacific.* The World Bank. https://documents1.worldbank.org/curated/en/506241590701178057/COVID-19-Impact-on-Tertiary-Education-in-East-Asia-and-Pacific.pdf

Chapter 3

Bridging the Higher Education Divide in Southeast Asia Through Open, Flexible and Distance eLearning (OFDeL): Now And Beyond 2030

Melinda dela Peña Bandalaria*

ABSTRACT

Higher education is considered a catalyst in accelerating the economic, political and sociocultural development agenda of the Association of Southeast Asian Nations (ASEAN). However, despite enabling mechanisms in some ASEAN countries, like financial assistance and scholarship grants to needy students, the level of access to tertiary education is still low, as evidenced by the school enrolment rate (SER) in the 10 ASEAN countries. Barriers to access include poverty or lack of financial means to cover the cost of higher education, discrimination of marginalised groups/sectors, student mobility, and physical access to tertiary-level institutions offering quality degree programmes. Open, flexible and distance eLearning (OFDeL), the mode of education system adopted by most open universities, is presented as a mechanism to address the higher education divide in the ASEAN region.

Keywords Distance education, higher education, online learning, open flexible distance e-learning, SoutheastAsia

* University of the Philippines Open University, the Philippines

INTRODUCTION

The importance of equitable access for all students on the basis of capacity (Article 2 of the First Protocol to the European Convention on Human Rights) to higher education in the Southeast Asian region is contained in the Kuala Lumpur Declaration, which the Association of Southeast Asian Nations (ASEAN) leaders signed in 2015. The declaration cites higher education as one of the catalysts in accelerating the region's economic, political and sociocultural development agenda (Lau, 2021). For ASEAN countries, "education is core to development and contributes to the enhancement of the [region's] competitiveness" (United Nations Educational, Scientific and Cultural Organisation [UNESCO] Bangkok, 2014, p. 1).

The 10 member countries of the ASEAN, consisting of Brunei Darussalam, Cambodia, Indonesia, Lao PDR, Malaysia, Myanmar, the Philippines, Singapore, Thailand and Vietnam, have a combined population of more than 679 million, with an average age of 29 (Worldometer, 2022) and with Indonesia accounting for the highest population and Brunei Darussalam with the lowest. The ASEAN population accounts for 8.58% of the world population, about 50% of which are in urban areas (Worldometer, 2022). ASEAN is also home to 1 in 11 of the world's 15–24-year-olds (Lau, 2021), the age range which includes the years that should be spent enrolled in higher education, implying that access to higher education in the ASEAN countries can significantly impact world data.

While it can be noted that "all ASEAN countries have provision for free and compulsory basic education covering at least nine years, such does not extend into tertiary years" (Southeast Asian Ministers of Education Organisation Regional Centre for Community Education Development [SEAMEO RCCED], 2019, p. 13). In fact, despite having about 20 million students in higher education, the enrolment rate averages only 40% across the region (Lau, 2021), implying that the cost associated with higher education is a major barrier to access. Hence, countries with a relatively higher incidence of poverty also show low enrolment figures at the tertiary education level. The other important component which should be considered in articulating access to higher education is the quality of available higher education programmes, which differs significantly across ASEAN countries (SEAMEO RCCED, 2019). It should be noted that quality education has been emphasised in the articulation of the United Nations Sustainable Development Goals, specifically Goal 4. The increase in student mobility due to the relatively freer manpower flow across ASEAN countries is an emerging issue at the higher education level. This is due to a lack of harmonisation in the course credits across higher education institutions (HEIs) in ASEAN countries. Vieira et al. (2020) also cite discrimination as another barrier to access, which people with physical disabilities experience. The discrimination can be in the form of a lack of access ramps in buildings and non-integration of the universal design for learning features in the teaching-learning process.

Considering the critical role of education in the region, this chapter examines the general picture of access to higher education in the countries in Southeast Asia, the factors affecting access to higher education, and the mechanisms by which OFDeL can bridge the higher education divide in the region. Timor Leste has been included in the discussion, although its membership in ASEAN has yet to be officially approved. Timor Leste's inclusion has been deemed necessary to provide a more or less accurate picture of higher education in Southeast Asia.

ACCESS TO HIGHER EDUCATION IN ASEAN MEMBER STATES

ASEAN has adopted Katarina Tomasevski's 4As Framework as a mechanism to promote access to tertiary education, which covers educational Availability, Accessibility, Acceptability and Adaptability (SEAMEO RCCED, 2019). Availability refers to sufficient educational institutions and programmes that include free education; Accessibility means no discrimination over gender, disability and other equity markers such as socioeconomic status and first in the family to participate in higher education, so as to facilitate inclusion of the most marginalised groups in education, implying the removal of financial barriers such as fees and schooling via distance; Acceptability pertains to the relevance and quality of education; and Adaptability considers the students' needs, the local context and the changing needs of society.

During 2000–2018, there has been an increase in enrolment in higher education in the region (UNESCO, 2020; SEAMEO RCCED, 2019). The overall increase in tertiary-level enrolment can be attributed to several factors, including economic development (UNESCO, 2020), a rise in middle-class aspirations (UNESCO, 2020) and the values attached to education among Asians (Breitenstein, 2013), the growth of private institutions (UNESCO, 2020), multiple pathways to access tertiary education and provision of financial support systems to address socioeconomic disparities (SEAMEO RCCED, 2019), and the growth of distance education institutions (UNESCO, 2020).

Participation in higher education can be considered an offshoot of the need for more skills and higher productivity, one measure of which is a country's Gross Domestic Product (GDP). A well-established relationship between GDP growth and higher education enrolment, as seen in Table 3.1, has been observed especially in emerging economies with a GDP per capita below USD10,000 (Lau, 2021). This is where countries in Southeast Asia can be classified, with the exception of Singapore (59,790), Brunei Darussalam (26,060) and, to some extent, Malaysia (10,230) (Table 3.1). The increase in higher education participation can also be considered one manifestation of the projection that the 21st century will be the Asian Century (ICEF Monitor, 2015).

Table 3.1 Tertiary school enrolment ratio (SER) and gross domestic product (GDP) per capita of the Association of Southeast Asian Nations (ASEAN) member countries

Country	Tertiary SER	GDP per Capita (Current Prices) 2020
Brunei Darussalam	32% (2020)	26,060
Cambodia	15% (2019)	1,610
Indonesia	36% (2018)	3,920
Lao PDR	13% (2020)	2,590
Malaysia	43% (2019)	10,230
Myanmar	19% (2018)	1,530
The Philippines	35% (2017)	3,320
Singapore	91% (2019)	59,790
Thailand	49% (2016)	7,190
Vietnam	29% (2019)	3,520
Timor Leste	18% (2010)	1,350

Source: United Nations Educational, Scientific and Cultural Organisation (UNESCO) Institute for Statistics (2022)

The increase in the level of tertiary education participation can also be attributed to the increase in the number of people in the middle class in ASEAN countries, which has resulted in the people's increased ability to provide tertiary education for their children to maintain or even further improve the family's financial status. This is very much related to Breitenstein's (2013) observation that education drives social mobility and is the only path to success, implying economic improvement; hence, Asian youths' purpose of studying is usually driven by the demands of their parents.

The high value placed on education is very much reflected in ASEAN countries, which has contributed to the increasing demand for higher education and the continued increase in population, especially those in the middle class.

From 1965 to 2000, the Gross Enrolment Ratios at the tertiary level in 10 ASEAN countries significantly increased (Table 3.2), indicating the expansion and increased participation rate in higher education. This trend is expected to continue, given the projection that 65% of the population in Southeast Asia will be in the middle class by 2030, with 60% of this group being under the age of 35 (United Overseas Bank FDI Advisory, 2021) and who will demand higher education opportunities. Martinus (2022) even projects that domestic

Table 3.2 Gross enrolment ratios at the tertiary education level in ASEAN member countries (1965–2000)

Country	1965	1975	1985	1995	2000
Brunei	N/A	N/A	N/A	7%	14%
Cambodia	N/A	N/A	N/A	2%	3%
Indonesia	3%	2%	7%	11%	N/A
Lao PDR	N/A	N/A	N/A	2%	3%
Malaysia	2%	3%	6%	11%	23%
Myanmar	1%	2%	N/A	6%	8%
The Philippines	19%	18%	38%	30%	30%
Singapore	10%	9%	12%	34%	N/A
Thailand	2%	4%	20%	20%	32%
Vietnam	N/A	N/A	N/A	4%	10%

Source: Adopted from UNESCO Bangkok (2006)

universities might not expand quickly enough to accommodate the increasing demand for quality higher education, which has become the impetus for many foreign academic institutions to establish their presence in ASEAN countries.

This expansion in participation in higher education can also be the result of the resources allocated by the ASEAN governments. This is in recognition of the key role of education in the region, which is placed at the core of development and as a major contributor to the enhancement of ASEAN competitiveness (UNESCO Bangkok, 2014).

Access to higher education in the ASEAN region has also been facilitated by the establishment of private HEIs, which have increased considerably as private sector investment has been favourably supported by the Private Education Act and decrees or laws. In Malaysia, for instance, a key policy to increase accessibility has been to support the formation of private tertiary institutions (SEAMEO RCCED, 2019). Hence, from 2010–2017, most ASEAN countries showed an increase in the number of private HEIs, as shown in Table 3.3, which has played a significant role in the development of the higher education system in the region.

Table 3.3 Number of private higher education institutions (HEIs) in ASEAN member countries

ASEAN Member Country	2010–2012	2015–2017	% Increase	% of Private HEIs in the country
Brunei	6	6	0	50%
Cambodia	46	72	56%	57%
Indonesia	2813	2431	(14%)	97%
Lao PDR	31	83	168%	49%
Malaysia	500	599	19.8%	97%
Myanmar	0	35	35%	17%
The Philippines	1,636	1,712	5%	88%
Singapore	47	30	(36%)	77%
Thailand	73	455	523%	87%
Vietnam	29	305	952%	83%
Timor Leste	N/A	N/A	N/A	N/A

Source: Welch (2021)

Except for Indonesia and Singapore, the number of private HEIs in all ASEAN countries increased during the period 2010–2017, with the highest percentage increase being in Vietnam. This can also be considered indicative of the rise of the middle class and their consequent capacity to provide for their children's private education. Except for Myanmar (17%) and Lao PDR (49%), private HEIs in all ASEAN countries account for more than 50% of the HEIs in each country, accounting for 97% in Indonesia and Malaysia.

In Cambodia, the increase in private and state-owned universities has transformed higher education in the country over the last 10 years because it has expanded the opportunities to access higher education for a larger number of students (SEAMEO RCCED, 2019). Enrolment in tertiary-level education has shown a sharp increase since 2010, especially after decades of civil war and the foreign occupation of the 1970s and 1980s. While the increase in tertiary-level enrolment and the number of private HEIs appear impressive, Cambodia still has one of the lowest enrolment ratios among ASEAN countries (see Table 3.1) (Dahles, 2017).

Another factor that has facilitated access to higher education is the provision of multiple pathways for secondary education graduates, including technical and vocational education and training graduates to continue in tertiary education (SEAMEO RCCED, 2019). These multiple pathways include bridging and continuing programmes in higher education, credit transfer and recognition of prior learning.

To facilitate the inclusion of students from low-income families and those with physical disabilities in the higher education system, financial support like scholarships, loan schemes and education funds have been made available to these groups. In Vietnam, for instance, members of ethnic and socioeconomically disadvantaged groups are provided with special measures such as grants, exemptions and subsidies to enable them to study for post-secondary education. The exact financial support mechanism is also available in Lao PDR, Myanmar, and Malaysia (SEAMEO RCCED, 2019). In the Philippines, the Universal Access to Quality Tertiary Education (Republic Act 10931) has been implemented since 2018, which provides free tuition for all students enrolled in government or state-funded colleges and universities

(Republic of the Philippines, 2014). Indonesia and Thailand, on the other hand, both have enabling policies to assist persons with disabilities to access tertiary education, with many universities participating in the initiative (Akmal, 2017).

The establishment of distance education institutions in ASEAN countries also contributed to increased participation in higher education. In the 11 member countries, Timor Leste included, there are 11 open universities whose primary mode of instruction is distance education (Table 3.4), which does not require students to come to the physical campus to complete their degree programmes. Thailand was the first to establish open universities: two were established during the 1970s, while Malaysia has the two youngest open universities, established in 2000 and later. Most open universities in ASEAN countries were established during the 1990s. It can be noted that these open universities accounted for 12.28% of the total enrolment in higher education in the ASEAN region during the period 2018–2020, and most probably account for the difference in the gross enrolment ratio and school enrolment ratio of a country.

UNPACKING ACCESS TO HIGHER EDUCATION

Despite the observed increase in participation in higher education, it is important to unpack what access to education, especially higher education, exactly constitutes. Admission to a formal degree programme at the tertiary level is the common definition of access; however, it should be noted that admission is not enough. As defined in the Glossary of Education Reform (The Great Schools Partnership, 2014), access:

> refers to the ways in which educational institutions and policies ensure—or at least strive to ensure—that students have equal and equitable opportunities by providing additional services or removing any actual or potential barriers that might prevent some students from participating in certain courses or programmes. (para. 1)

Some of these services include access to assistive technologies, equal opportunities to participate in educational programmes and activities, accommodations, Internet connection and so on, which are essential for students to continue being part of the programme. Hence, in addition

Table 3.4 Percentage of open university (OU) enrolment to total higher education (HE) enrolment in ASEAN countries and contribution to access to tertiary education, as implied in the country's gross enrolment and SERs

ASEAN Member Country	Number of OUs	Date Established	Percentage of OU Enrolment to Total HE Enrolment	Gross Enrolment Ratio	Tertiary SER
Brunei	0	N/A	N/A	32 (2020)	32 (2020)
Cambodia	0	N/A	N/A	13.09 (2015) 222,880 (2019)	15 (2019)
Indonesia	1	1984	8.3% (2020)	36.3 (2018)	36 (2018)
Lao PDR	0	N/A	N/A	16.91 (2015) 101,340 (2019)	13 (2020)
Malaysia	2	2000 (OU Malaysia) 2006 (Wawasan OU)	1.1% (2018)	43.1 (2019)	43 (2019)
Myanmar	2	1992 (Yangon University of Distance Education) 2000 (Mandalay University of Distance Education)	0.009%	13.53 (2012)	19 (2018)
The Philippines	2	1995 (University of the Philippines OU) 1990 (The Polytechnic University of the Philippines OU)	0.01% (2020)	35.5 (2017)	35 (2017)
Singapore	0	N/A	N/A	88.89 (2018)	91 (2019)
Thailand	2	1978 (Sukhothai Thammathirat OU) 1971 (Ramkhamhaeng University)	2.4% (2018)	49.3 (2016)	49 (2016)
Vietnam	2	1990 (Hanoi OU) 1990 (Ho Chi Minh OU)	0.47% (2018)	28.6 (2019)	29 (2019)
Timor Leste	0	N/A		18.15 (2010)	18 (2010)

***Sources:** The Global Economy (2019), UNESCO Institute for Statistics (2022) and Statista (n.d.)*

Note: Data for Singapore is for tertiary school enrolment, which is the number of students in tertiary-level education as a percentage of all people who have finished secondary school in the last five years. This is vis-à-vis gross enrolment ratio, which is the ratio of total enrolment, regardless of age, to the population of the age group that officially corresponds to the level of education.

to enrolment statistics, access to higher education should also look into graduation or programme completion rates. For the United Nations Educational, Scientific and Cultural Organisation, countries need to pay attention to drop-out rates (which measure the process) and graduation rates (which measure the outcome of their efforts) instead of merely looking into high enrolment rates (Vieira et al., 2020).

As can be noted from Table 3.1, SER in ASEAN countries can be clustered into four groups: (1) High, as in the case of Singapore with 91% SER, (2) Medium-High for Thailand and Malaysia, (3) Medium-Low for Indonesia, the Philippines and Brunei, and Vietnam, and (4) Low for Cambodia, Lao PDR, Myanmar and Timor Leste. It can be noted that this classification or grouping can correspond to the country's GDP and economic classification as follows: Singapore has been classified by the Asian Development Bank (2011) as a high-income economy; Indonesia, Malaysia, Thailand, and the Philippines as middle-income economies; and Cambodia, Lao PDR and Vietnam as low-income economies. Based on the GDPs, Myanmar and Timor Leste can also be considered low-income economies, while Brunei, considering the unique features of the country, may not fall into any classification.

Especially for Brunei, despite the high GDP of the country (29,060), its SER is only 32%, which is lower than that for Indonesia, Malaysia, the Philippines and Thailand, which have much lower GDPs. This is likely attributed to the number of programmes that students can choose from in the seven HEIs in the country and the financial capability of well-to-do families to send their children to study in universities outside the country that offer more degree programmes. This number is usually not reflected in the SER data of a country, as these are usually collected by the country's Ministry of Education in annual school censuses and compiled in education monitoring information systems (Baker & Halabi, 2014).

From these data, one can infer that access to higher education is a complex phenomenon and cannot be explained by one factor alone. In addition to poverty, other observed factors that prevent access to higher education are crises and emergencies, institutional barriers (high tuition fees and exclusive entrance examinations), geographic mobility and discrimination (Lau, 2021).

As indicated in Table 3.1, the poorer countries/economies or those with low GDP also have lower SER, as exemplified by Lao PDR, Cambodia, Myanmar and Timor Leste. Poverty is one of the reasons people do not participate in higher education, as families cannot afford to send their children to universities. Instead, some of them may have to work to support their families. Tertiary-education age level can be considered old enough to work or engage in economically productive endeavours or activities.

Crises and emergencies or peace and order conditions can also affect participation in higher education, as in the case of some ASEAN countries that have experienced such situations, like Myanmar and Timor Leste and, to some extent, the Philippines.

Institutional barriers to accessing higher education can also be considered the result or consequences of poverty. Low-income families cannot afford high tuition fees, especially those of private HEIs which dominate many ASEAN countries. During the period 2015–2017, about 88% of HEIs in ASEAN countries are private (Muftahu, 2020). In most cases, public or state-funded HEIs which offer subsidised education have competitive admission examinations because of limited places, and those who gain admittance are students with good preparation (which is also a function of being able to afford it). In Vietnam, for instance, admission to higher education is highly competitive and places great pressure on students. Due to this, entrance examination periods in the country have been dubbed "suicide seasons" due to the increasing number of student suicides after the announcement of university entrance examinations each summer. In 2012, only 30% of test takers passed the entrance exams. This system was abolished in 2015 to facilitate access to higher education (Trines, 2017).

Geographic mobility or distance from an HEI is another barrier to tertiary education participation. Almost 50% of the population in ASEAN countries are in rural areas, which can also be a function of their socioeconomic condition. In Thailand, 27% of all universities are located in Bangkok (which has 14% of the nation's population), 10% are in the northern region (where up to 18% of the population is located) and 19% are in the northeast region (which is home to 29% of Thailand's population) (Crocco, 2018).

While many ASEAN member countries provide financial support and other mechanisms to facilitate access of marginalised and disadvantaged groups to higher education, their full participation is prevented by discrimination, which affects their learning journey. Discrimination may include a lack of physical access by ramps in university buildings and, in the case of cultural minorities, limited access to the required preparations to handle university admission examinations or the necessary information about the opportunities available, such as scholarships and grants. In Cambodia, in addition to financial problems, other factors preventing high school graduates from participating in higher education include language barriers and lifestyle changes (Chhoeurm, 2021).

As pointed out, the definition of access or participation in higher education implies inclusion in programme completion or graduation. Hence, another indicator of access is the graduation or programme completion rates. Graduation, or the ability to complete a degree programme, can also be a function of the students' financial capability to participate in various academic activities and the course and programme completion requirements, which in most cases implies a cost. The lack of access to expensive learning materials, like books, can impact the students' academic performance and result in them dropping out of the course or getting out of the programme.

In Indonesia, more than 286,000 undergraduate students left college without a degree in 2014–2015. While this figure accounts for only 4.6% of the overall national enrolment, it is 20% of the total of new students admitted at the tertiary level during the corresponding year (Mulyadin, 2020).

In the Philippines, less than half of those who enter college or university reach their senior year, resulting in an average survival rate of 49%. Only three out of every five students in the fourth year of study graduate within that fourth year, resulting in an average graduation rate of 61%. The overall completion rate for the higher education system is about 30% (Philippine Business for Education, n.d.).

Singapore, for instance, consistently exhibits a high rate of graduation. In 2005, there was a total of 12,508 first-year intakes, and four years later, 11,947 graduated, registering a graduation rate of nearly 96% (Ministry of Education Singapore, 2015, as cited by Kent, 2017). Even in other higher education strands like polytechnic schools, art institutes and technical education, graduation rates were similarly high (above 90%). However, the programmes or courses of study are not all four years long. In 2011, of the 15,566 new university entrants, 15,236 graduated, representing a 98% graduation rate. During the last 10 years, Singapore observed an expansion in access to higher education without compromising graduation rates (Kent, 2017).

For underrepresented populations, Creighton (n.d.) cites several factors that can explain the low graduation rates, which are somehow related to barriers to participation. These are pre-entry attributes, goals and commitments, institutional experiences, and personal and normative integration. Pre-entry attributes refer to students' high-school rank and perceptions of their social adjustment on campus. If the students are not well prepared due to their secondary school education, the chance of dropping out of the programme is relatively high. Goals and commitment refer to students' perceptions of social support, which may facilitate an increased commitment to the institution and encourage the students to stay in the programme. Institutional experiences refer to discrimination, isolation and lack of support services, which do not positively contribute to learning and programme completion. Personal and normative integration refer to the extent to which a student is involved on campus, acclimatised to the academic culture of the institution, and connected socially to various components of the university community (i.e. faculty, administrators, student affairs professionals and peer groups) (Pascarella & Terenzini, 2005; Tinto, 1999).

In Thailand, the gross graduation ratio for tertiary education increased over the period 2001–2015, ending at 27% in 2015. Gross graduation ratio is the total number of graduates in the first degree expressed as a percentage of the total population of the age where they, theoretically, finish the most common first-degree programme (Knoema, n.d).

In Brunei, assuming a tertiary programme duration of four years, graduation rates for the 2013 and 2014 university entrants are 37.4% and 31.2%, respectively (Ministry of Education Brunei Darussalam, n.d.).

OPEN, FLEXIBLE AND DISTANCE ELEARNING TO BRIDGE THE HIGHER EDUCATION DIVIDE IN ASEAN COUNTRIES

Looking closely at both the drivers of access and the barriers to participation in higher education, an OFDeL system of education may be the strategy to bridge the higher education divide in ASEAN countries. Open education is a philosophy wherein the barriers to access and participation, like costs or tuition/school fees and admission requirements, are removed. Flexible learning, meanwhile, frees the teaching and learning process from the limitations of time, place and pace of study. On the part of the learner, flexible learning "may include choices in relation to entry and exit points, selection of learning activities, assessment tasks and educational resources in return for different kinds of credit and costs" (Naidu, 2017, p. 269); while on the part of the teacher, it can involve choices in the allocation of their time and the mode and methods of communication with learners. Distance education is the mode of instruction characterised by the physical separation between the students and the teacher and other education ecosystem elements usually found in brick-and-mortar universities. This also implies that learner support is also delivered to off-campus students. E-learning implies using modern information and communication technologies to bridge the physical distance between teachers and students and reduce the transactional distance that may be magnified by physical separation.

The following sections show the ways in which OFDeL can help bridge the education divide in higher education.

Reduction in the cost of education

Open education provides inclusive learning opportunities to various types of learners. Examples of open education initiatives are the Massive Open Online Courses (MOOCs) and open educational resources. MOOCs are free online courses available for anyone to enrol, which "provide an affordable and flexible way to learn new skills, advance your career and deliver quality educational experiences at scale" (MOOC.org, n.d., para. 1). In 2021, there were about 19,400 MOOCs that were made available by 950 universities, with 220 million students taking advantage of these open learning opportunities. One can also earn degrees and micro-credentials from MOOCs, as 70 MOOC-based degrees and 1,670 micro-credentials were offered in 2021 (Shah, 2021). Open programme is also another form of open education. It is exemplified by those offered by Open Education Resource (OER) Universitas, which assembles open online courses from OER and other open-access materials. As such, the content of the courses can be accessed for free, and learners can study ubiquitously. Students will only have to pay the assessment cost required for the certification and the award of equivalent credits.

The distance mode of delivering instruction also contributes to reducing the cost of education as students need not leave their homes and be on campus to study and get a degree. The usual costs associated with the conventional mode of instruction, like accommodation and transportation, are significantly reduced if not eliminated.

Ability to work and earn at the same time

The flexibility afforded by the OFDeL system may also allow students to work and study simultaneously. This provides them with the means to defray the cost of education, thus removing the barrier to access tertiary education. In OFDeL, students are given some degree of flexibility as to when to study the learning materials (learner-content interaction) and when to interact with teachers (learner-teacher interaction) and fellow students (learner-learner interaction) to facilitate learning. Hence, studying is done at learners' own pace, place and time, allowing them to engage in other productive activities such as working.

Discrimination prevention

Since students under the OFDeL system do not need to go to the physical campus, the possibility of being discriminated against can be avoided. Access to buildings without ramps is no longer a problem for students with disabilities, and those belonging to minority groups may not be marginalised.

Mobility of students

Since most OFDeL programmes do not require physical presence in the classroom and the education ecosystem is designed to cater to off-campus students, learners do not have to worry about transferring residence or place of work. Students can continue studying at their university remotely. OFDeL can also address the lack of harmonisation in course credits across universities since students need not transfer to another school when transferring locations.

OFDeL is a system of education usually adopted by open universities. As indicated in Table 3.3, there are 11 open universities in the ASEAN region, which can present a large potential that can be harnessed to significantly increase the level of participation in higher education in the region. This can contribute not only to the SER of the country (students in the age when they should be at the tertiary level) but also to the gross enrolment ratio, which includes the participation of those outside the regular age groups like adults or school leavers.

OFDeL can present a new business model, especially to conventional universities. The experience of doing remote teaching and learning during the Coronavirus Disease 2019 (COVID-19) pandemic may completely change the education system, such that more universities may consider offering courses and degree programmes in the flexible and distance e-learning mode of instruction. This can cater to different types of learners, including lifelong learners looking for opportunities to improve their qualifications for professional and personal advancement. In Thailand, for instance, even before the pandemic, universities were primarily concerned with competition from schools or training courses that use online learning technology (Mala, 2019). Employers may also see that graduates of an open university possess attractive attributes such as persistence, perseverance, a sense of responsibility and even independence, as these are all essential attributes for degree completion in the open university system.

CONCLUSION

ASEAN member countries consider education as essential not only for the social and economic mobility of individuals, but for the region's development and enhancement of its competitiveness. While there are drivers of access to higher education, they are not enough for the level of participation to penetrate across the socioeconomic profiles of citizens. Poverty still presents a major barrier to access and full participation in higher education, and the marginalised are still disadvantaged despite enabling strategies and policies to their benefit. This implies that the conventional higher education system is not entirely inclusive, and an innovative strategy, as in the case of OFDeL and the open university system, may be necessary. The experience in undertaking remote teaching and learning during the COVID-19 pandemic may be a trigger for OFDeL to be exclusive to open universities. It may also be a new business model even for residential campuses that consider a dual model of providing learning opportunities to different learners. This scenario may be the mechanism to bridge the higher education divide in the ASEAN region, which may not be too difficult to attain given the region's experience in the open university system spanning more than 50 years, which is just 10 years younger than what is considered to be the model of the open university system, the United Kingdom Open University. This implies the possibility of significantly increasing access to higher education in the ASEAN region.

REFERENCES

Akmal, A. (2017). Public policy and ICTs for higher education of disabled students in Indonesia. *KnE Social Sciences, 2*(4), 51–58. https://doi.org/10.18502/kss.v2i4.867

Asian Development Bank. (2011). *Higher education in dynamic Asia: Study reports.* https://www.adb.org/sites/default/files/publication/29407/higher-education-across-asia.pdf

Baker, D. P., & Halabi, S. (2014). School enrollment. In A. C. Michalos (Ed.), *Encyclopedia of quality of life and well-being research* (pp. 5695–5700). Springer. https://doi.org/10.1007/978-94-007-0753-5_2599

Breitenstein, D. (2013, August 4). Asian students carry high expectations for success. *USA Today.* https://www.usatoday.com/story/news/nation/2013/08/04/asian-students-carry-high-expectations-for- success/2615483

Chhoeurm, P. (2021, March 25). *The significance of higher education for Cambodian students.* Cambodian Education Forum. https://cefcambodia.com/2021/03/25/the-significance-of-higher-education-for-cambodian-students

Creighton, L. M. (n.d.). *Factors affecting the graduation rates of university students from underrepresented populations.* https://files.eric.ed.gov/fulltext/EJ987305.pdf

Crocco, O. S. (2018). Thai higher education: Privatization and massification. In G. Fry (Ed.), *Education in Thailand: An old elephant in search of a new mahout* (pp. 223–255). Springer. https://doi.org/10.1007/978-981-10-7857-6_9

Dahles, H. (2017). The politics of higher education in Cambodia. *International Institute for Asian Studies Newsletter*, 78. https://www.iias.asia/the-newsletter/article/politics-higher-education-cambodia

ICEF Monitor (2015, June 10). *Is Asia ready to be the next higher education superpower?* http://monitor.icef.com/2015/06/is-asia-ready-to-be-the-next-higher-education-superpower

Kent, D. C. (2017). A new educational perspective: The case of Singapore. *Penn GSE Perspectives on Urban Education, 14*(1), 1–5. https://files.eric.ed.gov/fulltext/EJ1160443.pdf

Knoema. (n.d.). *Thailand: Gross graduation ratio for tertiary education.* https://knoema.com/atlas/Thailand/topics/Education/Tertiary-Education/Gross-graduation-ratio-for-tertiary-education

Lau, J. (2021, June 24). Is South-East Asia higher education's next global hotspot? *Times Higher Education.* https://www.timeshighereducation.com/features/south-east-asia-higher-educations-next-global-hotspot

Licuanan, P. B. (2017). *The state of Philippine higher education* [Conference presentation]. Private Education Assistance Committee Conference.

Mala, D. (2019, January 4). Thai universities struggle to keep up. *Bangkok Post.* https://www.bangkokpost.com/thailand/general/1604990/thai-universities-struggle-to-keep-up

Martinus, M. (2022, April 26). ASEAN's consumers on the move: Tertiary education. *Fulcrum.* https://fulcrum.sg/aseans-consumers-on-the-move-tertiary-education

Ministry of Education Brunei Darussalam. (n.d.). *Brunei Darussalam education statistics and indicators 2014–2018.*

Ministry of Education Singapore. (2015). *Education statistics digest 2015.*

MOOC.org. (n.d.). *About MOOCs.* https://www.mooc.org

Muftahu, M. (2020). Demographic change and transition in Southeast Asia: Implications for higher education. *Universal Journal of Educational Research, 8*(2), 678–688. https://doi.org/10.13189/ujer.2020.080241

Mulyadin, T. (2020). *Student engagement and college grades in Indonesian higher education.* [Doctoral thesis, Ohio State University]. OhioLINK. https://etd.ohiolink.edu/acprod/odb_etd/etd/r/1501/10?clear=10&p10_accession_num=osu1577029456473232

Naidu, S. (2017). Editorial: How flexible is flexible learning, who is to decide and what are its implications? *Distance Education, 38*(3), 269–272. https://doi.org/10.1080/01587919.2017.1371831

Pascarella, E. T., & Terenzini, P. T. (2005). How college affects students. *A Third Decade of Research, 2,* 97–185. https://campusclimate.ucop.edu/_common/files/pdf-climate/Distance_learning_article-Pascarella_Terenzini.pdf

Philippine Business for Education. (n.d). *The state of Philippine higher education.* https://www.fnf.org.ph/downloadables/State%20of%20PH%20Higher%20Education.pdf

Republic of the Philippines. (2014, December 9). *Republic Act No. 10650.* Philippine Official Gazette. https://www.officialgazette.gov.ph/2014/12/09/republic-act-no-10650

Southeast Asian Ministers of Education Organisation Regional Centre for Community Education Development (SEAMEO RCCED). (2019). *Thematic study on right to education: Promoting of access to tertiary education in ASEAN.* ASEAN Intergovernmental Commission on Human Right. https://aichr.org/wp-content/uploads/2020/08/ASEAN-Thematic-Study-Report-on-the-Right-to-Tertiary-Education_Final_020819.pdf

Shah, D. (2021, December 1). By the numbers: MOOCs in 2021. *The Report.* https://www.classcentral.com/report/mooc-stats-2021

Statista. (n.d.). *Number of people enrolled in tertiary education in Asia-Pacific in 2019, by country (in 1,000s).* https://www.statista.com/statistics/1091404/apac-number-of-people-enrolled-in-tertiary-education-by-country

The Global Economy. (2019). *Singapore: Tertiary enrollment.* https://www.theglobaleconomy.com/Singapore/Tertiary_school_enrollment

The Great Schools Partnership. (2014). *The glossary of education reform.* https://www.edglossary.org/access

Tinto, V. (1999). Taking student retention seriously: Rethinking the first year of college. *NACADA Journal, 19*(2). https://doi.org/10.12930/0271-9517-19.2.5

Trines, S. (2017). Education in Vietnam. *WENR World Education News + Reviews.* https://wenr.wes.org/2017/11/education-in-vietnam

United Nations Educational, Scientific and Cultural Organisation (UNESCO) Bangkok. (2006). *Higher education in South-East Asia.* The UNESCO Asia and Pacific Regional Bureau for Education. https://files.eric.ed.gov/fulltext/ED494258.pdf

United Nations Educational, Scientific and Cultural Organisation (UNESCO) Bangkok. (2014). *Education systems in ASEAN + 6 countries: A comparative analysis of selected educational issues.* https://www.right-to-education.org/sites/right-to-education.org/files/resource-attachments/UNESCO_Education_Systems_in_Asia_Comparative_Analysis_2014.pdf

United Nations Educational, Scientific and Cultural Organisation (UNESCO) Institute for Statistics. (2022, October 24). *School enrollment, tertiary (% gross): South Asia, East Asia & Pacific.* The World Bank. https://data.worldbank.org/indicator/SE.TER.ENRR?locations=8S-Z4

United Overseas Bank FDI Advisory. (2021). ASEAN's rising middle class offers long-term potential. *UOB.* https://www.uobgroup.com/asean-insights/articles/aseans-rising-middle-class.page

Vieira, D., Mutize, T., & Chinchilla, J. R. (2020). *Understanding access to higher education in the last two decades.* UNESCO. https://www.iesalc.unesco.org/en/2020/12/23/understanding-access-to-higher-education-in-the-last-two-decades

Welch, A. (2021). *Private higher education in East and Southeast Asia: Growth, challenges, implications.* UNESDOC Digital Library. https://unesdoc.unesco.org/ark:/48223/pf0000380093

Worldometer. (2022, January 20). *South-Eastern Asia population (live).* https://www.worldometers.info/world-population/south-eastern-asia-population

Chapter 4

To Get Cracking: Discussing the Sustainability of Malaysia's Role as a Provider of Global Higher Education Through a Case Study of International Students

Sally Anne Param*

ABSTRACT

The number of students enrolled in higher education institutions (HEIs) outside their countries of origin has seen exponential growth. In this chapter, the role of Malaysia as one of the top study destinations in this region is premised. As a site for international student migration, Malaysia enjoys advantages on many accounts. However, this chapter intends to probe the actual experience of international students studying in the country. Complicated by the consequences of the Coronavirus Disease 2019 (COVID-19) pandemic and the urgent necessity of online learning, how do these students manage educational migration? Using a qualitative case study of seven international students from different countries, educational migration to Malaysia is explored. Based on familial choices to be here, these students face socioeconomic, cultural and physical changes that are very different from their lives back home. Navigating all these processes is part of the students' coping strategies to remain in Malaysia for the sake of higher education. The responses of the students in the study raise questions about the sustainability of international student migration in Malaysia. While only a snapshot of a much larger landscape of higher education, the micro-level issues faced by the students will eventually inform the future directions of international student migration to Malaysia.

* Sunway University, Malaysia

Keywords International, Malaysia, migration, student, sustainability

INTRODUCTION

The world is going to university. Used as the title of an article in *The Economist* (2015), the phrase highlights the phenomenon of higher education becoming internationalised. The role of higher education in today's society is much more sophisticated than the internal processes of going for classes or passing examinations. Globalisation has led to international students travelling across the miles to attend universities in other host countries and follow diverse-ranged curricula. This is part of the "emergent phenomena" in higher education today (Mulvey, 2020, p. 1).

Initially, only first-world countries or those commonly termed "Western" countries could boast of having international students (Pfaff-Czarnecka, 2020). This trend started changing when Asian universities began offering quality education at more affordable costs (Ota, 2018; Singh & Jack, 2018). Through the speed of social processes being disseminated and shared through digital mass media, the globalisation of higher education has enabled the influx of international students studying in Asian, and more specifically, Southeast Asian universities. Within Malaysia, local curricula are adapted and improved to make content broad and inclusive (Singh & Jack, 2018) or foreign programmes are franchised and custom-made to suit the local scene (Ahmad & Buchanan, 2017). These contexts enable the inclusion of international students so that they can pursue their degrees collectively with local students.

In light of these processes, this chapter contemplates the country's decision to become and maintain itself as a hub of short-term migration for international students. An article in the local newspaper questions the sustainability of local processes in attracting international students to the country (Rajaendram, 2021). In talking about policy changes and the incorporation of a new working model to replace an ineffective old one, the article uses the phrase "to get cracking"[1] to show how stakeholders need to work swiftly and

[1] The phrase is found in the first line of an article in *The Star* (Rajaendram, 2021) entitled *Policy changes, new learning model a must to attract international students, stakeholders say.*

bring change. "To get cracking" is aptly borrowed as a catchphrase in the title of this chapter, implying immediacy in the discussion of Malaysia's stance as a global provider of higher education. The rest of the chapter explores the sustainability of the nation's role in that capacity, assessed through international students' reasons for pursuing higher education locally.

Recent statistics show that Malaysia and Singapore are the only two Southeast Asian countries that have reached the Top 30 in university rankings, based on the metrics of government expenditure, investments, and research and development (Ministry of Education [MOE], 2015). Recent literature continues to quote how Malaysia has penetrated more traditional study-abroad destinations (Baas, 2019; Pfaff-Czarnecka, 2020). Despite current achievements, can Malaysia sustain its competencies to maintain the influx of international students? As a background setting, this discussion briefly touches on the readiness of the ASEAN region to understand both the context and implications of the globalisation of the knowledge economy. If international students are viewed as a sustainable commodity for the future, are there enabling "hidden" growth factors that have gone unnoticed?

This chapter delves into whether Malaysia is implementing long-lasting solutions to maintain the influx of international students. While this broad research statement frames the direction of this chapter, a small-scale qualitative study in the form of seven subjective voices of seven international students is also used. These individuals' comments on their lived experience as international students are mapped against the larger-scale discussion. The qualitative responses of this small group of students serve as a reflective check and balance to the country's larger aims and purposes of being a global provider of higher education.

LITERATURE REVIEW

Globally, the number of students enrolled in HEIs outside their countries of origin has seen exponential growth. Although the absence of recent statistics could be due to the consequences of COVID-19 on global interactions, enough recent literature indicates a burgeoning rise in student migration based on an emerging education-migration industry (Baas, 2019). Quantifiable data show that the number of students enrolled in an HEI outside their country of origin has grown from 4.5 million to 5.3 million from 2016 to 2017 (Hercog & van de Laar, 2016; Organisation for Economic Cooperation and Development, 2017). These staggering figures show that students are increasingly interested in diversifying their experience in higher education and studying abroad (Baas, 2019). This has led to an emerging industry that facilitates these students' study-abroad "mobility trajectories" (van Geel & Mazzucato, 2020, p. 120).

First-world nations were traditionally acclaimed hosts for international student migration in the past century. The traditional flow of international students had been from Asian nations to first-world countries like the United Kingdom, the United States and Australia (Mulvey, 2020; Singh et al., 2014). These countries were the staple hubs for higher education for many decades. The sudden shift in global patterns of education now highlights the prominence of Asian destinations, with students now selecting Asian universities as their preferred study location. Part of the "Rising Asia" imaginary, the "Asian academic fabric" is now growing, aided by "strongly .quantifying, market-oriented discourses" that boost "global competitiveness" and enhance "regional cooperation" (Pfaff-Czarnecka, 2020, p. 1403). Literature on international student mobility (ISM) has become so extensive that the abbreviation "ISM" is commonly used for convenience (Mulvey, 2020).

While Japan was previously the only Asian country with an influx of international students, changing tides indicate that more Asian universities are now attempting to offer foreign students a place to call home (McNamara & Ahrens, 2019). Evidence of this is found in the U21 Ranking of National Higher Education Systems (2020), where eight Asian countries are in the Top 30 list. From this index, only two nations are from Southeast Asia: Malaysia and Singapore (Universitas 21, 2020).

In Malaysia, the internationalisation of higher education is part of a regional movement to tap into globalisation and create economic revenue for the nation (Ministry of Higher Education [MOHE], 2011). Strategic alliances and networking opportunities have been promoted among regional educational institutions. In their thorough analysis of Malaysia's National Higher Education Strategic Plan 2007–2020, Munusamy and Hashim (2019) mention the influences of inter-regional cooperation such as the Asia-Europe Meeting, the Asia-Pacific Cooperation, and the Association of Southeast Asian Nations (ASEAN) in increasing the international flavour of each country's educational hub. The ASEAN University Network also promotes efforts to heighten the influx of international students to this region (Ota, 2018). By being "involved in the internationalisation agenda ... between collaborating nations and partners", educational sustainability is achieved (Munusamy & Hashim, 2019, p. 28). These scholars have enumerated four main reasons for the internationalisation of higher education—academic, political, sociocultural and financial—and claimed that the economic rationale is first in importance. While the old economy has to give way to a new model, the region has to network and collaborate with other members to sustain the income-generating industry of higher education (Tay, 2018).

Against this regional backdrop, Malaysia has seen its growth in accepting international students into local universities. In 2007, the government initiated the rationale for internationalisation in its policies, and the National Higher Education Strategic Plan was created (MOHE, 2007). That year alone, international student intake catapulted to almost 48,000 (Singh et al., 2014). Although the Ministry's 2020 projected goal was to have 200,000 international students (MOHE, 2011), the reality showed a shortfall, most likely exacerbated by the unpredicted emergence of what has been sourced as a zoonotic disease, Coronavirus Disease 2019 (COVID-19). National efforts continued nonetheless and, in 2020, records indicate that almost 96,000 international students were studying as undergraduates in Malaysia, both in government and private universities (MOHE, 2020).

Within the broader context of a burgeoning research field that examines the growing popularity of international students, this chapter aims to situate the research presented to explore the sustainability of Malaysia's role as a global higher education provider. Apart from enhancing the quality of education per se, educational *management* is needed. What are some of the factors that need to be considered in managing global higher education? Sady et al. (2019) advocate for universities to pursue a programme called Principles of Responsible Management Education, initiated by the United Nations, to gauge their level of competencies in sustaining students. Singh (2015) refers to the "need to understand the expectations of the international students" in Malaysia (p. 515). Tay (2018) recommends business plans that incorporate "safer and slicker services" (p. 206), while Ahmad and Buchanan (2017) call for "marketing practitioners and researchers" to research "the decision-making processes of international students" (p. 664). Studying the human element, such as international students' emotions, perceptions and attitudes, is also important (Ota, 2018). In the Netherlands, researchers refer to how teachers are prompt to impose negative sanctions on student absenteeism but fail to consider the emotional problems faced by migrant youths who are far from their home nations (van Geel & Mazzucato, 2020).

These are some of the macro-mezzo strategies Malaysia may need to enhance as a provider of quality higher education. In rethinking existing frameworks of sustainable practices that compete for the increase of foreign student enrolment, this chapter relies on a case study of international students. Qualitative responses from these students will help contemplate the larger issues of decision-making processes that lead to international student migration.

RESEARCH DESIGN

This chapter draws on a qualitative case study of seven international students, each from a different home nation, studying in private institutions in Kuala Lumpur, Malaysia. International students are generally considered individuals who have physically crossed an international border to enrol in education in a country other than their own (United Nations Educational, Scientific and Cultural Organisation Institute for Statistics, 2022). The students in the study were chosen randomly, each having to fulfil the criterion of being an international undergraduate student at a local private university. Each student needed to represent a different foreign nation as well. The countries represented in this research are China, Japan, the Philippines, Portugal, Sri Lanka, Indonesia and the United Arab Emirates (UAE). While students from China, Indonesia and the UAE are more commonly found in HEIs in Malaysia (Pfaff-Czarnecka, 2020), students from the other countries are not as common, thus adding a rich variance to this study. The conducted analysis of the students' views on student life in Malaysia did not differentiate the respondents by age, sex or type of study. The qualitative lens added strength to the students' detailed responses, allowing for students' attitudinal shifts or perceptions of well-being to be captured (King et al., 2019).

Each international student in this research was known to the researcher as a former student or a friend of a former student. This background of familiarity contributed positively to these students providing informed consent in being part of this research. The multiple COVID-19 lockdowns over the two years of 2020–2021 did not significantly hinder the initial stage of this research. Prior contact had already been established between the researcher and the students, and informal meet-ups had already taken place.

Despite this, the actual research process was carried out during COVID-19 lockdowns, and interviews had to be carried out via telephone calls and emails instead of face-to-face meetings. The interview questions were structured and operationalised prior to their distribution, and responses were encouraged to be open-ended and subjective. The students responded within two to three weeks, after which the responses were analysed. Two students chose to use a pseudonym in their responses, while the others maintained their actual names. The broad thematic structure was student experience, and the detailed questions dealt with students' backgrounds, why they chose to study in Malaysia, and what they liked or disliked about their experience as foreign students in a local environment. These student responses would be used to assess whether Malaysia can sustain its efficacy in increasing its international student population.

Due to the small sample size, this case study can never claim to be generalised and representative of the large population of international students. However, the data represent responses from seven different home nations that are diverse in lifestyle, language and culture. In that light, the research can claim to be a "snapshot" of foreign students' lived reality in Malaysia. This claim is indeed the strength of this qualitative piece of research, where authentic student responses captured verbatim added robustness to the validity of the data collection (King et al., 2019).

Together with interviews, the reflexivity tool of the "positioning practice" was also employed, allowing the researcher to contextualise the students' views against "broader institutionalised norms" (Alvesson et al., 2008, p. 485). This approach enabled the data to be analysed as interdependent and interconnected information within the larger context of international students' lived experiences. This is an important criterion in this study, as the students' voices were mapped against the larger structures that explored the sustainability of Malaysia's role as a global player in higher education.

FINDINGS

This section is divided into three sub-sections: (1) discussions on students' positive reasons for studying in Malaysia, (2) the challenges they face, and (3) a "hidden" factor behind their higher educational choices.

Positive reasons

Choice of major

Five students in this case study chose Malaysia due to its quality education. Chris from Indonesia said:

> I wanted to study film, and I found three universities in Malaysia that offer quality education in the study of film. I chose the one with more overall benefits.

Chris represents a growing percentage of student flow between Malaysia and Indonesia (Pfaff-Czarnecka, 2020). While proximity to his home nation and the similarity in language are the top reasons, Chris' example clearly shows that there are other factors drawing students.

Twinning options with first-world universities

Arslan from China, Ruby from Japan and Ariadne from the Philippines said they chose Malaysia as they have the option to obtain dual degrees.[2] This factor strongly echoes the findings by Ahmad and Buchanan (2017), where

[2] A "dual degree" here does not refer to two different fields, but rather to one qualification that carries a shared validity in both the host nation and the first-world country offering it—in this case, the United Kingdom.

international students chose a "branch campus" in Malaysia because the same degree programme is offered in a first-world country.

Migration

Daham from Sri Lanka chose quality education in Malaysia that would also enable him to migrate to another country:

> After studying options in all possible countries, Malaysia was the best as it allowed for both a pre-U programme and a two-year twinning degree programme for Medicine. Once I finish here, I can move on to complete the Medical degree in Australia.

These students confirmed findings from studies that refer to a higher level of quality education or specialisation field as causing student mobility. Often, studying abroad is considered a stepping stone towards future job market chances and migration to another country. A degree obtained in a host country's institution is often considered an investment towards finding a job after graduation, either in the host country or in another country (Hercog & van de Laar, 2017).

Family influence

Family is another reason why the students in this case study chose to study in Malaysia. Ariadne cited sibling influence, as she has older siblings who studied in the country and loved it. Daham chose Malaysia because both he and his parents were comfortable with the presence of the South Asian population here. Chris from Indonesia chose Malaysia because of the similarity in sociocultural elements: "It almost kinda feels like home," he said. In their research, Sundarrajh and Zulkfili (2019) also cite "external influence" as a reason international students choose to study in Malaysia, where family, friends or educational counsellors help them decide.

Other factors

Other reasons were also given by the students, although in brief. Good facilities are one of the reasons mentioned by all students, especially Patrick from Portugal. Patrick said the "state-of-the-art" facilities helped him cope better, as he compared his learning environment with his experience back home. Affordability is the other reason given by students like Chris and Fiza. Fiza from the UAE explained:

> I chose Malaysia by myself without the influence of my family ... I live in Dubai, where education is extremely expensive, so I wanted to look for cheaper options to get the same value of education.

What is observed from these findings is how the overall "package" to study locally has appealed to these international students. These student responses echo existing research that discusses contributing factors for the rise of international student traffic (Kelly et al., 2020; Mulvey, 2020; Singh & Jack, 2018). The responses also confirm that Malaysia has been positively responsive to the globalised rhetoric of a university education abroad and proved its ability to sustain its position as such. Yet, challenges also exist. These limitations may offset any significant boon previously lauded, thus questioning the host nation's ability to sustain its role.

Challenges

Sociocultural spaces

Before the students responded to the interview questions, they were informed that the research would probe into their overall well-being as international students and not just how they were faring academically. In their qualitative research on international students in a host country, van Geel and Mazzucato (2020) refer to how student well-being is "formed through interaction" with "a broader ecology composed of family, school and culture" (p. 122). In their research on the global influence of university curricula in Poland, Sady et al. (2019) find that training on intercultural skills was lacking compared to other areas. In this research, the students were questioned about their cultural interactions with locals. Ruby from Japan was happy with her experience:

> Unlike [the previous country she had studied in], there is more diversity in Malaysia, and I enjoy being exposed to the different cultures that are present.

Ruby even preferred Malaysia to her home country Japan. Ariadne from the Philippines echoed Ruby's sentiments:

> My life in Malaysia is pretty much defined by the people I am around with the most, and my Malaysian friends taught me to adapt very easily. I also share my Filipino culture with my friends, and so learning each other's culture has been positive.

However, other students in this case study did not share that positivity. Arslan, who is of mixed parentage of Pakistani and Chinese, said:

> Many people I meet on the streets don't speak good English, and sometimes communication is difficult. They are also wary of foreign students. I find this strange because I actually look like a local.

Daham's experience is similar:

> Those I study with are nice; we chat and discuss quite well in class or online. But when I visit different places (outside Kuala Lumpur), I meet people who are not friendly. They also don't speak English, so communication is difficult. I think they are not used to seeing different people in the country.

Both these students claimed that apart from their academic community, others they met were unfriendly and avoided talking to them. David felt the same, but because he recognised the symptoms of being an introvert in himself, he did not mind when people did not approach him to converse:

> Before COVID-19, I tried to cope with the lack of communication by taking a ride on the local LRTs for long hours. When I get off the train to go home, I feel better.

Chris said that while his Indonesian culture was very similar to Malaysia's, he felt that people here were not as accepting of foreigners as his people back home. Fiza shared the feeling of disconnect:

> I feel like there is definitely a sort of stigma surrounding international students that is a barrier each of us need to overcome when we come to Malaysia. I have noticed that many students are a bit hesitant to approach or talk to foreigners. This might be due to Malaysians' lack of knowledge regarding certain countries and cultures, perhaps?

Responses such as these indicate that academia alone is not what students prioritise in their lived experience in a host country. While generalised student-based narratives focus on positive outcomes like "educational progress" or "transferable skills", research shows that "interaction with local[s]" and "friendship[s]" are equally important for the personal well-being of international students (Singh & Jack, 2018, p. 618). The majority of the students in the present research sadly felt the lack of social acceptance and cross-cultural interactions.

COVID-19 lockdowns

All seven students claimed the multiple lockdowns did not hinder their academic progress. Most of them managed well and preferred the efficiency of online classes. Ruby from Japan and David from Portugal said they could re-listen to class recordings as revision, which improved their understanding. Daham said:

> In Sri Lanka, there was a digital disconnect and the timing for classes was haywire. Being here is an advantage.

Some students had to make adjustments in other ways. As a single child, Arslan admitted that "human interaction" was "the one greatest hurdle" he suffered as a lack. Chris missed the physicality of being with people, while Ariadne missed her cousin's grand wedding in the Philippines:

> Cancelling plane tickets back home and informing relatives we were not coming back was the hardest thing.

Since these adjustments are part of a global student phenomenon during the two unpredictable years of COVID-19, this othered feeling is less critical in the overall analysis of the students' well-being.

The "hidden" factor

Parents' skilled migration

Another factor why foreign students opt for Malaysia is the international careers of their parents. More than half of the world's population has shifted to new environments due to globalisation, causing new contemporary migration trends (Westendorp et al., 2021). Four international students in this case study have parents in senior employment positions in Malaysia. The expansion of the parents' companies in their home countries led to new branches or chains being set up globally, requiring their professional presence in host countries worldwide. The skilled migration of these professionals results in a demographic change in countries like Malaysia. This is becoming a common feature in modern societies where migration and a growing middle-class population go hand in hand (Van Geel & Mazzucato, 2020; Westendorp et al., 2021).

In the present case study, Arslan's mother is a financial analyst from China, Ruby's father is a manager of a Japanese manufacturing company, Ariadne's father is a civil engineer from the Philippines, and David's father is a regional manager from Portugal. While all four students cited many plus points of their choice in studying in Malaysia, the common thread they shared is that one of their parents is employed in Malaysia due to the economy back home that focuses on production, distribution or exchange. These parents are professionals in the knowledge industries, part of the global labour force of highly skilled personnel (Westendorp et al., 2021). In terms of education, skilled migration brings positive consequences to the host countries as professional parents often bring their children along. Such a phenomenon explains the temporary or semi-permanent migration of young people entering universities in destinations outside of their home nations.

This "hidden" element has sometimes gone unnoticed in the narrative of educational mobility. Recent literature has discussed student migration patterns to Europe and the Asia Pacific in the light of parental migration or students securing global professional employment for themselves (Baas, 2019; van Geel & Mazzucato, 2020). However, such data for Malaysia is still minimal. Most research on international students tends to focus on students' agency and why they choose Malaysia per se (Singh, 2015; Singh & Jack, 2018). This research, therefore, intends to shed light on the expansion of skilled migration of professional adults as the hidden factor behind some cases of international student enrolment.

This factor also shows that the students' decision-making processes are heavily shaped by their parents' choices in their work-based migratory destinations. In the proverbial allusion to "the apple does not fall far from the tree", the reference to characteristics that children emulate is more than just natural traits. In this context, what is mirrored is the unidentified inter-generational migratory pattern.

DISCUSSION

Scholars have identified fiscal reasons as the main factor why Malaysia prioritises the internationalisation of higher education (Munusamy & Hashim, 2019), and this chapter has discussed whether Malaysia can sustain its position as a robust provider. It seems that Malaysia has done well. In 2020, almost 96,000 international students were found to be studying as undergraduates in Malaysia, in both government and private universities (MOHE, 2020). If anything has made "digital responsibility" necessary, it has been the COVID-19 lockdowns and the necessity of digital learning (Tay, 2018, p. 206). Findings in this research have shown international students' satisfaction with the digital infrastructure and facilities provided by the universities they belong to. All seven students commented positively on the digitalisation of lectures and notes. Despite this praiseworthy point in the students' overall study experience, there is a questionable element to consider.

From a glimpse of the student narratives in this research, there is evidence that some students experienced feelings of being othered due to cross-cultural differences or biases. Research from other countries has shown how students can feel marginalised or ostracised by the host nation community (Ota, 2018; Sady et al., 2019; van Geel & Mazzucato, 2020). Local literature has also quoted such instances (Kelly et al., 2020; Singh & Jack, 2018). From their research, Singh and Jack (2018) find that "building [academic] competence" seems to be the only element a university focuses on to attract foreign students, when "building friendships and showing respect" need to be equally important (Singh & Jack, 2018, p. 621). Five students in the present research commented on how they felt excluded from the host society at different times and in different ways. These students claimed they were happy with their academic progress, but the lack of a common language and a sense of otherness created a social barrier. Reflexivity on the part of the researcher has helped define the emotive content across the shared responses.

If not addressed, this can result in growing dissatisfaction among international students, which can be further aggravated due to social media influence. Industry players need to be vigilant in viewing international students only as consumers, and instead attempt to increase their sense of social security.

Earlier existing research works surmise that Malaysia is not pushing hard enough to be competitive (Ahmad & Buchanan, 2017; Singh & Jack, 2018; Sundarrajh & Zulkfili, 2019) and other countries with less academic excellence but more social inclusivity may tip the balance in disfavour for Malaysia. The call for higher education leadership "to get cracking" can be alluded to in this context (Rajaendram, 2021). A "new model" to replace the old is necessary if the dissatisfaction with cross-cultural bias is not resolved. Although this may still be considered a minor issue, a delay in implementing a strategic resolution could result in the nation losing its position as an academic destination.

Another indirect area that Malaysia needs to sustain its hold on is the area of professional adult migration. Four students in the focus group have a parent who works as a professional expatriate in Kuala Lumpur. These four students also have their families living in Kuala Lumpur, while they and possibly their siblings study here. The presence of expatriates' children studying in Malaysia shapes the local educational industry, as it now has to facilitate foreign students in its structural implementation of the curricula. This shows a unique flow of experiences and changes in demography, all shaped by a chain of global economic factors.

In narrowing this discussion to the context of this chapter, it is evident that a globalised economy has shaped migratory patterns to the nation. It is safe to say that if Malaysia can sustain its open market concept, the economy can be a key driver in the sustainability of global higher education. In this research, David from Portugal chose to study in Malaysia as his father is a skilled migrant working here. Although David is still a sample who does not represent the milieu of the home countries of international students studying here, his presence in this research is proof enough of the power of the economy in drawing individuals and their families to host nations like Malaysia.

Policymakers need to recognise that the children of professionally skilled migrants can be part of the growing percentage of international students here. Government stakeholders and academics need to realise that they should work towards making higher education more feasible and conducive for the expatriate community. Research shows that professional migrant parents are known to take a deep interest in their children's education and want their children to be with them in the host country. This is now "becoming an international trend" (Ahmad & Buchanan, 2017, p. 665) and needs to be maximised. Building undergraduate opportunities for the expatriate community is an effective strategy for securing Malaysia's role as a key global higher education provider.

CONCLUSION

In tying the main strands of this chapter, Malaysia's role in sustaining global higher education has been the focus, with a case study of seven international students being used to compass that direction. While the country seems ready to manage the internationalisation of higher education, dramatically termed "Phase 4: Glory and Sustainability" (MOHE, 2007; Shariffuddin et al., 2017), reshaping cross-cultural acceptance and maintaining an open market system are pertinent areas Malaysians need to prepare for. Stakeholders, politicians, academics and everyone who is part of the nation's higher education blueprint need to reorient their executive plans as the country progresses into a globalised, urban and diverse nation. Malaysia must include sociocultural strategies to make international students feel welcomed and sustain its call for skilled migration.

Malaysia's academic space is only one aspect of national participation in the changing global environment. Shifting academic trajectories in higher education is not the only reason we need "to get cracking". This chapter also allows for a reflection on how shifting economies, the complexities of migration, and local attitudes towards cross-cultural inclusivity (or an unfortunate lack of it) should pivot and spur modernising Malaysia to make an overall adjustment towards global sustainability.

REFERENCES

Ahmad, S. Z., & Buchanan, F. R. (2017). Motivation factors in students decision to study at international branch campuses in Malaysia. *Studies in Higher Education, 42*(4), 651–668. https://doi.org/10.1080/03075079.2015.1067604

Alvesson, M., Hardy, C., & Harley, B. (2008). Reflecting on reflexivity: Reflexive textual practices in organization and management theory. *Journal of Management Studies, 45*(3), 480–501. https://doi.org/10.1111/j.1467-6486.2007.00765.x

Baas, M. (2019). The education-migration industry: International students, migration policy and the question of skills. *International Migration, 57*(3), 222–234. https://doi.org/10.1111/imig.12540

Hercog, M., & van de Laar, M. (2017). Motivations and constraints of moving abroad for Indian students. *Journal of International Migration and Integration, 18*(3), 749–770. https://doi.org/10.1007/s12134-016-0499-4

Kelly, A., Bennett, D., Giridharan, B., & Rosenwax, L. (2020). Post-degree intentions of female international undergraduate students studying in Malaysia: A qualitative study. *Journal of International Students, 10*(1), 145–158. https://doi.org/10.32674/jis.v10i1.855

King, N., Horrocks, C., & Brooks, J. (2019). *Interviews in qualitative research* (2nd ed.). SAGE Publications.

McNamara, V., & Ahrens, L. (2019). *Cambodia: Evolving quality issues in higher education international trends: Lessons from the literature.* https://www.academia.edu/11418365/Cambodia_Evolving_Quality_Issues_in_Higher_Education_International_Trends_Lessons_from_the_Literature

Ministry of Education (MOE). (2015). *Malaysia education blueprint 2015–2025 (higher education).* https://www.um.edu.my/docs/um-magazine/4-executive-summary-pppm-2015-2025.pdf

Ministry of Higher Education (MOHE). (2007). *The national higher education strategic plan beyond 2020.* https://www.ilo.org/dyn/youthpol/en/equest.fileutils.dochandle?p_uploaded_file_id=477

Ministry of Higher Education (MOHE). (2011). *Internationalisation policy for higher education Malaysia 2011.* http://eprints.utm.my/id/eprint/28548/1/Book%20-%20Internationalisation%20Policy%202011.pdf

Ministry of Higher Education (MOHE). (2020). *Statistik pendidikan tinggi 2020: Kementerian pengajian tinggi.* https://www.mohe.gov.my/muat-turun/statistik/2020/492-statistik-pendidikan-tinggi-2020-03-bab-1-makro-institusi-pendidikan-tinggi/file

Mulvey, B. (2020). "Decentring" international student mobility:The case of African student migrants in China. *Population, Space and Place, 27*(3), e2393. https://doi.org/10.1002/psp.2393

Munusamy, M. M., & Hashim, A. (2019). Internationalisation of higher education in Malaysia: Insights from higher education administrators. *AEI Insights: An International Journal of Asia-Europe Relations, 5*(1), 21–39. https://mjir.um.edu.my/index.php/AEIINSIGHTS/article/view/31647

Organisation for Economic Cooperation and Development. (2017). *Education at a glance 2017*. OECD iLibrary. https://doi.org/10.1787/eag-2017-en

Ota, H. (2018). Internalization of higher education: Global trends and Japan's challenges. *Educational Studies in Japan: International Yearbook, 12*, 91–105. https://doi.org/10.7571/esjkyoiku.12.91

Pfaff-Czarnecka, J. (2020). Shaping Asia through student mobilities. *American Behavioral Scientist, 64*(10), 1400–1414. https://doi.org/10.1177/0002764220947753

Rajaendram, R. (2021). Policy changes, new learning model a must to attract international students, stakeholders say. *The Star*, https://www.thestar.com.my/news/education/2021/11/07/policy-changes-new-learning-model-a-must-to-attract-international-students-stakeholders-say

Sady, M., Zak, A., & Rzepka, K. (2019). The role of universities in sustainability-oriented competencies development: Insights from an empirical study on Polish universities. *Administrative Sciences, 9*(3), 62. https://doi.org/10.3390/admsci9030062

Shariffuddin, S. A., Razali, J. R., Ghani, M. A., Wan Shaaidi, W. R., & Ibrahim, I. S. A. (2017). Transformation of higher education institutions in Malaysia: A review. *Journal of Global Business and Social Entrepreneurship (GBSE), 1*(2), 126–136.

Singh, J. K. N., & Jack, G. (2018). The benefits of overseas study for international postgraduate students in Malaysia. *Higher Education, 75*(4), 607–624. https://doi.org/10.1007/s10734-017-0159-4

Singh, J. K. N., Schapper, J., & Jack, G. (2014). The importance of place for international students' choice of university: A case study at a Malaysian university. *Journal of Studies in International Education, 18*(5), 463–474. https://doi.org/10.1177/1028315314523990

Singh, M. K. M. (2015). Socio-economic, environmental and personal factors in the choice of country and higher education institution for studying abroad among international students in Malaysia. *International Journal of Educational Management, 30*(4), 505–519.

Sundarrajh, S., & Zulkfili, N. (2019). Factors influencing international student decision of university selection in Malaysia. *International Journal of Education, Learning and Training, 4*(1), 11–26.

Tay, K. L. (2018). *Perspectives on social and business sustainability: Reflections and thoughts.* Partridge.

The Economist. (2015). *The world is going to university.* https://www.economist.com/leaders/2015/03/26/the-world-is-going-to-university

United Nations Educational, Scientific and Cultural Organisation Institute for Statistics. (2022). *Internationally mobile students.* https://uis.unesco.org/en/glossary-term/internationally-mobile-students

Universitas 21. (2020). *Ranking of national higher education systems 2020.* https://universitas21.com/sites/default/files/2020-04/U21_Rankings%20Report_0320_Final_LR%20Single.pdf

van Geel, J., & Mazzucato, V. (2020). Building educational resilience through transnational mobility trajectories: Young people between Ghana and the Netherlands. *YOUNG, 29*(2), 119–136. https://doi.org/10.1177/1103308820940184

Westendorp, M., Remmert, D., & Finis, K. (Eds.). (2021). *Aspirations of young adults in urban Asia.* Berghahn Books.

Chapter 5

English Language Legacies, Policy and Practice in Malaysian Educational Systems: Reverberations in Higher Education

Stephen J Hall

ABSTRACT

Language policy within the Malaysian educational system is highly centralised, yet tensions are evident in the complexity of varied community languages, the unifying use of the national language, and the advocacy of the English language as an expanding lingua franca for global business. The legacy of the past sets the scene for national language planning in Malaysia. Often, views of local identity are presented as a contest between the national language and the English language, linked to expressions of subtractive bilingualism. On an interactional level, there is widespread plurilingualism (Hall, 2018) in which speakers code-switch. Yet, this is often downplayed in educational policy and practice, while lessons may be missed from past initiatives, such as English for Teaching Mathematics and Science (ETeMS). Educationalists possibly miss opportunities for motivation through linguistic inclusivity, which could involve the multiple identities of Malaysian learners (Lee et al., 2010). Such choices involve starting from the National Philosophy of Education (NPE) (Ministry of Education [MOE], 2001, 2017) and the Malaysian Educational Blueprints (MOE, 2013, 2015) to develop educational leaders' and practitioners' sense of linguistic self. It will be suggested that one can draw on lessons from the past to develop linguistically inclusive language education in educational sectors, which feed into higher education. This overview will show how the recent history of a bilingual centralised planning change and reversal of policy reverberates through the system, inclusive of higher education, where the English language predominates. Approaches based on Malaysian research and current practices will be suggested for the post-pandemic future.

Keywords Digital literacy, languages in Malaysia, Malaysian education, pedagogy for the future, plurilingualism

INTRODUCTION

Any change to prepare future-ready university graduates in Malaysian higher education will build on developments in the Malaysian secondary system. The Malaysia Education Blueprint, which underpins educational system design, states that graduates need to have knowledge, thinking skills, leadership skills, be bilingually proficient, be ethical and spiritual, and embrace a sense of national identity (MOE, 2015). Individual creative and critical thinking skills, as described in the Blueprint, align with skills which employers see as necessary to be future ready (Bowles et al., 2019). The aspirational Blueprint—which has as 1 of the major 11 shifts, effective bilingualism—is delivered through a highly centralised system, which could be seen as more than guidance when one examines the details of the prescriptive Malaysian national primary and secondary school curricula and assessment systems (Vethamani, 2007). These systems provide the delivery framework for the majority of student learning experiences before students encounter higher education. This chapter is based on the premise that national planning and implementation of educational strategies impact the qualities that students bring to tertiary education in Malaysia and possibly in other nations with centralised education (Pandian, 2002).

It has been argued that higher education in Malaysia is shaped by centralised planning at all levels, with an underlying national philosophy and national economic plans shaping the education of students who enter higher education (Dzulkifli, 2015). Yet, questions remain as to how effective nationwide top-down planning and change are for meeting the needs of changing workplaces for global English language skills, teamwork, critical and creative thinking skills, and other transnational competencies (Pearson Learning, 2021). The challenges may be more apparent when there are major changes and policy reversals related to the importance of English and the national language of Malaysia (Bahasa Malaysia) in a multilingual and multicultural setting. One such case study illustrating challenges, and possible indicators for the challenges of change, is the major shift and later reversal of directives regarding the use of ETeMS (Mohamad Nor et al., 2011). A further example is the implementation of the Common European Framework of Reference for Languages (CEFR) (Little, 2006). This chapter examines this change process for ETeMS and CEFR, suggesting alternative approaches for embarking on language policy changes in highly centralised systems, such as that of Malaysia and its Association of Southeast Asian Nations (ASEAN) neighbours.

Malaysia's secondary schooling system has been described as highly centralised and framed within the context of the Malaysian Philosophy of Education and subsequent planning, implemented at the national, state and educational district levels (Stephen, 2013). Decisions, even at the classroom interaction level, are often couched within terms of reaching objectives, which are part of the Malaysia Education Blueprints (MOE, 2013, 2015) and linked to ranking. While teachers can control and determine what happens at the chalk front, much is determined by centralised goal setting and school leadership, creating tensions which will be described. English language teaching in the multicultural and multilingual setting of Malaysia provides a complex example of change possibilities and limitations for both macro-planners and those who nurture educational empowerment: classroom practitioners.

In order to be future ready, we consider in this chapter possibilities which build on the legacy of the ETeMS changes, the Malaysian Educational Blueprints and how these impact the future of language learning in the plurilingual (Hall, 2018) setting of diverse Malaysia. We also critically examine the process in which major policy changes for the teaching and learning of English within the subject areas of mathematics and science were introduced and then reversed. It is suggested that this period of change provides examples and approaches which need to be reviewed, should planners embark on further nationwide language developments aiming at dual language teaching and learning. This chapter uses observation and research into the challenges within the ETeMS and CEFR initiatives to argue that ownership of change at the local level remains crucial to meaningful bilingual and multilingual language empowerment. We turn to the Blueprints which underpin this highly centralised system.

THE LEGACY OF BLUEPRINTS

Understanding the state of Malaysian education and language policy begins with a consideration of the national philosophy, which underpins the Malaysia Education Blueprints and all plans for the highly centralised implementation of education, including the Dual Language Policy and the adoption of the CEFR for Malaysia, an ongoing initiative which will be described later in this chapter.

The NPE was formulated in 1988 as the philosophical guide to all educational endeavours in Malaysia. The NPE reads:

> Education in Malaysia is an ongoing effort towards further developing the potential of individuals in a holistic and integrated manner, so as to produce individuals who are intellectually, spiritually, emotionally and physically balanced and harmonious, based on a firm belief in and devotion to God. Such an effort is designed to produce Malaysian citizens who are knowledgeable and competent, who possess high moral standards, and who are responsible and capable of achieving high level of personal well-being as well as being able to contribute to the harmony and betterment of the family, the society and the nation at large. (MOE, 2008, p. ix)

Dzulkifli (2015) summarises how the NPE contains four vital aspects. The first dimension focuses on developing individual potential as a holistic person. The second dimension explicitly expounds on the balance of intellectual, spiritual, emotional and physical well-being in line with religious beliefs. In the subsequent sections, moral aspects and competencies for Malaysian citizenship are linked to individuals' capabilities in family life and Malaysian society. The first goal focuses on individual potential in a holistic way, and this links to many of the qualities which some have espoused as necessary in future-ready secondary leavers and graduates, namely individual originality and creativity (Pearson Learning, 2021). All of these aspects in the NPE intertwine in practice with learners' multiple identities, which Malaysians have as speakers of two to six languages, as this chapter will explore. The dimensions of the national philosophy underpin all subsequent plans and reports, from curriculum implementation documents to the Malaysia Education Blueprints.

The National Education Policy (MOE, 2001) principles underpinning the Blueprints are substantively aligned with more recent statements from global perspectives, with the exception of the religious aspect, from the Organisation for Economic Cooperation and Development goals for future learning (Hughson & Wood, 2020) and similar statements from Pearson Learning (2021), who as one the world's largest learning materials providers, have many vested interests in understanding the dynamics of the future global educational market place. There are other examples of principled alignment between the Malaysian Philosophy of Education and the qualities of future-ready graduates, the details of which are beyond the scope of this chapter. The challenge remains with aligning the individual agency of learners with national and global needs so as to empower both learners and teachers as self-directed language learners within a highly centralised system.

It is useful to consider a case study of how any contiguous planning for the future must be within the context of national language politics. We will do this by examining a period of change which impacted many, with the dimmed lens that one may not always learn from the past. We will examine how preparing future-ready bilingual or plurilingual learners can be impacted by policy changes such as the ETeMS, a substantive national policy implementation and reversal within the Malaysian Second Language curriculum. The centrally directed and well-funded policy change clearly showed the capacity of centralised planning to deliver widespread educational change in the short term.

A CASE OF POLICY SWITCHES

The Malaysian English as a Second Language (ESL) curriculum has undergone a series of changes before and after the launch and implementation of the Malaysian Education Blueprint 2013–2025 (MOE, 2013). In 2016, the

Kurikulum Standard Sekolah Rendah or the Standard Curriculum for Primary Schools, first introduced in 2011, was modified. Secondary syllabus change followed soon after. The context of the wider support for the curriculum positioning of English was one of the directional changes, exemplified in ETeMS changes. More recently, greater continuity can be seen in a number of Dual Language Policy initiatives, such as the success of the current Highly Immersive Programme (HIP) (Kamsin & Mohamad, 2020), an ongoing medium-scale initiative beyond the scope of this overview, but worthy of consideration when we turn to conclusions later in this chapter. ETeMS was one of the most sweeping changes, and its reversal serves as a case study for the delicacy and challenges of balancing national and community identity, local languages and more global needs.

Malaysia has seen how national language planning and preparation of wider future workplace changes must be clearly situated in the complex dynamics of multicultural and multilingual Malaysia. As planning needs to continue to focus on the central roles of the widely used national language and the global need for English language skills, there remains the challenge of inclusivity of the nation's cultural complexity and diversity. Political stances based on cultural positioning and identity rhetoric infuse much debate about language policy choices such as ETeMS, and it has been argued that political factors often drive change without consideration of long-term effects (Wen et al., 2018). The shape and direction of language teaching in the national education system are firmly in the hands of centralised national government, which is sensitive to voters' voices.

With political power and educational planning being highly centralised in Malaysia, the roles of the Prime Minister and the Minister of Education are central to planning for future generations; in fact, the position of the Minister of Education is often a precursor to the highest leadership role, as education is viewed as essential to national development and decision-making. A prominent case study of how planning with a global or ASEAN perspective in mind can be impacted by language-based politics can be seen in the introduction in 2002 and the later reversal of the ETeMS policy in 2010. This series of events is worth examining, as it highlights tensions which are yet to be fully resolved in Malaysia's preparation of future-ready global citizens. The reverberations continue with much public discourse and assertions related to national identity, cultural positioning (Alatas, 2021) and the importance of global English.

The linguistically complex Malaysian situation is also worth reflecting upon, as it is illustrative of what is seen by some as a contest of priorities between the English language as an international lingua franca, inclusive of its use in ASEAN (Kirkpatrick, 2012) vis-à-vis the identity marking and utility of the national language (Coluzzi, 2017). Rather than acknowledging a complex multilingual reality, the question of resourcing has often prompted varied national identity stances, some with an either-or situation in which fluent bilingualism or multilingualism is seen by some as creating a subtractive rather than an advantageous situation. In other words, this stance is that if one resources or prioritises a language, one will disadvantage the other and create language learning difficulties (Jimenez, 2020). In the multilingual and multicultural complexity of Malaysia, other languages, of which there are 137 (Eberhard et al., 2019), do not feature with much prominence in what is still a debate often voiced as a duality; a dichotomy between prioritising the national language and the English language, with Tamil and Chinese medium schools being *generally* accepted as an integral norm. In prioritising national and international needs, the educational planning focus has much smaller-scale programmes for other languages (How et al., 2015) in comparison to the bilingual approaches based on the widely accepted, unifying role of Bahasa Malaysia vis-à-vis the international utilitarianism of the widely spoken English language. The challenge is that the multifaceted language resources which multilingual learners bring with them into the education system are not drawn on or considered in pedagogy, sidestepping segments of the students' inner linguistic world.

Changing the medium of instruction for core subjects in primary and secondary schools to English from the national language in the ETeMS switches had many ramifications, especially when, for some Malaysians, the national language and English are third and fourth languages in their repertoire. The case of ETeMS illustrates the role of language politics, which all future language policy planners in Malaysia will need to consider when preparing students for a global marketplace in which English remains a prominent means of communication within ASEAN and beyond (Kirkpatrick, 2012).

ETeMS was introduced into Malaysian public schools in 2002 for national language schools, as well as within the smaller number of Chinese and Tamil medium schools. The objective was to develop greater English language proficiency in what was viewed by many as a situation of declining standards. Older Malaysians lamented the period when English was the medium in schools in the 1960s, before changes in the medium of instruction in the mid-1970s. Fast forward to the beginning of the new millennium and the then-Prime Minister Tun Dr Mahathir who, in 2002, spoke of the need for Malaysians to gain more knowledge and exposure in English through the dominant language of the Internet, mathematics and science (Mohamad Nor et al., 2011). In his advocacy of ETeMS, the then-Prime Minister mentioned that English was a medium of instruction with prominent trading partners and traditional educational partners, as well as the predominant language of digital literacy, a situation which remains unchanged today.

As a national agenda, the switch to English as a medium for two core subjects showed how the public education system could mobilise considerable technological, print and training resources when driven by a politically agreed scenario for change. Teacher training used the approach of teaching through English, a pedagogic approach similar to the widely used, practised and researched Content Integrated Language Learning (Goris et al., 2019). In other words, the approach was in line with other global initiatives to align content learning with English language learning. Interestingly, research notes that the ETeMS approaches involved considerable teacher training which "emphasises conceptualising lessons in English, but at the same time allowing students to receive instructions in their mother tongue" (Majid, 2011, p. 37). It could be argued that the practicalities of the English language and the national language working together were articulated more obviously in the ETeMS project than in earlier approaches, such as a nationwide, rural in-service teacher training that this author had been part of (Hall, 2012). I participated in a National Colloquium by the Malaysian English Language Teaching Association (MELTA) on ETeMS held in December 2007, in which positive feedback and some challenges were reported. Overall, English language teachers, researchers and planners viewed ETeMS as a workable strategy to broaden the exposure and usage of English in classrooms other than those with the English language as a subject. A national MELTA meeting also expressed hope that once the policy was implemented through all the primary and secondary levels, it would impact the increasingly prominent Programme for International Student Assessment (PISA) ranking and align with government aims to increase the language, mathematics and science ranking in the international survey of 15-year-old secondary school students. It was argued, however, that given how much time curriculum change takes to impact outcomes (Graves, 2008), a change process as ETeMS would only be measurable after a full cycle of primary and secondary learners went through the new medium for the core subjects.

The MELTA meeting also expressed the view that increased interaction in the English language would create more articulate writing and presentations at universities, both in Malaysia and for the considerable number of Malaysian university students aiming for an overseas tertiary education. A memorandum was sent to the MOE advocating effective bilingualism through continuing the policy, while noting that such a change as ETeMS relied on further enhancement of teachers' own proficiency and confidence in the changes. The challenge was that benefits from any curriculum changes, especially in language acquisition, would take time to come into effect (Marsh, 2007). Observers noted a systemic problem in that the initiative did not include building on earlier English language teacher training of previous projects for teacher proficiency and pedagogy, missing opportunities to scaffold teacher development (Selamat et al., 2011).

Time was unexpectedly limited, impeding any in-depth research into the effectiveness of this nationwide initiative to enhance the use of English in the national education system. In 2010 with a political change, after much public debate, the Malaysian government decided to revert to the teaching of mathematics and science in the national language. It was decided that, beginning 2012, national schools would teach mathematics and science in Bahasa Malaysia, with Chinese and Tamil in other vernacular national-style schools with their own mediums of instruction. The publicly stated rationale was that concept learning in the national language would be easier.

The national lesson with the contested reversal of nglish for mathematics and science is that changes in a highly centralised system are dependent on the political will to change. Little research exists on how resources were deployed and redeployed, and how the bilingual or plurilingual teaching of mathematics and science impacted learners' own language skills acquisition, although some studies describe challenges related to teacher upskilling (Mohamad Nor et al., 2011). There was a relatively short time to fully analyse curriculum change, although some difficulties in implementing and accepting teaching and learning were reported (Selamat et al., 2011).

There was, and still is, much public debate on the politics of balancing the national language as a unifying language across many indigenous, heritage and community languages, while enhancing global English as the second language for transnational business and education (Alatas, 2021). In January 2020, after Dr Mahathir resumed governance, he advocated a return to ETeMS:

> Malaysia will once again use English to teach Mathematics and Science subjects, said Prime Minister Mahathir Mohamad. Tun Dr Mahathir, who is also the acting Education Minister, said the use of English and mastery of the language in Malaysia's education system must be promoted. ("English to be used to teach maths, science again, says Malaysian PM Mahathir", 2020)

However, as political changes displaced Dr Mahathir as a language policy changemaker, there were few public statements supporting the reversal of the reversal.

The case of ETeMS makes it clear that effective bilingual policies which operate in many countries such as Canada (Cummins, 2014) will only occur if there is a policy change which includes acceptance of effective bilingualism as adding value to national needs and not subtracting from the national language as an important communitive tool and identity marker. There are limitations in the view which sees fluency in a second or additional language as subtractive bilingualism when the majority of the world is bilingual or multilingual (Baker, 2001). The view that one language detracts from another has little basis in research into the widespread bilingualism and multilingualism of the world (May, 2016). The MOE has addressed the limited subtractive bilingualism view (Jimenez, 2020) with programmes which draw from the principles of the Malaysia Education Blueprints, including the Dual Language Policy and HIP, which have been described elsewhere (Jiew, 2017; Kamsin & Mohamad, 2020). The main objective is to create a highly immersive, language-rich environment that promotes the use of English in all schools in Malaysia (MOE, 2017).

Significantly, in a move away from a centralised control model, the actors in the implementation of HIP in Malaysian schools are the school heads, teachers, pupils, parents and community, who should work hand in hand to enhance pupils' proficiency in the English language (MOE, 2017). Each of them is assigned specific roles and responsibilities in safeguarding the continuity of the programme. As such, the Dual Language Policy adopted and led by schools rather than a centralised top-down approach of ETeMS has seen effective bilingualism improvements, as reflected in assessments and surveys. The challenge which still remains is that core secondary subjects remain in the national language for government schools, while most university content is being taught in English. The reversal of ETeMS did, however, lead to an examination of how to sustain English language proficiency with the incorporation of principled approaches in the Malaysia Education Blueprint 2013–2025, and subsequent programmes such as the Dual Language Policy, HIP and the CEFR. We will turn to the CEFR, as one of these recent initiatives.

ASPIRATIONS FOLLOWING THE MALAYSIA EDUCATION BLUEPRINT

The Malaysia Education Blueprint 2015–2025 (Higher Education), published by the Ministry of Education in 2015, delineates the need for all students in Malaysia to be proficient in Bahasa Melayu and English, and also encourages students to learn one additional global language. Describing the positioning of Bahasa Melayu, the national language, and English at the same level defines the recognition given to the role of the English language in developing knowledge and communication skills among students, especially those with university and global aspirations. The phrase "bilingually proficient" is prominent (MOE, 2015, p. 32). The Blueprints, therefore, clearly set the scene with the foundation for English and the national language being developed at the same level.

The Blueprints were followed in 2016 by a national adoption and alignment with the CEFR (Council of Europe, 2001). The MOE in Malaysia launched a synergistic assessment system under the CEFR-aligned ESL curriculum. This development saw a move to principles of greater local school autonomy with attention to school-based processes (Sidhu et al., 2018), a significant step towards progressive recognition of the importance of individual achievement through learner-centredness, highlighted as an essential aspect within the CEFR. We will now consider the implementation of the framework.

The CEFR framework, drawing on decades of European-wide language learning and teaching, is designed with two overarching functions. First, for action with "a common basis for the elaboration of language syllabuses, curriculum guidelines, examinations, textbooks, etc. across Europe" (Council of Europe, 2001, p. 1); and second, as a framework for reflection providing "the means for educational administrators, course designers, teachers, teacher trainers, examining bodies, etc., to reflect on their current practice with a view to situating and coordinating their efforts and to ensuring that they meet the real needs of the learners to whom they are responsible" (ibid.). This notion of responsibility to learners is especially significant as the documentation aims at a democratised learner-centric approach to language learning, rather than a centralised assessment mechanism for nationalised planning and ranking achievement. Omar and Sinnasamy (2017) describe how the implementers at the classroom level are possibly left with challenges with the learner-centred competency scale being used for high-stakes assessment, but not that the sense of school-level ownership is greater than in earlier initiatives.

Little (2011), an CEFR analyst, states that planners, teachers and learners "should use the CEFR to develop curricula that are tailored to our learners' needs, explicitly accommodate learner initiative and control, and define learning outcomes (and perhaps also aspects of the learning process) in terms of 'can do' descriptors" (p. 388). In an earlier work, Little (2006) notes that the CEFR-aligned, school ESL curriculum is one that develops learner autonomy with the competency statements for learners and teachers built into the CEFR. Learners are led by teachers to self-assess themselves so that they, as language learners, develop increasing independence and greater individual responsibility for their own learning. The process is dependent on teachers guiding, mentoring and scaffolding, so as to enable English language learners to identify learning targets, self-monitor progress, and become more individually responsible and responsive to meet their language acquisition needs. As such, the principles of the CEFR link to qualities which are encouraged for future-ready graduates as enumerated in international studies describing communication skills, flexible thinking and learner self-directness (Bowes et al., 2019).

ADOPTION AND ADAPTION OF THE CEFR IN TEACHING AND LEARNING

The adoption of the CEFR in Malaysia, with processes which were not widely documented, appears to be for other reasons than these central aims of the CEFR as a self-directed, learner competency scale. This author witnessed advocacy by large-scale overseas providers linking the CEFR to possible improvements in the PISA ranking through textbook provision by British commercial interests. The local MELTA and consultation groups called on the Ministry to suggest that the framework should be a guide rather than an assessment system, and that proposals to change texts in primary and secondary schooling to British-written textbooks should be reconsidered on the grounds of possible cultural misalignment. This author has been part of earlier processes of selection for varied texts at secondary and primary levels, but it appears that with the adoption of a unified CEFR framework and imported texts that central decision-making process was at play, exhibiting all the signs of what Hofstede (2001) has termed "Power Status". One could suggest that the choice of the CEFR as a national approach demonstrates how the need for standardisation can lead to implementation which may not account for wide variations in Malaysia's linguistic landscape. This process may not be unique to one nation (Hulstijn, 2007; Trim, 2012). Such highly centralised planning and directive process, while facilitating measurement of outcomes, could pose challenges to fostering flexible responses which align local language learning contexts to global needs.

The adoption of the CEFR was initially unreported until contracts were awarded for national textbooks from a British publisher for primary and secondary English language learning and for the CEFR-based teacher testing and training across all levels. The drive to align English language teaching with the CEFR included teacher testing, teacher in-service training, along with the adoption of texts level by level across primary and secondary. Students for higher education in Malaysia are therefore prepared with secondary schooling English language with input which may have few links to their own linguistic and cultural background. However, the role of greater empowerment at local levels was subsequently addressed by aligning the framework with School-Based Assessment (SBA).

The adoption of the CEFR resulted in fundamental changes to teaching, learning and assessment, including the integration of innovative SBA. This aimed at a shift from the traditional stance of assessment of learning to assessment for learning that emphasises both peer and self-assessment as necessary components for the development of autonomous language learners, as described earlier. As such, the development aligned with the Malaysia Education Blueprint plans with emphasis on greater learner autonomy, as also espoused in the CEFR, namely more autonomous, future-ready graduates.

SBA attempted to balance centralised planning with local assessment (Othman et al., 2013). The development linked to the CEFR was a move towards more formative assessment, away from traditional summative assessment, at a time when global concerns linked with skills ranking and assessment were much in the minds of educational planners. Ong (2010) describes assessment across subjects in secondary schools, detailing how two modes of SBA had been implemented in schools in the first decade of this millennium. These are monthly and end-of-term summative tests carried out by teachers in schools without reference to official standards imposed by the Malaysian Education Syndicate, and trials or mock examinations conducted in schools to prepare students for high-stakes examinations. This test-centric process continues to this day, perhaps inverting planning intentions by providing students with much practice in being assessment orientated to expected norms, rather than developing learner competencies in global English language communication.

One of the major challenges in moving from highly centralised changes, as was seen in ETeMS and the adoption of the CEFR, is developing the mindset and skills for more local autonomy with SBA (Malakolunthua & Sim, 2010). In a study of English language teachers by Majid (2011), it was found that SBA was viewed as very multidimensional and that teachers faced difficulties in using the formative assessment embedded in the implementation of the CEFR-aligned changes. This assessment for learning is central to the framework and, as mentioned earlier, aligns with global calls for more autonomous learners. Other studies note that there was little evidence of peer and self-assessment required for developing autonomous learners with issues of time constraints, classroom enrolment, heavy workload, and lack of training limiting self-assessment and reflection (Ghazali, 2017; Veloo et al., 2016). It could be suggested that addressing the constraints teachers mentioned in these studies is important for any change to be effectively implemented to create greater learner autonomy and future-ready graduates.

CHALLENGES

Teachers' proficiency and motivation for teaching English to achieve the goals of the National Education Blueprint and the CEFR remain problematic, according to researchers (Kepol, 2017; Sidhu et al., 2018). Kepol notes that diverse teaching and learning needs include the complex language mixes that learners bring to classrooms, including Malay dialects, uncertainties about the role of English, and community issues of access to culturally relevant materials. Implementation of the aims of the Blueprint is also linked to technological support, the latter being a huge challenge amplified by the Coronavirus Disease 2019 or COVID-19 pandemic. Integral to implementing the admirable aims of centralised planning are the gaps between rural Malaysia and urban-centric planning.

One of the continuing challenges is the mismatch between teacher development programmes and bilingual or multilingual teachers' needs due to centralised planning and processes, whereby top bureaucrats, often in urban settings, designate what teachers ought to be doing (Dyer et al., 2004). The last two decades of Malaysian English language teacher development have seen a series of projects which did not fully build on each other with a focus on sustainability and continuity to enhance the Malaysian Blueprint goals (Stephen, 2013). This author was part of such a project in which empowerment of sustainable local expertise in the face of native speakerism was a real challenge (Hall, 2012). Hiew and Murray (2021) analyse a framework for critiquing English language teacher development projects which involved overseas teacher-educators in Malaysian districts. They note that the benefits of considerable investment in both primary and secondary sectors would be fuller if there was supportive continuity for bilingual or multilingual teacher mentoring and a focus on sustainable, localised expertise. The researchers highlight the importance of local identification with language choice, in contrast to language policies being enforced from centralised ruling. They describe a further challenge when resources and local expertise which have been developed for effective learning for both Bahasa Malaysia and English are not built on and shared within the community's own cultural dynamics. More inclusive developments could involve the heritage and indigenous languages that many young Malaysians bring into primary school classrooms.

IDENTITY COMPLEXITIES

A universal challenge is the alignment of centralised educational planning with the implementation within learning environments, usually classroom-based—although for the last two years, online. Within all the changes to make the role of English language teaching more aligned with the 21st century, a key challenge is implementation, which depends on the quality of teaching and learning and interaction within classrooms. Teacher quality also relates to a teacher's own sense of identity as a citizen of the nation and perhaps to whether being bilingual, multilingual or "plurilingual" is recognised and incorporated into the dominance of centralised planning, with frameworks within which teachers must perform. In Malaysia, this could possibly be extended to an acceptance of code-switching within classrooms; this widespread reality can also be termed "translanguaging" or "plurilingualism". This complexity is being increasingly researched, but possibly underacknowledged as an effective pedagogical tool, even if it is a classroom reality at many levels in Malaysia (Hall, 2018; Paramesvaran & Lim, 2018; Shah & Adnan, 2020).

The space to openly engage in what is already happening in terms of using the national language and heritage and community languages in classroom interaction has few supporting statements in centralised documentation. There are, however, efforts to broaden HIP, and developments in this area could intensify with a greater focus on teacher training and recognition of the nation's linguistic complexity.

Challenges—such as using languages other than English in English teaching to implement language syllabus changes, such as the CEFR goals—could be related to teacher and learner issues of identity and articulating the acceptance of multiple identities, part of being bilingual or multilingual (Lee et al., 2010; Lee et al., 2021). A further issue is the recurrence of some rhetoric as a choice between a national language and English as the global lingua franca, which is, at times, couched in terms of the possibilities of cultural loss with the dominance of English (Azman, 2016). Yet, this is in a situation when multilingualism is the global norm (May, 2016) and English is the lingua franca across ASEAN for governments, being widely used in education, tourism, shipping and finance, to name but a few domains. It is possible that active cultivation of multilingual classroom realities with a pedagogy which acknowledges code-switching could lead to a clearer positioning of English and the national language (Albury, 2017), thereby benefitting bilingual or multilingual language acquisition as advocated in the National Education Blueprint.

CONCLUSION

To move forward with a more inclusive framework could entail embracing an approach where the two dominant language choices of the national language and English are seen as repertoires for differing situations, in much the same way that Malaysians easily code-switch between languages (Albury, 2017). Specifying domains of usage and teaching accordingly is after all a norm, as there are English for Academic Purposes, English for Tourism, and English for airline pilots' courses, which use specific, cost-effective resources for targeted situations. Such an approach to English language development, even within higher education, would then entail recognising that although English is espoused as a second language in Malaysia, for many, it is one of several language choices, often like a foreign language, and really dependent on who is being addressed and for what specific purposes.

English is part of wider choices along with the national language, which may be used in some settings in a regionally specific dialect. There are many other active languages in Malaysia which are part of learners' mindsets and identities. Eleven languages are considered institutional, with six used in institutions of knowledge dissemination. There are 137 languages in Malaysia, including heritage languages from Indian, Chinese and Thai sources, such as Punjabi and Foochow; indigenous languages from the pre-Malay original inhabitants, such as Semai and Bidayuh; and the so-called vernacular school languages of Mandarin Chinese and Tamil (Eberhard et al., 2019). One could see parallels in other ASEAN countries, where many dialects and languages other than the unifying national norm exist, as in Indonesia. National and community-specific identities are often multilayered and celebrated at festivals, yet less focused on as a linguistic resource and a range of communicative competencies which inform students' identities, language choices and learning.

In Malaysia, the importance of language choices linked to multiple identities has been described at secondary and tertiary levels of education as being part of Malaysian students' sense of self, linked to learning motivation across content areas (Lee et al., 2010; Shah & Adnan, 2020). There is less research at tertiary levels, although Too (2017) describes the complex challenges and settings of transition and motivation, when learners move from the predominantly national language, secondary school context to the English language-dominant tertiary levels. In a more specific, small-scale focus, Ting et al. (2017) study the language vitality of Malaysian languages. They focused on the use of Bahasa Malaysia for national unity and English as the second language for cross-community communication, and made links to positive self-images, namely students' representation of their individual identities. The small-scale study was in the under-researched area of vernacular languages. Vernacular languages may be defined as languages used in national-type schools, where the schools have other languages than Bahasa Malaysia as the medium. The scenario is, therefore, one in which learners' own linguistic repertoires remain an untapped resource if the situation is approached as a simplistic, dualistic one of English and the national language in contestation, as occurred with the policy changes of ETeMS.

It is worth noting that more than the two lingua franca languages of Bahasa Malaysia and English can be heard every day in Malaysian universities, outside of language clubs and societies, illustrating the complex linguistic landscape that many may take for granted. A small-scale study by Ying et al. (2015) of five primary Malaysian students from vernacular Tamil and Chinese schools gauged the vitality of Tamil and Mandarin. The findings indicate that Bahasa Malaysia and English do not have high vitality, while the vernacular languages do, namely acceptance, usage and expressed value.

More in-depth research into students' sense of multiple identities could enhance a deeper understanding of Malaysia's linguistic complexity and the contexts of language learning, so as to position the acquisition of the national language and the English language for globally communitive graduates within the linguistic complexity of Malaysia.

Malaysia's linguistic complexity and its commitment to the national language of Bahasa Malaysia and English as a second language pose many challenges as ASEAN moves forward with English as a lingua franca. Yet, at this time, the multilingual skills which learners have are often not seen as a resource for pedagogy which draws on learners' complex cultural identities. At this time of great digital disruption and a return to whatever the new normal will be, graduates will require a strong sense of belonging in a community in which they can develop a range of self-directed skills and communicative competence. The nation has demonstrated in the past with ETeMS and the adoption of an international system in the CEFR that language learning changes are very possible, if there is political will. The sustainability of upskilling in the national language and empowering learners with English as a global lingua franca may, however, need to consider the resources that learners themselves bring to language learning, as complex, multilingual and multicultural citizens.

REFERENCES

Alatas, S. M. (2021, November 29). Debates on language have divided our society. *Malaysiakini.* https://www.malaysiakini.com/columns/601035

Albury, N. J. (2017). Mother tongues and languaging in Malaysia: Critical linguistics under critical examination. *Language in Society, 46*(4), 1–23.

Azman, H. (2016). Implementation and challenges of English language education reform in Malaysian primary schools. *3L: The Southeast Asian Journal of English Language Studies, 22*(3), 65–78.

Baker, C. (2001). *Foundations of bilingual education and bilingualism* (3rd ed.). Multilingual Matters Ltd.

Bowles, M., Bowes, N. I., & Wilson, P. T. (2019). Future-proof human capabilities: Raising the future employability of graduates. *International Journal of Business and Social Science, 10*(9), 10–21.

Ghazali, N. H. C. M. (2017). The implementation of school-based assessment system in Malaysia: A study of teacher perceptions. *Geografia-Malaysian Journal of Society and Space, 12*(9), 104–117.

Coluzzi, P. (2017). Language planning for Malay in Malaysia: A case of failure or success? *International Journal of the Sociology of Language, 2017*(244), 17–38.

Council of Europe. (2001). *Common European Framework of Reference for Languages: Learning, teaching, assessment.* Cambridge University Press.

Cummins, J. (2014). Rethinking pedagogical assumptions in Canadian French immersion programs. *Journal of Immersion and Content-Based Language Education, 2*(1), 3–22. https://doi.org/10.1075/jicb.2.1.01cum

Dyer, C., Choksi, A., Awasty, V., Iyer, U., Moyade, R., Nigam, N., Purohit, N., Shah, S., & Sheth, S. (2004). Knowledge for teacher development in India: The importance of 'local knowledge' for in-service education. *International Journal of Educational Development, 24*(1), 39–52.

Dzulkifli, A. R. (2015). *Nurturing a balanced person: The leadership challenge.* USIM Press.

Eberhard, D. M., Simons, G. F., & Fennig, C. D. (Eds.). (2019). *Ethnologue: Languages of the world* (22nd ed.). SIL International.

English to be used to teach maths, science again, says Malaysian PM Mahathir. (2020). *The Straits Times.* https://www.straitstimes.com/asia/se-asia/english-to-be-used-to-teach-math-science-again-says-malaysias-mahathir

Goris, J., Denessen, E., & Verhoeven, L. (2019). Effects of content and language integrated learning in Europe: A systematic review of longitudinal experimental studies. *European Educational Research Journal, 18*(6), 675–698. https://doi.org/10.1177/1474904119872426

Graves, K. (2008). The language curriculum: A social contextual perspective. *Language Teaching, 41*(2), 147–181. https://doi.org/10.1017/S0261444807004867

Hall, S. J. (2012). Deconstructing aspects of native speakerism: Reflections from in-service teacher education. *The Journal of Asia TEFL, 9*(3), 107–130.

Hall, S. J. (2018). Plurilingual positioning and its effectiveness in classroom interaction. In P. Heard (Ed.), *Great thinkers, great minds: Sunway University professorial lecture series* (pp. 43–67). Sunway University Press.

Hiew, W., & Murray, J. (2021). Enhancing Huber's evaluation framework for teacher professional development programme. *Professional Development in Education*, 1–15. https://doi.org/10.1080/19415257.2021.1901236

Hofstede, G. (2001). *Culture's consequences: Comparing values, behaviors, institutions, and organizations across nations.* Sage Publications.

How, S.Y., Chan, S. H., & Abdullah, A. N. (2015). Language vitality of Malaysian languages and its relation to identity. *GEMA Online Journal of Language Studies, 15*(2), 119–136.

Hughson, T. A., & Wood, B. E. (2020). The OECD learning compass 2030 and the future of disciplinary learning: A Bernsteinian critique. *Journal of Education Policy, 37*(4), 1–21. https://doi.org/10.1080/02680939.2020.1865573

Hulstijn, J. H. (2007). The shaky ground beneath the CEFR quantitative and qualitative dimensions of language proficiency. *The Modern Language Journal, 91*(4), 663–667.

Jiew, F. F. (2017). The evaluation of highly immersive programme (HIP). *International Journal of Academic Research in Business and Social Sciences, 7*(2), 437–449.

Jimenez, A. (2020). *Subtractive bilingualism: Encouraged by English-only in schools, affecting first language.* [Master's thesis, California State University]. Digital Commons @ CSUMB. https://digitalcommons.csumb.edu/caps_thes_all/879

Kamsin, S. R., & Mohamad, M. (2020). The implementation of highly immersive programme (HIP) speaking activities in Malaysian schools: A literature review. *Creative Education, 11*(9), 1783–1794. https://doi.org/10.4236/ce.2020.119130

Kepol, N. (2017). Quality Malaysian English degree teachers: Examining a policy strategy. *Malaysian Journal of Learning and Instruction, 14*(1), 187–209.

Kirkpatrick, A. (2012). English in ASEAN: Implications for regional multilingualism. *Journal of Multilingual and Multicultural Development, 33*(4), 331– 344. https://doi.org/10.1080/01434632.2012.661433

Lee, H.Y., Hamid, M. O., & Hardy, I. (2021). English and regional identity in ASEAN. *World Englishes,* 1–15. https://doi.org/10.1111/weng.12571

Lee, S. K., Lee, K. S., Wong, F. F., & Ya'acob, A. (2010). The English language and its impact on identities of multilingual Malaysian undergraduates. *GEMA Online Journal of Language Studies, 10*(1), 87–101.

Little, D. (2006). The Common European Framework of Reference for Languages: Content, purpose, origin, reception and impact. Language Teaching, *39*(3), 167–190.

Little, D. (2011). The Common European Framework of Reference for languages: A research agenda. *Language Teaching, 44*(3), 381–393. https://doi.org/10.1017/S0261444811000097

Majid, F. A. (2011). School based assessment in Malaysian schools. The concerns of the English language teachers. *US-China Education Review*, 393–402.

Malakolunthua, S., & Sim. K. H. (2010). Teacher perspectives of school-based assessment in a secondary school in Kuala Lumpur. *Procedia Social and Behavioral Sciences, 9*, 1170–1176.

Marsh, D. (2007.) *Implications for the performance of Malaysian teaching of mathematics and science.* Conference organised by the Education Ministry's Teachers Education Division and ELTC Centre for Teaching Mathematics and Science Seremban.

May, S. (2016). Bilingual education: What the research tells us. In O. Garcia, A. Lin, & S. May (Eds.), *Bilingual and multilingual education: Encyclopedia of language and education* (3rd ed.) (pp. 1–20). Springer. https://doi.org/10.1007/978-3-319-02324-3_4-1

Ministry of Education (MOE). (2001). *Falsafah pendidikan kebangsaan: Matlamat dan misi (National education philosophy: Goal and mission).* Curriculum Development Centre.

Ministry of Education (MOE). (2013). *Malaysia education blueprint 2013–2025.*

Ministry of Education (MOE). (2015). *Malaysia education blueprint 2015–2025 (higher education).*

Ministry of Education (MOE). (2017). *Bahagian perancangan dan penyelidikan dasar Pendidikan (Edisi keempat).* Dasar Pendidikan Kebangsaan.

Mohamad Nor, F., Aziz, M. A., & Jusoff, K. (2011). Should English for teaching mathematics and science (ETeMS) in Malaysia be abolished? *World Applied Sciences Journal* (Special Issue), *12*, 36–40.

Omar, H. M., & Sinnasamy, P. (2017). Between the ideal and reality: Teachers' perception of the implementation of school-based oral English assessment. *The English Teacher, 38*, 13–30.

Ong, S. L. (2010). Assessment profile of Malaysia: High-stakes external examinations dominate. *Assessment in Education: Principles, Policy & Practice, 17*(1), 91–103. https://doi.org/10.1080/09695940903319752

Othman, I., Md Salleh, N., & Mohd Norani, N. A., (2013). The implementation of school based assessment in primary school standard curriculum. *International Journal of Education and Research, 1*(7), 1–10.

Pandian, A. (2002). English language teaching in Malaysia today. *Asia-Pacific Journal of Education, 22*(2), 35–52. http://doi.org/10.1080/0218879020220205

Paramesvaran, M. D., & Lim, J. W. (2018). Code-switching practices in a Malaysian multilingual primary classroom from teacher and student perspectives. *Indonesian Journal of Applied Linguistics, 8*, 254–264. http://doi.org/10.17509/ijal.v8i2.13273

Pearson Learning. (2021). *The future of education: 5 skills employers look for now and in 2030.* https://www.pearson.com/en-au/insights-and-news/the-future-of-education/5-skills-employers-look-for-now-and-in-2030

Selamat, A., Esa, A., Saad, S. S., & Atim, A. (2011). Teaching and learning mathematics and science in English in primary schools in the state of Johor, Malaysia. *Journal of Education, 16*(2011), 61–73.

Shah, D. S. M., & Adnan, A. H. M. (2020). Formal schooling and the process of identity construction: Experiences of Malaysian youths in 'bad' schools. *International Journal of Modern Education, 2*(4), 78–89. http://doi.org/10.35631/IJMOE.24007

Sidhu, G. K., Kaur, S., & Chi, L. J. (2018). CEFR-aligned school-based assessment in the Malaysian primary ESL classroom. *Indonesian Journal of Applied Linguistics, 8*, 452–463. http://doi.org/10.17509/ijal.v8i2.13311

Stephen, J. (2013). English in Malaysia: A case of the past that never really went away. *English Today, 29*(2), 3–8.

Ting, S. H., Marzuki, E., Chuah, K. M., Misieng, J., & Jerome, C. (2017). Employers views on the importance of English proficiency and communication skills for employability in Malaysia. *Indonesian Journal of Applied Linguistics, 7*(2), 315–327.

Too, W. K. (2017). English language teaching and policies at the tertiary level in Malaysia. In E. S. Park & B. Spolsky (Eds.), *English education at the tertiary level in Asia: From policy to practice* (pp. 109–129). Routledge.

Trim, J. (2012). The Common European Framework of Reference for Languages and its background: A case study of cultural politics and educational influences. In M. Byram & L. Parmenter (Eds.), *The Common European Framework of Reference: The globalisation of language education policy* (pp. 14–36). Multilingual Matters.

Veloo, A., Ramli, R., & Khalid, R. (2016). Assessment practices among English teachers in Malaysian secondary schools. *International Journal for Infonomics, 9*(4), 1220–1227.

Vethamani, M. E. (2007). The ebb and flow of English language education in Malaysia. In M. E. Vethamani & R. Perumal (Eds.), *Teaching English in Malaysia: A special 25th MELTA anniversary publication* (pp. 1–10). Sasbadi Sdn Bhd.

Wen, S.W., Chibundu, I. S., & Chua, S. P. (2018). Debating vernacular school system in Malaysia: A comparative analysis of multilingual local newspapers. *SEARCH: The Journal of the South East Asia Research Centre for Communication and Humanities, 10* (2), 87–114.

Ying, H. S., Heng, C. C., & Abdullah, A. M. (2015). Language vitality of Malaysian languages and its relation to identity. *GEMA Online Journal of Language Studies, 15*(2), 119–134.

Chapter 6

Attaining Equity and Diversity in the Massified System of Higher Education: A Qualitative Study of the Malaysian Context

Muhammad Muftahu*

ABSTRACT

The purpose of this chapter is to examine the impact of Malaysia's higher education growth on equity in access and diversity among the population of attending students in recent decades. A study was conducted, where data were collected through semi-structured interviews with middle and senior managers from a leading Malaysian public university to elicit their views on equity and diversity in their university. The findings indicate that the equity and diversity of students are affected as higher education in Malaysia becomes more prevalent—that is, massified. While higher education institutions (HEIs) have attempted to keep up with the rate of massification and so boast a varied student population in terms of student backgrounds, this study finds that obstacles in gaining admittance to higher education continue to persist for people from non-traditional backgrounds. The issue of higher education access for students from disadvantaged backgrounds requires specific attention, as it indicates the levels of socioeconomic inequity. This study is beneficial in that examining the institutionalisation of higher education from the viewpoint of students on diversity and equity provides insights and understandings through which higher education might achieve greater diversity and equity among the HEI student population. The further

* Universiti Sains Malaysia, Malaysia

massification of higher education should be implemented with more strategies and initiatives at the ministerial (that is, governmental) and institutional levels that equably increase the diversity of the student population.

Keywords Diversity, equity, higher education, massification

INTRODUCTION

It is well-established that education is critical for the social and economic growth of a country. Developing nations have acknowledged the essential nature of higher education development to satisfy current global labour market demands. As the need for higher education provision increases, many higher education systems worldwide have expanded extensively and undergone wide and deep structural changes. In the last two decades, the higher education gross enrolment rate worldwide has almost doubled, from 19% to 38% between 2000 and 2018 (United Nations Educational, Scientific and Cultural Organisation [UNESCO] Institute for Statistics, 2020). This worldwide increase, however, shows wide regional disparities. According to the United Nations Educational, Scientific and Cultural Organisation (UNESCO), Southeast Asia, Latin America and the Caribbean have seen a great increase in their gross enrolment rate. Meanwhile, Sub-Saharan Africa has had the slowest increase in participation rates, and the growth has been insufficient to match rising demand (UNESCO Institute for Statistics, 2020).

Enrolment expansion has put enormous pressure on national governments to deal with various issues related to extending higher education boundaries, particularly in terms of the structure of their HEIs. According to Chan (2016), some HEIs have made significant adjustments to their curriculum, teaching and assessment procedures to ensure their students graduate with the essential knowledge, skills and capacities to compete in the global economy.

However, massifying the student population in higher education is a double-edged sword. On the one hand, massification has opened up considerable prospects for a more significant number of individuals, enabling students to continue their studies, and its popularity has contributed to addressing the issues associated with growing demand (Chan & Lin, 2015). For instance, the Malaysian government has been implementing new higher education policies to address the industry demands for graduates through innovative laws and practices and by deploying novel approaches that assist students in acquiring the skills and knowledge required for graduation (Shariffuddin et al., 2017). On the other hand, a more extensive university system may have detrimental consequences on the labour market such as student overcrowding, thereby impacting educational quality which, in turn, may increase educational inequality (Bai, 2006; Wu, 2011). Kamanzi et al. (2021) indicate that higher education expansion has brought about an increase in inequalities in terms of the social origins of attending students. This means that although higher education systems can diversify the student population through expansion, there are potential repercussions on the equality of access for potential students.

The expansion in the number of students attending higher education in Malaysia—that is, its massification—is crucial for determining how the country's higher education system may be strengthened to satisfy the demands and expectations of the global labour market. However, to date, little is known about the impact of the massification of the student population on equity and diversity in the Malaysian context. This study thus aims to examine this topic and identify issues and challenges in the implementation of policies and practices in Malaysian HEIs concerning student enrolment expansion. It aims to suggest measures to enhance equity and diversity in terms of student participation from different socioeconomic and cultural backgrounds, in line with the United Nations Sustainable Development Goals.

LITERATURE REVIEW

Higher education in Malaysia

Malaysia has witnessed a massive higher education expansion since the establishment of its first public university, Universiti Malaya, in 1959. The university received 322 students in its inaugural year (Khoo, 2005). Today, Malaysia houses 20 public universities and 467 private HEIs operating in a multiethnic, multicultural and multilingual society with a population of over 32.5 million (Tapsir, 2019). In addition, there are 36 polytechnics and 105 community colleges (Ministry of Higher Education [MOHE], 2021). This higher education provision has enabled a large number of Malaysians to have access to tertiary education. Over the last four decades, the Malaysian higher education system has significantly increased tertiary enrolment rates to approximately 44% of citizens between the ages of 17 and 23, compared to only 14% in the 1970s and 1980s (Tapsir, 2019). In 2019, there were 567,625 students enrolled in public universities, 96,362 in polytechnics, 26,118 in community colleges, 328,978 in private universities, 88,530 in university colleges, 187,733 in colleges, and 28,103 in overseas branch campuses (MOHE, 2020). A similar rising trend can be found in Technical, Vocational Education and Training (TVET). In 1980, Malaysia's TVET was barely 4%. It rose from 11% in 1995 to 22% in 1998 after legalising private HEIs. By the turn of the millennium, TVET had surpassed 30% in Malaysian higher education. It rose further to 45% in 2018, with over 1.3 million students (UNESCO Institute for Statistics, 2020).

Massification of higher education globally

The term "massification" was first used by Trow (2006) to denote mass enrolment in a national system. In higher education, massification is commonly used to mean higher education that is available to all who qualify, thus resulting in very large numbers of students entering universities and a proliferation of HEIs to cater for these student numbers (IGI Global, 2021). The transformation of the higher education system in many countries from exclusive or elite education to mass-scale education can be considered a response to new demands in socioeconomic development (Selyutin et al., 2017).

Higher education massification can be advantageous in many ways. In developing countries, it is seen as a strategy to improve HEIs (Chan & Lin, 2015) and combat the intense global competition and challenges in higher education. In China, for example, Mok and Jiang (2016) find that the massification of higher education has provided increasingly more access to junior colleges and universities, subsequently producing a growing number of college graduates looking for jobs in the labour market. Similarly, Noui (2020) indicates that higher education massification has improved students' institutional environment and enrolment profiles. For example, massification has led to an increase in the number of female students and the social and geographic diversity of students in higher education.

However, excessive credential issuance and stagnating work opportunities may result in the devaluation of higher education and graduate unemployment (Noui, 2020) and may intensify educational inequality (Mok & Jiang, 2016). In addition, a study involving universities in Ethiopia has found that higher education massification resulted in a decline in teaching quality (Akalu, 2017).

Massification has also proved to be challenging financially. This is due to the tremendous expectations and pressures placed on higher education to develop the human resources required by nations for international competition (Dunrong, 2015). In terms of finance, four massification models are commonly adopted: (1) American, (2) Western European, (3) Southeast Asian, and (4) Latin American. Malaysia has adopted two of these models, the Southeast Asian and the Latin American ones, relying on private-sector tuition fees and philanthropic contributions to expand the country's higher education system (Thian, 2014).

Equity in higher education

Clancy and Goastellec (2007) argue that approaches to higher education access have evolved through three historical phases. Initially, universities were only available to those from specific backgrounds, whether relating to gender, religion or racial origin—a concept referred to as "inherited merit" by these authors. Then, universities became more widely available to those from all backgrounds. This gave birth to the notion of "equal rights" in the 20th century, which prohibited explicit discrimination against certain sections of society. However, reality demonstrates that admission into higher education remains extraordinarily difficult for underprivileged populations despite the absence of formal restrictions. The final stages in this evaluation were marked by a variety of affirmative action or favourable discrimination rules and practices.

Access to higher education has risen to the top of the priority list for those working to improve HEIs and their systems. However, many countries have residents who cannot continue their education after high school, particularly those from disadvantaged and marginalised socioeconomic groups. In Kyrgyzstan and Tajikistan, for instance, there is a significant rural-urban divide despite a rapid expansion in the countries' higher education system (Hughes, 2018). Similarly, in Malaysia, unequal access to higher education continues to be a severe problem (Ghasemy et al., 2018). Barriers to achieving equity in higher education include financial and economic restrictions that hinder potential students from enrolling in such institutions (Ilie & Rose, 2016). To reduce enrolment barriers for students from low-income and disadvantaged backgrounds, governments and international organisations such as UNESCO have recommended a variety of frameworks and designs for policies and interventions to increase access to higher education for all qualified people, with a particular emphasis on underprivileged or marginalised populations. The government of Malaysia is also tackling this issue and partnering with international organisations engaged in higher education.

Diversity in higher education

According to Phillips (2019), diversity in higher education often appears in one of four categories: (1) diversity in representation, (2) diversity in climate and inter-group relations, (3) diversity in curriculum and scholarship, and (4) diversity in institutional values and structures. It is also commonly associated with multiculturalism, and both elements have become important forces in higher education.

A positive approach to diversity guarantees that all enrolled students receive the same benefits from HEIs regardless of their backgrounds. Additionally, the learning opportunities available to students are boosted, increasing their competitiveness. Despite the numerous benefits of diversification, many HEIs worldwide have found the implementation of diversity in their student populations to be a huge challenge. Diversification raises questions about the responsibilities of HEIs to meet the expectations and needs of diverse students of various races, ethnicities and faiths, as well as students with a wide range of views, attitudes and socioeconomic backgrounds—all of which may have an impact on teaching and learning methodologies and practices.

A further issue concerns students' differing perceptions of diversity. In relation to students, diversity refers to selection and is determined by accessibility, location, programme offerings, reputation and cost (Tremblay et al., 2012). Diversity also has a limiting connotation regarding the institutions to which students have easy access. Thus, systemic variety within a national system is irrelevant if the only institutions students have reasonable access to are all the same (Organisation for Economic Cooperation and Development, 2009).

METHODOLOGY

The massification of higher education in Malaysia to achieve equity, diversity and equality in institutional expansion serves as the methodological foundation of this study. The research framework is critical and interpretative. This strategy was chosen to allow for a comprehensive analysis of the issues surrounding the massification of higher education.

A qualitative case-study methodology was used for this social science-based study, allowing researchers to conduct in-depth examinations and investigations of social situations, events or interactions (Creswell, 2003; Maxwell, 2004; Mullen, 2005), including how people conceptualise values and alignments (Creswell, 2003; Silverman, 2004). According to Chiang et al. (2015), the qualitative research method allows researchers to understand in detail the experience of their research participants. Examples of case studies include descriptive, evaluative and explanatory studies. The case study can investigate a contemporary phenomenon in depth and within its real-life context, especially when the boundaries between phenomenon and context are not clearly evident (Yin, 2009). Comparison case studies and evaluative case studies, on the other hand, aim to explain phenomena by identifying patterns within or across cases, while explanatory case studies attempt to draw judgements about the phenomena. In this particular instance, neither of these alternatives is acceptable.

Interviews

Interviews were one-on-one, interpersonal question-and-answer sessions that the interviewer facilitated and controlled (Okoro, 2003). The interview process was often performed orally, with the interviewer immediately posing questions and the interviewee vocally responding. Researchers were seen as active participants in purposeful conversations (Salkind, 2010). The interviewer would document comments in writing, audiotape them on a recorder, or both (McNamara, 2022). Interviews were typically performed once; however, the second round of interviews would be undertaken depending on the depth and quality of the interviews in the first round. The interview questions for this study were developed after conducting a literature review and analysing data from other studies.

The instrument's dependability was established using selected literature to achieve a degree of consistency in data collection based on the study's objectives. Experts were consulted on the interview questions to provide feedback and recommendations for improving the tools and data-gathering technique.

Participants

The participants in this study were drawn from a Malaysian public university. While no standard sample size exists for qualitative research (Lincoln & Guba, 1985), a minimum of five samples is seen as appropriate to facilitate data gathering (Strauss & Corbin, 1990) due to the massive data volumes and intricate technicalities of qualitative research. Given the nature of the study, participants were chosen using purposive sampling, a widely used technique for identifying and selecting information-rich cases related to the phenomenon of interest (Palinkas et al., 2015). Qualitative research strengthens the researchers' capacity to make wide selections of suitable participants whose intellectual temperament and closeness to the study location make them well suited to provide analytical replies to interview questions (Creswell, 2003). The study's participants were chosen at the discretion of the HEI and included senior and mid-management level university employees. The participants comprised three males and two females.

Data collection and data analysis

The study acquired primary data through interviews and secondary data through a review of documents about the policy and execution of higher education massification in Malaysia. All interviews were conducted in English, and fieldwork took place in the selected university from January to March 2021. Each interview lasted between 30 and 60 minutes, and all interviews were recorded and transcribed verbatim. The data were analysed using thematic analysis, a technique for identifying, analysing, organising, describing and reporting themes found within a data set (Braun & Clarke, 2006, as cited in Nowell et al., 2017) during the document analysis.

FINDINGS

Four themes were identified from the data analysis based on the objectives of the study, each of which will be discussed in turn:

(1) Massification of higher education for inclusivity.
(2) Equity of access to higher education.
(3) Diversity in higher education.
(4) Barriers to access to higher education.

Massification of higher education for inclusivity

Over time, higher education in Malaysia has witnessed changes in the patterns of enrolment and has therefore become concerned about educational quality in light of equal access to higher education and ensuring the employability of graduates.

The study participants expressed various perspectives. According to one study participant, massification is motivated by a desire for inclusion. He believed massification should focus on universal access to higher education because the profile of students enrolled in higher education has changed. Accordingly, HEIs should be more receptive to students from diverse backgrounds:

> I think [massification] is about inclusivity. We have to acknowledge that the profile of our students will change, and we need to provide opportunities for everybody to gain access to higher education. That's the reason why lifelong learning is an agenda, so more people will benefit. [We] also have to make sure that universities are not bordered ... [so that] everyone can have access to knowledge. (I/01)

One participant acknowledged that the Malaysian government has implemented various initiatives to make education inclusive:

> I think ... education has become an important part of the [country's] agenda [since Independence]. I think the government has put efforts into ensuring the quality [of education] ... [so that] people in the country get better education ... increase their employability ... [and have the] opportunity to gain a better life. This is one of the main points why the Malaysian government would like to expand ... in providing more education. (I/05)

The study participants mentioned various benefits resulting from the government's inclusivity efforts. According to one participant, massification would help the growth of higher education in Malaysia for the future rather than the present:

> It is more about the future ... in the past, there [was] a division between education for ... lifelong learners and ... normal people after high school. It's just beginning. (I/01)

Another participant indicated that the massification of higher education would result in more career prospects for both domestic and international students and instructors, and assist in meeting the expectations of Malaysian students:

> It opens [up] job opportunities ... not only [for] international students but also ... international lecturers. Education is a business and we have high demand, and we don't have enough higher education [institutions] to accept all these students. It's income-generating. (I/04)

Equity of access to higher education

Technological advancement

The technology-driven Fourth Industrial Revolution (4IR) is a major aspect that HEIs need to pay attention to in expanding access. 4IR has accelerated change in higher education in teaching, management and ways of cultivating talent.

As one participant commented, access to higher education is vital in the upskilling and reskilling of the country's human resources in the era of 4IR:

> With the disruption of the Fourth Industrial Revolution and so on, I think people need to re-tool and reskill. Therefore, they need to have access to higher education. We, as a university, must allow them to have access. (I/01)

Seamless access to knowledge

The findings indicate that the massification of higher education will benefit the exchange of information by ensuring equitable access. The implication in the following respondent's comment (I/02) is that higher education should accommodate the needs and situations of students from diverse backgrounds. However, the process of providing access should be simple so that students can access higher education with ease, allowing them to expand their knowledge in their own time and at their own pace. As one participant noted, if entry is made complex, it may be thought that the institution is not acting sufficiently as a change agent for society. The respondent's comments are as follows:

> Access should be at ... our and the users' convenience. That's why we should ask ourselves, "What is our offering and in what form do we offer our process?" [Otherwise,] we are not doing enough to change society. (I/02)

Intervention according to special needs

Interventions to facilitate access to HEIs should be reflected in the delivery of teaching and learning programmes, such as by using local languages—for example, Malay—to meet the requirements of students who may be limited in their English language proficiency. A participant remarked that while his institution has a lofty aim as a "research university", this should not prevent it from offering necessary resources to aid students in their learning:

> [Students] need degrees, but ... we know English will be an issue. [So,] we have to use Malay ... or the local language and dialect, [like] the *Orang Asli* dialect. Some might ask, "We are a research university; why do we need [to do all] that?". We have to work on this. The course structure ... shouldn't hinder people from accessing [education]. If we can do this, then ... we are an advocate of knowledge. We are not to be stopped by our status as a research university. (I/02)

Policies for access to higher education

The participants acknowledged that the Malaysian government has implemented several policies and initiatives aimed at increasing access to higher education, such as subsidising study costs to promote opportunities and help students pursue higher education at all levels, from foundation to postgraduate. One participant remarked that her institution adheres to the policies but also has its own set of policies to increase access. HEIs with university status are granted increased autonomy to control admissions, allowing them to be more creative in offering admission to the university:

> Public [universities] ... are subsidised by the government ... to give opportunities to Malaysians to further study, from the foundation [level] to ... postgraduate level. That's why there are lots of policies [by the Ministry] ... We follow whatever policy is given. We sometimes try to come up with our own policy, especially when we get special status. Then, the Ministry rewarded us and wanted the university to handle our own intake. We are the only one in Malaysia [to do that]. (I/04)

Fee discounts

The university employs some strategies to recruit students from diverse backgrounds, especially those who are disadvantaged or less wealthy. One of the strategies is to provide a discount on university tuition:

> We can give [school fee] discounts [because] ... we want [students] to be able to come in. (I/01)

One of the participants emphasised that tuition rates are discounted for students with athletic backgrounds, older citizens, and those from specific cultural backgrounds:

> At the moment, we have tuition fee discounts for [students with] sports background ... senior citizens and [those with specific] cultural backgrounds. (I/04)

Minority or less privileged groups

Findings from the interviews indicate that the *Orang Asli* were considered a minority group in the university, and their enrolment has increased little over time. According to one of the participants, additional efforts should be made to enrol students from this societal group in post-secondary education. One participant's comment exemplifies this:

> The [*Orang Asli*] are still considered a minority. Maybe [there is] a slight increase [in their intake], but [it's] not that apparent. We still need to work harder to bring them in. (I/01)

Diversity in higher education

Student profile

Responses from the participants indicate that in recent years, there has been an increase in the range of the backgrounds of students enrolled in the university. For example, in the past, distance education programmes were available to adult learners with job experience. Today, the student profile at the university has shifted to include a more significant proportion of younger students. One study participant commented the following:

> We used to feel that only lifelong learners [did] ... distance education ... That used to be the norm. But now, in general, ... the student profile is getting younger, and there is definitely a change. (I/01)

To increase the diversity of the student profile, one participant stated that her institution provides extra options for students from varied backgrounds, including those with *Sijil Tinggi Persekolahan Malaysia*[1] (STPM) and matriculation credentials, as well as those with other academic credentials:

> [T]his university ... give[s] opportunities to Malaysian students who [did] STPM and matriculation, to get ... students [from] different academic backgrounds. (I/04)

Intake channels

The university achieved student diversity by varying its intake channels. According to one participant, her university established a variety of unique admission methods to this end. International students are admitted through a global intake, whereas domestic students are admitted through a Class 1 intake. Additionally, there are channels dedicated to older citizens and students from diverse cultural and athletic backgrounds, and an offshore programme. These initiatives have increased the diversity of students enrolled at the university:

> In this university, we have special intakes. [W]e have an international intake [and] a Class 1 [intake]. The students pay the full fees in their first year, but they study as [per] normal with other students ... We also have alternative channels for senior citizens, [and students from] different cultural backgrounds [and] sports backgrounds. We also have an offshore programme, a ... channel for those [who] work. We introduced these to [improve] diversity in terms of the admission of students. (I/04)

---

1 *Sijil Tinggi Persekolahan Malaysia* or the Malaysian Higher School Certificate is a pre-university examination for Malaysian students, often required for admission to local universities.

Another participant, however, reported that while diversity is increasing on her university campus, most international students come from a limited geographical region. The majority of existing international students, according to her, are from Middle Eastern and African nations. Only a small number of international students are from other countries. Most of them come to the institution for a brief term of study through foreign student exchange programmes. In contrast, local students represent a varied cross-section of Malaysia's major races, including the *Orang Asli*:

> Diversity is there ... we can see so many students from different backgrounds on campus. But we can see that the majority is from certain areas only. We want a more diverse combination, [from] all countries ... but, of course, not all international students want to pursue full-time studies in Malaysia, [as they] rather come on a short-term basis like on [the] exchange programme. [W]e can't get hold of full-time students for the Bachelor's or Master's programmes, not as many as from the Middle Eastern, African countries. If we narrow down the [the concept of diversity] to the local students, we have all races in this university ... Malay, Chinese, Indian and all the native races, compared to other universities that focus more on the *Bumiputera*[2] races. (I/05)

Various academic backgrounds

Another strategy adopted to boost student diversity is admitting undergraduate students from a variety of academic backgrounds. According to one participant, their university can expand diversity through this technique as it enjoys complete autonomy. The university's diversity policy, which remains in force, has become a model for some other universities:

> In 2009, we were the only university to introduce diversity [in our admission policy]. [We received students from] lots of academic backgrounds, equivalent to STPM and matriculation. Before 2009, intake was under the centralised UPU[3] for undergraduates. After 2009, we gained autonomy [and] introduced diversity. [That] remains our policy in this university ... and we can see some universities following [suit]. (I/04)

---

[2] *Bumiputera* is a Malay term that translates to "Son of the Soil" and refers to the Malay and *Orang Asli* peoples.

[3] UPU stands for *Unit Pengambilan Universiti* or University Central Unit, which is responsible for coordinating the application and placement of students in local universities and colleges.

Barriers to access to higher education

Quotas

The findings of this study indicate that quotas are a significant impediment to students obtaining entrance to higher education. Specific programmes, according to one of the participants, require lab or studio space, placing restrictions on student enrolment:

> [While] we can accept applications at any time and any level, [there are] barriers ... due to quotas. How many students per programme can the school accept? Some programmes require a studio or a lab base, so [there are] limitations. (I/05)

Only a limited number of students may access higher education even though enrolment has increased, as the Ministry of Higher Education (MOHE) has established a cap or quota on student admissions. While students with a variety of academic backgrounds may enrol, there are still several restrictions:

> The number of applications increased, but we have limited seats ... [due to] quotas ... We can take [students with] various academic backgrounds, but [the intake is] limited to 10% [due to policy set up by the Ministry]. (I/04)

However, according to one participant, the various intakes in her university have no bearing on MOHE's student admission quotas for public mainstream pupils. If any particular school in the university can expand their enrolment, they may do so:

> [Admission] depends on the capacity of the schools. If schools can take more [students], then they can. (I/04)

Entry requirements

Admission standards, including English language proficiency, a cumulative grade point average (CGPA) and interviews, can also act as a barrier to those pursuing higher education. Students' applications must demonstrate that students possess the necessary academic credentials and adhere to certain requirements, as explained by one study participant:

> [There are] so many barriers [such as] ... English [fluency], CGPA, even interviews for programmes. [However,] the main thing ... is that [the

> students'] academic backgrounds meet the minimum requirements. We have no issue accepting student applications on programmes that can accept students directly without interviews. (I/05)

The participant, however, claimed that removing the requirement may create problems for the institution. She argued that the institution has already established the admission standards for each programme, and that the university may face complications if a school or centre eliminates fundamental admission standards such as English:

> There are programmes that do not require English [as part of the admission]. When the School of Arts removed the requirement [of English proficiency], students from all kinds of backgrounds [joined the school]. Of course, schools want better and higher-quality students to produce theses. If students don't understand English, how can they communicate? We need to produce theses in English or Malay, not their native language. (I/05)

Availability of lecturers

Supervisors are required to oversee the work of students in research-based programmes for thesis completion. Even if students complete all admission standards, they may still be denied admission if an appropriate supervisor is unavailable:

> In terms of research, [access depends] on the availability of supervisors. Even though a student meets all the requirements, we can't offer them a place if a supervisor is not available. How can we offer a place when someone can't supervise them? This would jeopardise the student's time and fees, and that won't be fair to them. (I/05)

In summary, the findings have revealed some positive impacts of massification on equity and access to the university and HEIs in general. Among the positive impacts mentioned are increased growth of higher education, better representation of students from different backgrounds, and better career prospects. Nevertheless, there is also a host of issues and challenges. These include a lack of participation by indigenous groups, a lack of diversity among international students, and the existence of barriers that hinder efforts towards equity of access and diversity. The major issues mentioned are quotas, entry requirements and availability of lecturers.

DISCUSSIONS AND CONCLUSIONS

This study sought to examine the impact of higher education massification on equity and diversity, and explore issues and challenges in the institutional implementation in Malaysia. Four themes emerged from the findings: (1) massification of higher education for inclusivity, (2) equity of access to higher education, (3) diversity in higher education, and (4) barriers to access to higher education.

The responses obtained from the participants in this study demonstrate that there are a number of strategies or initiatives implemented by the Malaysian government to increase equity and diversity. The initiatives observed by the participants can be generally grouped into two levels—ministerial and institutional. At the ministerial level, two major initiatives were mentioned: (1) the national lifelong learning agenda, and (2) differentiated intake channels. At the institutional level, initiatives that have been implemented, as remarked by the participants, include school fee discounts, interventions according to special needs, and extra options for student admissions. The participants also reported that their university has the autonomy to be creative in expanding access for students, since the institution is of university status.

These initiatives have resulted in a range of positive impacts on the composition of the student population. The higher education massification in the country has increased the number of students enrolled in HEIs, providing somewhat greater access to students from a range of backgrounds and so increases the level of inclusivity. Similarly, the student profile has shifted from being elitist in nature to a more varied one. These points were noted by some of the study participants, lending support to the quantitative findings regarding the rising trend of student enrolment in Malaysian HEIs reported in previous studies (MOHE, 2020; Tham, 2011). The massification efforts, according to the study participants, have also enabled a greater number of students to have better career prospects and increased the supply of skilled graduates needed by industries. These findings are consistent with the findings by the Department of Statistics Malaysia (2020, 2021), which demonstrate an increasing trend in graduate employment since 2018. In short, it may be said that higher education massification in Malaysia has some positive impacts on access and inclusivity and indirectly contributes towards the country's socioeconomic and human capital development.

However, there are also shortfalls in the massification efforts, as observed by the participants. One of the study's key findings is that while the population of local students in the university is diverse, there is little diversity among international students. As reported by one of the participants, most international students come from a limited geographical region. This observation is in line with Statistica (2022), which reports that the majority of international students in Malaysia come from Asian countries such as China, Indonesia and Bangladesh, with very few from Europe. Similarly, there are still gaps in diversity in terms of local students. For instance, underprivileged groups were seen by the study participants to be underrepresented. Some structural barriers were also identified, namely the ministry-imposed quota system, entry requirements, and availability of teaching staff for research students.

These aforementioned barriers can become significant impediments to students obtaining entrance to higher education. Even though the various initiatives aimed at massifying higher education can be said to have a significant influence on increasing student access and reducing disparities, there still appear to be considerable differences in participation by students from different socioeconomic backgrounds. It also needs to be noted that the imbalance between access, equity and diversity is not unique to Malaysia. Bulbul (2021) reports that in many countries, significant disparities exist in higher education participation rates among different social and cultural groups.

Greater efforts must therefore be made to boost equity and diversity in the higher education system. As pointed out by Yaacob et al. (2019), there needs to be more attention from the government to intervene in diversity issues and provide functional mechanisms that encourage stakeholders to enhance quality education, such as embracing learners from diverse backgrounds and instilling a global mindedness among students through their studies.

Finding avenues for students from disadvantaged socioeconomic groups in Malaysia is critical in fostering equity in higher education, since discrepancies in access to various disciplines have far-reaching repercussions for intergenerational fairness. We concur with Mohd Salleh and Yahya (2011), who argue that it is imperative that a much larger number of young people—especially those belonging to underprivileged classes or living in rural areas—get the benefits of higher education to prevent the dangers of increased socioeconomic stratification, with the gap between the "haves" and "have nots" widening further.

Varied student choices will contribute to a diverse higher education system that can help students sharpen their critical thinking and analytical skills, and succeed in an increasingly multicultural and interconnected world. A system that embraces diversity can also break down stereotypes, reduce bias, and enable schools to fulfil their role in opening doors for students of all backgrounds (United States Department of Education, 2016).

Access is also contingent on various overlapping concerns. According to Bulbul (2016), socioeconomic and sociocultural factors—especially income status, the education level of parents, and living areas—are determinants of higher education attendance and continuation for young adults in many countries. It is therefore important that a holistic approach is adopted in the government's efforts to facilitate access.

In addition, barriers to access need to be urgently addressed. For instance, admission standards to programmes can act as a hindrance to pursuing higher education. Arguably, as noted by Mohd Salleh and Yahya (2011), in an ideal society, excellence is best promoted by policies that select society's most creative and motivated members for advanced education. However, selection based on prior achievement may be unfair to those without sufficient opportunities and exposure in pre-tertiary education, resulting in discrimination and further disparities. This is especially the case with respect to indigenous people, the *Orang Asli*. According to Wan (2020), despite continuous efforts and investments over the years, education gaps persist between the *Orang Asli* children and non-indigenous ones.

Diversification of the student body can be fostered through various admission channels that provide educational opportunities for individuals with a range of academic and career experiences. Financial support is also critical in increasing university access for a broader range of students; thus, course fee discounts may be granted to underprivileged populations to assist and support their study completion.

Despite initiatives by the government and HEIs to improve diversity, this study and findings from past literature suggest that only limited progress has been made. There is a need for action to enable increased enrolment of students from diverse backgrounds, and HEIs and academics must be receptive to facilitating student access. This is especially critical given the disruption to teaching and learning caused by the Coronavirus Disease 2019 outbreak (Muhammad, 2020). There may be a need for some degree of tolerance at the point of entry without compromising quality. As Mohd Salleh and Yahya (2011) point out, combining tolerance at the university's point of entry with rigour at the point of exit might offer a solution to this dilemma.

Efforts towards equity and diversity must also be all-encompassing. Thus, there is a need to address the nationality imbalance in terms of international student enrolment. Benchmarking best practices by leading countries that champion higher education equity and diversity, such as New Zealand, the United States and Japan (Forbes, 2012), might assist Malaysian HEIs in their endeavour to facilitate access effectively and holistically.

In conclusion, all students must have an equitable opportunity to enrol in tertiary education. To this end, higher education stakeholders must be aware of the growing diversity of the student bodies, their backgrounds, and the academic problems they encounter. Disadvantaged students require more help throughout their studies to bridge the growing divide between the university entry and departure points. With entry "loosened" due to policies and relaxed admission criteria, additional academic support for disadvantaged students may be needed to ensure their academic success.

As HEIs continue to expand access by admitting more students than ever before, it is critical for institutions to establish institutional structures and processes to ensure and promote equity, diversity and inclusivity. It is also critical for institutions to ensure that quality and excellence in offering a transformational educational experience for all students are not jeopardised when access is extended. Attaining this balancing act in an era of massification is crucial to ensure that expansion results in equal access for students from all backgrounds while maintaining quality and excellent standards.

REFERENCES

Akalu, G. A. (2017). Higher education 'massification' and challenges to the professoriate: Do academics' conceptions of quality matter? *Quality in Higher Education, 22*(3), 260–276.

Bai, L. M. (2006). Graduate unemployment: Dilemmas and challenges in China's move to mass higher education. *The China Quarterly, 185*, 128–144.

Braun V., & Clarke V. (2006). Using thematic analysis in psychology. *Qualitative Research in Psychology, 3*, 77–101. https://doi.org/10.1191/1478088706qp063oa

Bulbul, T. (2021). Socio-economic status and school types as the determinants of access to higher education. *Egitim ve Bilim, 46*(205), 303–333.

Chan, R. Y. (2016). Understanding the purpose of higher education: An analysis of the economic and social benefits for completing a college degree. *Journal of Education Policy, Planning and Administration, 6*(405), 1–40.

Chan, S. J., & Lin, L. W. (2015). Massification of higher education in Taiwan: Shifting pressure from admission to employment. *Higher Education Policy, 28*(1), 17–33.

Chiang, I-C. A., Jhangiani, R. S., & Price, P. C. (2015). *Research methods of psychology* (2nd Canadian ed.). BCcampus. https://opentextbc.ca/researchmethods

Clancy, P. & Goastellec, G. (2007). Exploring access and equity in higher education: Policy and performance in a comparative perspective. *Higher Education Quarterly, 61*(2), 136–154.

Creswell, J. W. (2003). *Research design: Qualitative, quantitative, and mixed methods approaches* (2nd ed.). Sage Publications.

Department of Statistics Malaysia. (2020). *Ministry of economy: Department of statistics Malaysia.* https://www.dosm.gov.my

Department of Statistics Malaysia. (2021). *Ministry of economy: Department of statistics Malaysia.* https://www.dosm.gov.my

Dunrong, B. (2015). Shifting demographics in higher education in Asia. *International Higher Education,* (47), 14–15. https://ejournals.bc.edu/ojs/index.php/ihe/article/download/7957/7108.

Forbes. (2012). *Global diversity rankings by country, sector and occupation.* https://images.forbes.com/forbesinsights/StudyPDFs/global_diversity_rankings_2012.pdf

Ghasemy, M., Hussin, S., Megat Daud, M. A. K., Md Nor, M., Ghavifekr, S., & Kenayathulla, H. B. (2018). Issues in Malaysian higher education: A quantitative representation of the top five priorities, values, challenges, and solutions from the viewpoints of academic leaders. *SAGE Open, 8*(1), 1–15.

Hughes, A. (2018). Barriers to entering higher education: Rural students' perspective. *Journal of Information Technologies and Lifelong Learning, 1*(2), 22–27.

IGI Global. (2021). *What is massification of higher education?* https://www.igi-global.com/dictionary/massification-of-higher-education/69992

Ilie, S., & Rose, P. (2016). Is equal access to higher education in South Asia and Sub-Saharan Africa achievable by 2030? *Higher Education, 72,* 435–455.

Kamanzi, P. C., Goastellec, G., & Pelletier, L. (2021). Mass university and social inclusion: The paradoxical effect of public policies. *Social Inclusion, 9*(3), 32–43.

Khoo, K. K. (2005). *One hundred years: The University of Malaya.* Universiti Malaya Press.

Lincoln, Y. S., & Guba, E. G. (1985). *Naturalistic inquiry.* Sage.

Maxwell, J. A. (2004). Causal explanation, qualitative research, and scientific inquiry in education. *Educational Researcher, 33*(2), 3–11.

McCowan, T. (2016). Three dimensions of equity of access to higher education. *Compare: A Journal of Comparative and International Education, 46*(4), 645–665.

McNamara, C. (2022). General guidelines for conducting research interviews. Management Library. https://managementhelp.org/businessresearch/interviews.htm

Ministry of Higher Education (MOHE). (2020). *Higher education statistics 2019.*

Ministry of Higher Education (MOHE). (2021). *Department of polytechnics and community colleges.* https://mypolycc.edu.my

Mohd Salleh, N., & Yahya, F. (2011). Issues on accessibility and equity in the Malaysian higher education: The roles of distance education—An overview. *Gading Business and Management Journal, 15,* 41–48.

Mok, K. H., & Jiang, J. (2016). *Massification of higher education: Challenges for admissions and graduate employment in China.* Centre for Global Higher Education.

Muhammad, M. (2020). Higher education and COVID-19 pandemic: Matters arising and the challenges of sustaining academic programs in developing African universities. *International Journal of Educational Research Review, 5*(4), 417–423.

Mullen, C. A. (2005). *Fire & ice: Igniting and channeling passion in new qualitative researchers.* Peter Lang Publishing.

Noui, R. (2020). Higher education between massification and quality. Higher Education. *Evaluation and Development, 14*(2), 93–103. https://doi.org/10.1108/HEED-04-2020-0008

Nowell, L. S., Norris, J. M., White, D. E., & Moules, N. J. (2017). Thematic analysis: Striving to meet the trustworthiness criteria. *International Journal of Qualitative Methods, 16*(1), 1–13.

Okoro, R. U. (2003). Research methods in educational studies. International *Journal of Business and Social Science.*

Organisation for Economic Cooperation and Development. (2009). *Creating effective teaching and learning environments: First results from TALIS.* https://www.oecd.org/education/school/43023606.pdf

Palinkas, L. A., Horwitz, S. M., Green, C. A., Wisdom, J. P., Duan, N., & Hoagwood, K. (2015). Purposeful sampling for qualitative data collection and analysis in mixed method implementation research. *Administration and Policy in Mental Health and Mental Health Services Research, 42*(5), 533–544.

Phillips, A. (2019). The quest for diversity in higher education. *Pepperdine Policy Review, 11*(4).

Salkind, N. (2010) *Encyclopedia of research design.* SAGE Publications.

Selyutin, A. A., Kalashnikova, T. V., Danilova, N. E., & Frolova, N. V. (2017). Massification of the higher education as a way to individual subjective well-being. *The European Proceedings of Social and Behavioural Sciences.*

Shariffuddin, S. A., Razali, J. R., Ghani, M. A., Wan Shaaidi, W. R., & Ibrahim, I. S. A. (2017). Transformation of higher education institutions in Malaysia: A review. *Journal of Global Business and Social Entrepreneurship, 1*(2), 126–136.

Silverman, D. (2004). *Doing qualitative research.* (2nd ed.). SAGE.

Statistica. (2022). *Number of international students studying in higher education institutes in Malaysia in 20222019, by country of origin (in 1,000s).* https://www.statista.com/statistics/866731/international-students-in-malaysia-by-country-of-origin

Strauss, A., & Corbin, J. (1990). *Basics of qualitative research: Grounded theory procedures and techniques.* Sage Publications.

Tapsir, S. H. (2019, May 14). Harmonising public and private higher education. *New Straits Times.* https://www.nst.com.my/opinion/columnists/2019/05/488452/harmonising-public-and-private-higher-education

Tham, S. Y. (2011). *Exploring access and equity in Malaysia's private higher education.* Asian Development Bank Institute.

Thian, L. B. (2014). *Institutional factors that contribute to educational quality at a private higher education in Malaysia* [Doctoral thesis, Universiti Malaya].

Tremblay, K., Lalancette, D., & Roseveare, D. (2012). *Assessment of higher education learning outcomes: Design and implement.* Organisation for Economic Cooperation and Development. https://www.oecd.org/education/skills-beyond-school/AHELOFSReportVolume1.pdf

Trow, M. (2006). Reflections on the transition from elite to mass to universal access: Forms and phases of higher education in modern society since WWII. In J. J. F. Forest & P. G. Altbach (Eds.), *International handbook of higher education* (pp. 243–280). Springer.

United Nations Educational, Scientific and Cultural Organisation (UNESCO) Institute for Statistics. (2020). *Education: Gross enrolment ratio by level of education.* http://data.uis.unesco.org/index.aspx?queryid=3812

United States Department of Education (2016). *Advancing diversity and inclusion in higher education.* https://www2.ed.gov/rschstat/research/pubs/advancing-diversity-inclusion.pdf

Wan, Y. S. (2020). *Education policies in overcoming barriers faced by Orang Asli children: Education for all.* Institute for Democracy and Economic Affairs. https://www.ideas.org.my/publications-item/policy-paper-no-66-education-policies-in-overcoming-barriers-faced-by-orang-asli-children-education-for-all

Wu, C. (2011). High graduate unemployment rate and Taiwanese undergraduate education. *International Journal of Educational Development, 31*(3), 303–310.

Yaacob, A., Awang-Hashim, R., Valdez, N. P., & Yusof, N. (2019). Illuminating diversity practices in Malaysian higher education institutions. *Asia Pacific Journals of Educators and Education, 34,* 1–16.

Yin, R. K. (2009). *Case study research: Design and methods* (4th ed.). Sage Publications.

Chapter 7

Resilient Southeast Asian Education Through Humane and Compassionate Pedagogical Framework: An Autoethnography in Online Teaching and Learning Amid COVID-19 Health Crisis

Rafael Ibe Santos*

ABSTRACT

The worldwide pandemic that paralysed the delivery of tertiary education in 2020 has forever changed the way we conduct teaching and learning. Responses and remedies from universities were blended, remote or online in approach, often placing a great burden on the part of students and their families. Suffice it to say, schools and educators alike failed to see the human aspect of the whole scholastic enterprise, setting aside, for instance, the myriad struggles learners faced—from physical to psychological and mental conditions that affected performance. The interpretivist-constructivist study in this chapter explores the common themes that reflect students' predicament and learning experiences relative to remote schooling during the academic year 2020–2021, based on three sets of autoethnographic narratives. At the same time, it looks at the possible implications of such stories on education theory, practice, curriculum, virtual learning and teacher training. Using a qualitative design, the analysis reveals that college students clamour for understanding, empathy and adequate scaffolding in a consistently positive learning environment, highlighting the centrality of supportive approaches

* University of Asia and the Pacific, the Philippines

and methodologies in a fully remote context. The research further finds that students—susceptible to unpleasant circumstances wrought by the global health crisis—can and will thrive in challenging situations if pedagogy is grounded in empathy. The study points to a paradigm that combines the philosophies of Jean Piaget and Lev Vygotsky, resulting in a humane and compassionate pedagogical approach that could assist tertiary education in playing a pivotal role in Southeast Asia's social and economic recovery.

Keywords Autoethnography, humane and compassionate pedagogy, learning experience, narratives, online learning

INTRODUCTION

As the migration to virtual schooling either partially or fully became inevitable because of the Coronavirus Disease 2019 (COVID-19), the United Nations Educational, Scientific and Cultural Organisation (UNESCO) outlined a list of recommendations for countries to adopt (2021). Aside from modifying scholastic objectives and prioritising the social aspect of the whole academic experience, governments were urged to ensure adequate support for vulnerable learners and their families. Echoing UNESCO, the Organisation for Economic Cooperation and Development (OECD, 2021a) underscores the need to aid learners in navigating virtual platforms while supporting them in terms of their overall well-being and mental health. This expectation broadens the traditional role of educators to include so-called task crafting and cognitive crafting (Dutton & Wrzesniewski, 2020). Task crafting involves modifying "the type, scope, sequence, and the number of tasks," while cognitive crafting implies a change in the way functions are interpreted (para. 2). "Noticing the suffering of students and responding with compassion," as explained by Dutton and Worline (2020), is not in the job description of faculties, but it has become "an inevitable reality of the work of teaching" (para. 8).

This expanded role must now include empathising and caring for learners, and aside from course delivery, factors wrought by the health and education crisis must be considered. This form of vigilance helps ensure students are in their best shape, and able to assimilate knowledge and develop skills. Full awareness of college students' mental and physical conditions, coupled with morale-boosting and motivating instructional techniques, could lead to a more positive curricular experience (Taştan et al., 2017). This can translate into active virtual engagement and better academic performance (Aguilera-Hermida, 2020). All of this further points to teacher training that transcends technical know-how and delivery strategies to ensure assistance is received by those who are vulnerable. As OECD (2021b) has noted, academics must "become active agents for change, not just in implementing technological and social innovations, but in designing them too" (pp. 5–6). Following OECD and UNESCO, the training of educators requires learning how to stand alongside their pupils in this new normal by exhibiting sensitivity and concern.

That we are experiencing "a pedagogical and instructional challenge" in addition to a technical debacle is not an overstatement (Ali, 2020, p. 22). Besides ensuring continuity of delivery and technological skills adeptness among faculties (AlSaqqaf & Ke, 2021), schools are presented with the need to look at a myriad of well-being issues encountered by undergraduates. The Hope Center for College, Community, and Justice (2021) in the United States reports that as of spring 2021, more than half of college students experienced low to moderate anxiety, while a third complained of moderate to severe depression. According to experts, undergraduates cannot excel academically if their mental and psychological concerns are not properly addressed (Freberg & Angelo, 2021). The worldwide response has been on creating a supportive environment for learners. For instance, United Kingdom-based primary and secondary schools have found it a matter of priority to meet pupils' emotional and mental health and well-being (Sharp et al., 2020). Academics have also gone out of their way to find solutions to "learning gaps" via interventions such as "small-group or one-to-one sessions" (Sharp et al., 2020, pp. 9 & 40). The situation in higher education, however, appears to be lagging. Studies show that the COVID-19 lockdown has negatively impacted the mental health of British university students (Savage et al., 2020) and thoughts of suicide have increased among young adults (O'Connor et al., 2021). Increased risks of depression and anxiety have also been noted (Kwong et al., 2021). In fact, about 34% of young British people consider their mental health as having gotten "much worse" due to the pandemic's "huge amount of extra strain" (Mind, 2021, para. 1), yet supportive and sensitive curricular strategies for undergraduates seem lacking. The answer by Britain's higher education institutions (HEIs) includes flexible teaching and learning arrangements, technological backing, mental health talks, and on-campus wellness programmes, except for direct interventions from professors. Despite offering a whole range of mental and emotional support, British HEIs appear to emphasise self-help wellness programmes and leave out teacher-initiated assistance that may aid students in coping with remote schooling (Lane, 2021). A few universities extend welfare services such as counselling in addition to self-care resources (University of Oxford, 2021; The University of Manchester, n.d.).

The situation among the members of the Association of Southeast Asian Nations (ASEAN) is also far from ideal when it comes to aiding students to cope with academic demands amid the COVID-19 threat. Scrambling towards the resumption of scholastic activities following periods of disruptions, education officials found themselves focusing on continuity of schooling and exhausting available modalities for delivery without considering the challenging environments confronting pupils. In Malaysia, connectivity issues and continuance of classes, although characterised by some flexibility in schedule and instructional approaches, overshadowed concerns for learners' wellness (Izhar et al., 2021). In the same vein, Indonesia, the Philippines, Thailand and Vietnam also rushed towards their own versions of virtual classes that involved broadcasts and Internet-based tools and platforms (Joaquin et al., 2020). Invariably, there was an emphasis on transitioning to study-from-home arrangements, adjustment to online or technology instruments and training for their use. Noticeably absent were responsive and sympathetic pedagogical practices among academics.

The prevalence of mental health issues among college students in Cambodia, Laos, Malaysia, Myanmar, Thailand and Vietnam has been noted (Dessauvagie et al., 2021). Researchers in Malaysia, for their part, have found a surge in mental health disorders during the pandemic (Mohd Kassim et al., 2020; Wong et al., 2021). Other Malaysian scholars echo similar findings and emphasise that online arrangements in college have been causing anxiety, stress and depression among students, thus pointing to a more flexible style in pedagogy (Thandevaraj et al., 2021). Local psychologists have also noted that a spike in depression and anxiety-related disorders among teens and children has been due to "confinement, social isolation and uncertainty" (Tan, 2020, para. 77). Lack of skills could also complicate students' situation since not everyone is used to "self-directed learning" (Tichavsky et al., 2015, p. 6). Despite the mental health challenges facing ASEAN undergraduates, coupled with an unfriendly and unpredictable educational ecosystem, there exists a propensity to ignore their circumstances. Overwhelmed with "stress and anxiety" and depression that is as high as 71%, Malaysian university students also have to deal with "information and work overload" (Al-Kumaim et al., 2021, pp. 5–6). Also observed is a proclivity among academics to rush syllabus implementation to satisfy institutional requirements (Al-Kumaim et al., 2021). Thandevaraj et al. (2021), for instance, report "cognitive exhaustion" in Malaysia (p. 1299). The sentiment against overwhelming online course requirements has been a major issue in the Philippines as well. Student leaders from top universities, complaining of the "lack of environments conducive to learning at home and the effectiveness of the online lectures", emphasise that too much workload increases students' burden (Bagayas, 2020, para. 4). A study by Tee et al. (2020), who have found "moderate-to-severe anxiety" among a quarter of respondents and "moderate-to-severe depression" among one-sixth of the participants at the onset of the COVID-19 pandemic, provides a strong basis for such reactions (p. 390).

The foregoing highlights the need to explore teaching frameworks that address learners' cognitive and non-cognitive needs and concerns. This study is a direct response to the seeming neglect of the learning difficulties encountered by students in a health crisis. Thus, I will explore in this chapter the benefits of humane and compassionate pedagogical frameworks in an online learning environment complicated by a health crisis such as the COVID-19 pandemic. In this interpretivist research, I provide a background on Jean Piaget and Lev Vygotsky's constructivist teaching and learning philosophies, retrace the genesis of compassionate education, and explain the methodology employed. I then focus on common themes that mirror students' predicament and learning experiences during the academic year 2020–2021 remote schooling, by examining three sets of self-ethnographic narratives. Conclusions and implications of the findings on education theory, practice, curriculum, virtual learning and teacher training—all pivotal in Southeast Asia's social and economic recovery—are then discussed.

BACKGROUND: CONSTRUCTIVISM IN PIAGETIAN AND VYGOTSKYAN PEDAGOGICAL TRADITIONS

Constructivism—which, according to Yilmaz (2008), has implications on pedagogical practice—views education as an "interpretive, recursive, and nonlinear process by active learners interacting with the surroundings of the physical and social world" (Fosnot, 2005, as cited in Rao, 2018, p. 25). It is a philosophy that gives more value to input from the learner than the teacher, who must act as a facilitator. Bélanger (2011) explains that "[t]eaching, from a personal constructivism perspective, involves providing experiences that induce cognitive conflict and hence encourage learners to develop new knowledge schemes that are better adapted to experience" (p. 28). The role of the teacher, then, is to provide realistic activities involving a lot of group interaction. In this situation, learners develop self-regulation and independence.

Constructivist education is anchored on the concepts of John Dewey and William James, as well as the principles of Piaget, Vygotsky, Jerome Bruner and Ernst von Glasersfeld. Yilmaz (2008), citing the work of Richardson (2003), considers constructivist pedagogy as "the creation of classroom environments, activities, and methods that are grounded in a constructivist theory of education" with goals that focus on the development of "deep understandings" (p. 165). Here, while not the central figure, the educator is actively engaged in ensuring a curriculum that spurs concept development and "deep" understanding as the goal of instruction, rather than behaviours which are achieved through "authentic" tasks (Fosnot 1996, as cited in Yilmaz, 2008, p. 165). Yilmaz (2008) adds:

> As a theory, constructivism is neither a stimulus response phenomenon nor a passive process of receiving knowledge; instead, as an adaptive activity requiring building conceptual structures and self-regulation through reflection and abstraction, learning is an active process of knowledge construction influenced by how one interacts with and interprets new ideas and events. (p. 165)

There are at least two major theories under educational constructivism, namely cognitive constructivist theory of learning and sociocultural constructivist theory of learning. Cognitive constructivist theory of learning traces its roots to the principles of Jean Piaget, a Swiss psychologist, while sociocultural constructivist theory of learning is attributed to Lev Vygotsky, a Russian developmental psychologist.

Cognitive constructivism emphasises the idea of active learning. Such a learning is characterised by active thinking that allows for the interpretation and construction of meaning. It is a process of building knowledge and solving problems via various interactions with the world, indicating directedness and independence in intellectual development. Based on his experiment involving his children, Piaget introduced the concepts of assimilation and accommodation which demand active learners and not passive ones. This is because, as posited by Piaget, problem-solving skills cannot be taught but rather discovered. Assimilation occurs when a piece of information is stored in the learner's schema. Growth happens as the child adjusts to the environment, known as accommodation, which facilitates the revision of existing knowledge in the brain. A period of confusion, when the brain cannot assimilate or understand new knowledge, is called disequilibrium—the very opposite of equilibration. In the latter, the child has accommodated most of the new information and stored it in their schemata, indicating substantial intellectual growth.

The Vygotskyan orientation emphasises the sociocultural aspects of learning. Lave and Wenger (1991) assert that the sociocultural theory requires a "legitimate, peripheral participation in communities of practices" (Bélanger, 2011, p. 30). Under this theory, each learning event is always situated in "the context of people's experience and of their specific participation in the world around them" (p. 30). Related to this approach in education is the idea of scaffolding, drawn from Vygotsky's Zone of Proximal Development theory. The concept teaches that learners are on a journey towards intellectual maturation, and that particular level of growth can be reached with support and intervention. Such scaffolding is not done arbitrarily or at random; rather, it is extended following a determination of learners' level of competence. This involves making the necessary adjustments in pedagogical philosophies and giving support. As knowledge acquisition improves, the extent of scaffolding is lessened and eventually eliminated to promote autonomy.

THE SHIFTING FOCUS OF COMPASSIONATE EDUCATION

The concept of humane pedagogy traces its roots to the early 1800s, which saw the advancement of compassion in dealing with living and non-living things (Burnett, 2000; Unti & DeRosa, 2003). Impressed upon young minds was the value of kindness and empathy exhibited through respect for human rights, animal welfare and the environment (Academy of Prosocial Learning, 2016; Institute for Humane Education, 2021). Over the centuries, this notion metamorphosised, somehow finding its way into the whole-person pedagogy terrain. From the traditional emphasis on the humane treatment of people, animals and nature, it gave rise to various agendas and paradigms. The so-called 21st-century competencies (21CC) frameworks (e.g. Partnership for 21st Century Learning or P21), for instance, emphasise "respect of cultures, religions, and lifestyles" as well as environmental literacy and social and cross-cultural skills, which all point to respect for others (Battelle for Kids, 2019, pp. 6 & 23–24). The Assessment and Teaching of 21st Century Skills, aside from emphasising 21CC, feature personal and social responsibility and citizenship, all of which encompass respect for human rights and the preservation of natural and cultural resources (Binkley et al., 2012). All of these are likely an offshoot of the humane approach or some aspects of it.

From the metamorphosised version of whole-person education, humane pedagogy is again finding its place in academia in light of growing concerns for students' mental health. Sporting a new coat, its focus has shifted from compassion as shown by pupils to one by teachers toward their learners. A pedagogy that is rooted in empathy, this approach can be adopted at all levels. It is captured in a curriculum that is mindful of the circumstances of learners and is flexible and adaptive without sacrificing scholastic standards. Dutton and Worline (2020) observe: "Noticing the suffering of students and responding with compassion isn't ... part of the job of teaching. Yet, paradoxically, it is an inevitable reality of the work" (para. 8). Here, we see a further transformation of educational philosophy—now more than ever emphasising student-centredness (Danker, 2015) of understanding and compassion.

Dutton and Worline (2020) believe that educators, armed with the compassionate approach, are likely to sense signs of pain and suffering and interpret such misery as "worthy of ... attention and empathy" (para. 5). Additionally, employing compassionate practice results in "feeling concern for the suffering of others" so that certain actions are taken "to address or alleviate suffering" (para. 5). Citing various practices by academics, Dutton and Worline add that to show compassion, deadlines can be revised. Assignments can also be altered to ensure "connectedness" among learners to counteract the feeling of isolation, especially for individuals deprived of strong family support (para. 6). Giving short assessments frequently instead of a few long tests and disregarding the lowest scores are also advised. Topics relevant to real-life situations, such as those dealing with the pandemic, are also recommended.

STUDY METHOD: AUTOETHNOGRAPHY ON ONLINE EDUCATION

The autobiographical narrative technique, adopted from Hamdan (2012), provides a methodological grounding for this chapter as it is "highly" suitable for education studies (p. 586). In this enquiry, I rely on my reflective teaching notes or "retrospective viewpoint[s]" (Hamdan, 2012, p. 586). The goal is to interpret the past—that is, the narratives relative to the teaching of four classes in media and technology and three English classes in the academic year 2020–2021. Such stories chronicle struggles and viewpoints regarding professional practice. Introspections were sourced from two published syllabi in Canvas, a web-based learning management system, as well as feedback, namely the semestral evaluations, learning products and emails. These "privileged" and "personal experience methods" provide a "significant form of knowledge" that is useful "on a variety of topics relevant to teaching ... in order to expand knowledge" (Hamdan, 2012, p. 587).

Pertinent activities, notably requirements in the media and English courses during the entire school year (August 2020–May 2021), were revisited. Notes on the perspectives of freshmen enrolled in three English classes and junior college students enlisted in four media courses were also examined. The latter was extracted from course evaluations and unsolicited feedback such as emails and learning products. From these, three categories of autoethnographic narratives were formed and then analysed to ascertain teaching and learning experiences in a remote context. From the narratives, strategies that were lauded by the students and that reflected Piagetian and Vygotskyan principles were identified and explored, substantiating the same with studies and practice by other experts in the field of (remote) education.

Professors may solicit the participation of their students in cases that are deemed "essential ... as in issues of program evaluation or pedagogy" (Ferguson et al., 2004, p. 64). In this study, direct participation from students such as answering surveys was not necessitated. Moreover, the study commenced only after the culmination of the classes involved. Nonetheless, permission to reference the participants' narratives was secured via email, and formal consent was readily granted electronically. To protect confidentiality, "generic descriptors" (i.e. use of the generic "student") were utilised in citing comments without changing the data substance (Ferguson et al., 2004, p. 65). Conflict of interest and methodological issues were addressed by ensuring that the "power inequities" between learners and faculty did not come into the picture (p. 56). This was done by commencing the research at the culmination of classes and after the submission of grades.

Autoethnographic entries, which do not necessarily reflect the perspectives of the university, represent three categories. The first comprises evaluations and emails reflecting anonymised comments from course evaluations and electronic messages from freshmen. The second consists of practice and Canvas entries representing self-reflections and reconstruction of the teaching and learning activities (TLAs) and assessment tasks. The last category—learning product comments—is a record of learning product narratives pertaining to the handling of classes. From this collection, TLAs were identified. Results were analysed and interpreted using narrative analysis, one of the traditional five qualitative enquiry approaches. Narrative enquiry, using mostly interviews and observations, may include documents, films, and other texts and reflective teaching notes, as in the case of this study (Butina, 2015). Following Butina (2015), the narratives perused fit well in this categorisation. References to students' comments or remarks were not exhaustive but were used to illustrate learning experiences.

This study concerns how three sets of autoethnographic narratives capture and reflect teaching and online learning experiences. The sub-problems are the following:

(1) What is the scope of each of the three autoethnographic narratives?
(2) How are teaching and learning experiences reflected in the narratives?
(3) What are the implications of the teaching and learning experiences in terms of pedagogical theory relative to practice and curriculum, virtual learning and teacher training?

STUDY RESULTS: COURSE EVALUATIONS AND EMAIL NARRATIVES

In this section, I refer to retrospective notes with regard to feedback on the remote conduct of three English courses and four media subjects based on two course evaluations and emails.

Course evaluations

The following is a reflection noted on the first-semester course evaluations:

> I, personally, felt as if my professor was just a *little too harsh* at times. He *does not accept the excuses of technical difficulties* or [WiFi] problems as I recall one of my classmates having to go out to buy data to take the exam once. Having no [WiFi] at home was not an excuse as he announced in advance that there was an exam which I understand but even then, he *expects us to go out and buy data when for some people going outside just isn't an option. There was not much flexibility* in this course, and it honestly was *very suffocating* (italics mine). (Santos, 2020b, p. 1)

Another student complained of "TOO much work" that was "overwhelming", adding that they "may have [been] overestimated ... we actually had one activity that we could not accomplish" (capitalisation in the original) (Santos, 2020b, p. 1). Regarding my teaching approach, the following was observed:

> During the first few days I was able to understand the lesson[s] ... but during the next few modules we had to do our own reading and [group work] based [on] what we understood from our OWN learning. [We] had papers and other things to submit but ... many of us struggled this semester (capitalisation in the original). (Santos, 2020b, p.1)

Sentiments highlight coping issues or the failure to consider the enormity and complexity of requirements, or both. Undeniably, curricular planning was done as if learners were not languishing in a myriad of complications associated with virtual schooling. Although it was previously resolved that kindness and flexibility would be shown, the preceding comments prove otherwise. Hinted by the comments is a clamour for academics who constantly feel for those placed under their care. Providing "positive emotional content" and reducing online tasks are some ways this is expressed (Al-Kumaim et al., 2021, p. 15). Self-reflections point to the value of putting oneself in the shoes of mentally and emotionally battered undergraduates.

Midway through the first term, major adjustments were made following Piagetian and Vygotskyan principles in teaching which highlight a balance between independent learning and supportive approaches (Scott, 2021). Changes proved helpful. While there were "several papers that were required throughout the semester", reported a freshman, "they ... [helped] enhance my skills and challenge me. Group [work] done also allowed me to interact" (Santos, 2020b, p. 1). Still, another saw "a really encouraging and motivating personality" in their professor, adding, "I love his attitude so much as he never fails to be super considerate and makes his students smile with his lectures." The change in tone reveals experiences and expectations in virtual school. Acquisition of skills outweighs the volume of tasks, while a longing for socialisation, as Aguilera-Hermida (2020) highlights in her study, is expressed. Preceding thoughts also provide clues regarding the value of sensitivity and understanding in handling collegiate learners. A lot is expected of instructors. Delivering just the right amount of relevant, interactive content within a supportive and positive environment goes a long way. Constructivist approaches, designed to develop critical thinking and independence in distance education (Brown, 2014), deserve adequate scaffolding (Scott, 2021), especially for the vulnerable. As we deal with individuals who get easily overwhelmed, it helps to constantly inquire how everyone is faring. Hearing them out sincerely and then thinking of ways to assist them can provide comfort (Pearson, 2020).

Email narratives

Narratives from emails indicate a contrast from students' recollections of a strict, unbending and inconsiderate professor. A freshman (Student 1) noted a teacher who was "reasonably strict … with our conduct and with teaching lessons" but "also understanding" (Santos, 2020a, p. 1). Deadline extensions, responding to emails on weekends and "for keeping an open mind and for putting in the time … to answer all questions" were observed by Student 2 (p. 2). Positive learning experiences were captured in such expressions as "a completely safe space", "felt safe", "freedom to ask questions and make mistakes" and "encouraged" (p. 3–5). Some referenced remarks are provided in Table 7.1.

Table 7.1 Selected email excerpts from first-semester students

Student	Comments
3	"very considerate when it comes to deadlines and requirements"
4	"very interactive"; "you grant extensions"
5	"the countless ... considerations on the deadlines"; "learned and improved"
6	"admired the time and effort to be responsive especially during weekends"
7	"giving and finding time almost every day, even during weekends, to answer ... questions and address our concerns"; "patience"; "you make sure we adjust ... no student is left behind"
8	"it is very helpful that you make things easier for us by helping and guiding us with the lessons and activities"

Comments reflect the sensitivity to and understanding of students' situations in a remote context, demonstrated through the adjustment of deadlines (Appendix A) and the teacher's regular presence through promptness in sending feedback or addressing concerns. Again, there is a clamour for adequate and regular support and empathy, pointing to social constructivism in teaching. Undergraduates look up to their professors even in small matters, such as aiding them in understanding a lesson further or clarifying assessment guidelines. These are not entirely new, but the fact that they are put under a spotlight indicates a changing ecosystem in tertiary education. Professors are perceived as allies when they show consideration towards those they teach.

Second-semester evaluations narratives

A responsive and supportive pedagogy was observed in the second term of the 2020–2021 academic year based on evaluation narratives (Table 7.2). A commitment "to keep my mind open" after listening to freshmen's feedback during the first semester paid off (Santos, 2021a, p. 3). Vowing to "keep listening to the comments and consider ways to help them cope and complete the requirements, without lowering [the] standards" was in the right direction (p. 3). For instance, Student 1 reported having "enjoyed" how their concerns were responded to "fairly quickly" and was grateful for the "recordings of … lectures in different formats" (p. 3).

Table 7.2 Selected comment excerpts from second-semester course evaluations

Student	Remarks
2	"fun activities ... allowed us to showcase our skills"
3	"really enjoyed ... group works"
4	"gives feedback on our works and replies quickly to our concerns which is very helpful"
5	"very easy to work with"; "wants his students to pass"; "helps us [pass]"
6	"very enjoyable"
7	"probably the course where I learn[t] the most ... [t]hough the pacing was relatively fast, it is ... one of the top courses"
8	"very enthusiastic teacher ... I could see how much he cared for us"
9	"whole course ... a great experience!"
10	"students are able to apply the lessons ... despite this online learning setup"
11	"pacing of the course ... seems very rushed and overloaded with requirements [but] ... [he is] considerate and tried to find ways for us to complete"
12	"very engaging"
13	"really understanding and flexible with submission dates"
14	"understanding and patient ... fun and easy to learn from him"
15	"my favourite ... this term because he seems ... he really cares about his students ... I found the course ... very fun and educational"
16	"very considerate in giving deadlines and grades"
17	"knows how to make the assignments less heavy"
18	"activities ... were practical ... we could use the skills we learn[t] in other subjects and in real life"
19	"topics are interesting"; "activities ... enjoyable"; "oftentimes, the tasks are overwhelming"
20	"course was flexible and was very much generous"; "was communicative towards students"

Emerging from the retrospective narratives is that students in a virtual setup thrive when true learning takes place and professors commit to extending real and adequate support even beyond instructional hours. Deubel (2003, as cited in Dennis et al., 2007) subscribes to such Vygotskyan approach in teaching and believes that an academic's "attitude, motivation, and true commitment toward instruction delivery via distance education programs" spell the difference in terms of quality of learning (p. 43). This observation is consistent with a study by Sunway University scholars on the impact of social support on one's coping capabilities. Lian and Geok (2009) have found that a person's ability to cope in early adulthood is influenced by perceived social support and, in the case of this study, empathy and understanding from educators. Flexibility with deadlines, kindness, consideration, understanding, patience and care are associated with supportive pedagogical strategies. Words and phrases like "interesting", "enjoyable", "fun", "enthusiastic", "great experience", "very engaging", "teaching methods", "overall delivery" and "being able to learn from the teacher" demonstrate positive educational experience. Support is related to constant communication and promptness of feedback to concerns. Finally, collaborative work that entails interactions is underscored, suggesting that it enhances the learning experience. Experiences of students point to humane and compassionate practices in pedagogy. Quality instruction is already a given in a remote context, but educators are expected to give more during and beyond teaching time by demonstrating care, concern and compassion. This combination reflects Piaget and Vygotsky's constructivist principles.

PRACTICE NARRATIVES AND CANVAS REFLECTIONS

Practice narratives

A curricular strategy that considers students' predicaments is captured in the following practice narrative entry:

> At the start of ... the online learning setup, I decided ... to focus on being cordial and accommodating. (Some students had prior knowledge of my strictness in my previous classes, while others were warned of a "terror" instructor). Given the difficulty being encountered by many in online learning, I resolved to abandon my usual intimidating demeanour

> ... My tone had to sound friendly and positive and made it my regular practice to give positive comments. It was made clear in class that comments and suggestions were very much welcome. Lectures ... had to be refined to ensure an interactive and fun learning with the integration of games ... These created a positive learning atmosphere and made students confident to reach out to their teacher for any concerns. (Santos, 2021b, p. 1)

This approach represents a further change in my overall curricular strategy for 2020–2021, one that resulted in and ensured a welcoming and encouraging atmosphere. Ultimately, it made a big difference in students' scholastic experience. Records of two media classes during the second mini-term from March to May 2021 showed a stark difference in academic performance compared to the 2019–2020 batches. Among the 2020–2021 enrolees, six garnered almost perfect scores as against a few in the previous year. Ten students scored between 94% and 98%, while the majority had final grades of 81%–93%, even though the course was completed online. While this is not the concern of this study, it provides hints of the impact of a caring method in remote delivery. Blazar and Kraft (2017) stress that "high-quality teachers" who "provide emotionally supportive environments" are most likely to see their students succeed in terms of "social and emotional development" (p. 146).

Retrospective notes indicate that motivation was a prominent tactic. The narrative record states, "All classes were given a guarantee that it was alright to make mistakes and that all students were viewed as being capable of performing well" (Santos, 2021b, p. 1). In cases where students had stopped submitting assignments due to their conditions, assurances were given that their ability to complete tasks mattered more than promptness.

Motivating students to succeed was a regular strategy. Goals and expectations for the class were clearly explained at the beginning of each mini-term. This was followed by a conditioning technique that emphasised students' capacity towards success, being assured that they would be able to manage well. Each class was often treated with motivational spiels about the possibility of performing well, grounded on consistency and discipline. Such were oft-repeated, especially when deadlines were nearing and when there were signs that others were struggling to comply with institutional standards. Checking the welfare of the learners was made on a regular basis while lines of communication "were open, and concerns would always be accommodated" (Santos, 2021b, p. 1). Support was assured and deadlines would be adjusted, if warranted.

Given the challenges of distance schooling, students' perspectives had to be considered; thus, input regarding the course was proactively solicited (Appendix B). Platforms for such dialogue included regular synchronous sessions, email and question-and-answer time via the Mentimeter application (Appendix C), which provided a safe space and anonymity. As regular synchronous meetings were expected in place of face-to-face sessions (Gherghes et al., 2021; Valdez, 2021), I ensured regular synchronous meetings were conducted. Online engagements were appreciated because they were a substitute for face-to-face arrangements, showing the learners' need for support through lectures and the teacher's constant online presence.

Practice narratives show five curricular approaches: (1) a positive and conducive learning environment, (2) constant motivation and certainty of early success, (3) regular checks on learners' welfare, (4) constant solicitation of feedback, and (5) sufficient synchronous meetings and interactions. These are consistent with the second-semester course evaluations and email narratives. These constructivist methods have proved to have enhanced educational experience.

Canvas narratives

Canvas entries show the creation of non-restrictive constructivist learning environments (CLEs), which represent learning spaces and other resources set up for independent learning (Ahmad et al., 2015). From a macro perspective, CLEs come in the form of projects, while from a micro perspective, they constitute instructions for requirements (Santos, 2021c). The activities are not restrictive but serve as jump-off points for active and independent learning to the truest spirit of constructivism (McLeod, 2019). Guidelines are negotiable, and their execution depends on individual or group preference without sacrificing academic standards. Tasks can be accomplished according to one's pacing within certain parameters to ensure submission within reasonable timeframes.

During the second semester, independence was exercised in the podcast project. Recording and editing were accomplished using any web-based applications, while choices of themes, music and other elements were not dictated. The same was applied to a visual project, allowing freedom of choice regarding design elements. The days and hours were made flexible in the media fasting, which traditionally followed a strict timetable. Giving much latitude not only ensured self-expression and independent knowledge construction but, more essentially, resulted in a more relaxed experience which helped alleviate or mitigate anxiety.

Consistent with a non-restrictive approach, the use of various modes of representation became the norm. Options for information presentation included Microsoft Word .doc, Microsoft Word .docx or PDF (for written work), MP3 (for audio files), MP4 or MPEG-4 AVC (for audio and video), and PNG or JPEG (for still images). All of these are congruent with constructivism's goal of providing experience in and appreciation for multiple perspectives as per Honebein (1996), which is non-restrictive and ideal in a virtual ecosystem. The constructivist approach worked well for many, but some necessitated scaffolding via additional guidance and individual/group coaching. Chambers et al. (2021) quote Mike Roberto, a trustee professor at Bryant University, as saying that "the rigors of the course work" can be maintained while showing empathy and understanding at the same time (para. 10). Undergraduates, according to the professor, tend to be more "motivated and engaged in courses where faculty demonstrated empathy for their circumstances" (ibid.).

Aside from teacher-student interaction, participation through student-student interaction and curation of individual experience characterised all requirements. Pair and group tasks, such as an interview project, afforded virtual socialisation. Three forms of interactions were performed: (1) data-gathering via interview, (2) collaboration for data interpretation, and (3) actual presentation (Santos, 2021d). Likewise, the audio project was accomplished in pairs to encourage interactions, while a group report on media topics facilitated further interpersonal communication. Such socialisation was crucial during the pandemic to mitigate social isolation, which heightened anxiety and depression (Filho et al., 2021).

Flexibility and support were key pedagogical practices throughout the digital learning experience in 2020–2021, seen through deadline extensions, resubmissions (chances to improve work), easing of guidelines, and submission of additional or related make-up to assist underperformers. These are again reflective of the Vygotskyan orientation, with mindfulness of learners' situations—such as coping difficulties due to virtual schooling complications and connectivity problems—being the primary reason. For some students, satisfying class requirements was difficult enough because of anxiety and other mental health issues. American professors underscore the need for flexibility in a COVID-19 learning terrain and believe in the value of proficiency rather than mere scores. Educators are enjoined to empathise with those lacking "the support systems, emotional maturity, or coping skills necessary to thrive during this unprecedented time" (Chambers et al., 2021, para. 25).

Eliminating certain assessments was another way of practising flexibility. In the first semester, minor tasks were dropped, emphasising the completion of a major writing project instead. During the second semester, two photography tasks were disregarded, while a scheduled assessment for two sections was skipped as feedback indicated coping issues and high stress levels. An interview task, which required a video conference with experts, permitted other data-gathering methods. The choice of interviewees was also expanded, so long as the interview was accomplished properly and communication skills were developed. Those who performed poorly during the second semester were given a chance to submit tasks related to the core concepts, boosting scores without disregarding standards. This demonstrates a balance between accountability and compassionate pedagogy, emphasising participation such as articulation of thinking in class (Chambers et al., 2021). Pushing college learners too hard and focusing on minute details are counterproductive during a pandemic. The better route is approaching assessments with empathy and focusing on core topics instead of many tests (Chambers et al., 2021).

Four methods were employed in the conduct of all online classes based on autoethnographic entries: (1) non-restrictive constructivist learning environments, a philosophy by Piaget (Ludwig, 2002), (2) the use of multiple modes of representation, (3) intentional virtual interactions, a social constructivism by Vygotsky (Kozulin et al., 2003), and (4) flexibility and support, a feature of Vygotsky's educational theory. These are a show of empathy, especially to individuals who struggled emotionally or mentally because of the pandemic.

LEARNING PRODUCTS NARRATIVES

Presented in this section are selected unsolicited comments made in the digital portfolio, whose content and design were decided by pre-organised groups. Of the eight groups, three narrated their educational experiences. Previous autoethnographic notes indicated giving assurances regarding available help and support without lowering scholastic standards. Independent and active learning were balanced with scaffolding.

Student 1 wrote: "Your constant reminder of not lowering your standards but instead helping us reach them made me believe in myself ... it did not make me complacent, but it pushed me to strive harder" (Santos, 2021b, p. 1). Table 7.3 contains comments regarding learning experiences that reflect preferred pedagogical techniques.

Table 7.3 Selected remarks from learning products

Student	Remarks
2	"your willingness to teach us to understand the lessons better and extend deadlines made this course easier for us"
3	"course was not the easiest to accomplish"; "countless questions were always answered"
4	"patient and considerate"
5	"consideration on our ... situation will forever be appreciated"
6	"scared because of your subject" but "realised that you were a very considerate teacher and helped me become a better student"
7	"whether it is through email or class discussions, you always managed to quell our never-ending clarifications and concerns"; "we never had a teacher quite as interactive and engaging like you, and we are ultimately blessed for that ... thank you for your time and consideration"
8	"thank you for being understanding [of] our situation, adjusting the deadlines to meet our needs, and always replying to our concerns"
9	"one of the things I am grateful for is that you were so patient and understanding ... taking the time to always reply to my countless messages and for the consideration that you showed us"
10	"for making sure we are okay and checking up on us from time to time"
11	"whenever you ask[ed] about our situation or check up on us [;] it was much needed"
12	"you always think of ways to help us ... or by regularly asking us about how we feel about the course and how you can make our experience better"; "You helped me a lot, and I learn[t] a lot from your class. I am grateful to have a teacher like you who is passionate about what he teaches. It has been a meaningful year, and I am glad that you are here to make it happen"
13	"definitely fun and memorable experience"; "highly appreciate[d] the effort you exert[ed] to help us and understand our situation"
14	"this course was not easy at all but with you as our professor, it made us more determined and inspired because of your hard work and diligent effort"; "thank you for all the efforts ... to make this course fun and bearable"

This form of support affected motivation levels and encouraged better engagement. Checking students' welfare at every synchronous meeting by calling them individually was appreciated. Students felt well supported by their teacher's availability and prompt response to their concerns. One way of showing support to my classes is being swift in addressing concerns even late in the evening and on weekends. Often, an email is responded to within minutes after it was sent.

Preceding narratives presented six teaching and learning strategies that are reflective of a fusion of both Piagetian cognitive constructivism and Vygotskyan social constructivism. These are: (1) helping students reach their goals without lowering the standards, (2) exercising patience, (3) being understanding and considerate about deadlines and concerns, (4) checking on learners and inspiring them through fun and interactive learning, (5) giving prompt feedback, and (6) having a constant online presence or availability. Comments show that teachers deal with humans who desire support and encouragement. As Selvanathan et al. (2020) have found, college students resent inaccessible and unavailable instructors, particularly during a pandemic.

DISCUSSION

The latest COVID-19-related studies (Chaturvedi et al., 2021; Wang et al., 2021), which highlight mental health issues of students, serve as a call to all stakeholders in education to recalibrate, if not abandon, instructional paradigms that are often devoid of humanity and compassion. Literature cited (see Al-Kumaim et al., 2021; Izhar et al., 2021; Thandevaraj et al., 2021) highlights a scholastic approach that is inflexible and designed to deliver content so that students could be promoted to the next level and satisfy institutional standards. All of this happens in an emergency situation that confines and deprives students of fuller self expression and an enjoyable learning experience. Ironically, for the most part, we encounter a teacher-centric pedagogy that is lacking, if not completely devoid of, scaffolding strategies—a practice that I must abandon after hearing from my students. In such a short time, students must perform according to the parameters set by their professors without consideration of the circumstances of the former. That approach prevailed during the pandemic even though many students were suffering from various psychological, emotional and mental issues that could potentially hamper learning (Bagayas, 2020; Tan, 2020; Thandevaraj et al., 2021; Tichavsky et al., 2015).

This autoethnographic study shows there is a better way. Every college instructor, if they want to produce excellent students with skill sets that the real world demands, must hold fast to their individual and scholastic standards, while balancing them with understanding and compassion. While instructors must expect, even demand, utmost compliance to the set curricular standards, they ought to also walk alongside their struggling learners, coach them toward success despite the pandemic, and regularly give them small nudges of positive remarks. Other tactics that would boost motivation levels and push students to work harder would go a long way. This compassionate online approach is doable.

Resilience among students does not always happen without support from their professors. Expecting them to be able to stand on their feet, especially during a troubling time like the COVID-19 crisis, will be too much of a burden. Developing resilience among ASEAN students means recognising, first and foremost, our role as educators—purveyors of not only essential content but also supportive instructional environments and approaches. Dennis et al. (2007) agree and call on academics to "embrace the factors that motivate" and "predict the success of ... students and reflect the practices of successful online instructors in online teaching" (p. 43).

IMPLICATIONS OF THE STUDY

This study presents a framework of education that works efficiently in an online context. I am of the view that the Piagetian and Vygotskyan versions of constructivism are ideal in a remote setup because of the amount of freedom extended to learners (cognitive constructivism) and the balance achieved with scaffolding or support (social constructivism) whenever needed. This is not an either-or proposition. Regarding practice and curricula, as already emphasised, support strategies are crucial. Efforts tend to gravitate towards the capacity and readiness to embrace a less-interaction to zero-socialisation online arrangement, usually requiring too much independent learning and mere compliance to the requirements enshrined in the syllabus.

It is not enough to merely require active learning/thinking because, as far as ASEAN college students are concerned, such approaches cannot and will not work on their own. Students need more than just a list of objectives, activities and assessments. These are incomplete, especially in light of the COVID-19 pandemic. Focusing now on virtual learning, courses must be designed with compassion in mind. Given our students' mental and psychological state, it is critical to institutionalise academic ease through flexible deadlines and manageable requirements without sacrificing course goals. Instructors and administrators are urged to deliver more than usual, encompassing a learner-friendly curriculum that is mindful of the learners' challenges. Forms of scaffolding such as giving constant encouragement, checking on the welfare of students, and adjusting assessment requirements so that students' needs and concerns are accommodated or understood will go a long way in ensuring progress and intellectual development. Based on this autoethnography, educators are expected to apply support strategies that demonstrate care and compassion, especially during a crisis.

I turn now to teacher training. In this prevailing health and education crisis worldwide (OECD, 2021b), it is not uncommon to emphasise the importance of Internet connectivity, adeptness in using web-based apps and other instruments, and institutional support for teacher training and coping strategies for students in ensuring the continuity of the scholastic enterprise. While all of these are timely and appropriate responses to mitigate the effects of the COVID-19 pandemic on learning, support for teacher training and coping strategies for learners is often not given as much attention as the use of technology and mastery of online navigation. In fact, teacher training focuses mainly on adapting to the so-called new normal, basically how to transition from in-person instruction to a blended or fully online approach. It is high time that training goes beyond handling technology and implementing the syllabus. The paradigm highlights the training of the self. Faculties must compel themselves into adaptive and empathetic methods, and HEIs are called upon to make these available to every educator. Cranton and Cohen (2013) lament that real faculty development is a neglected domain in education. They find a propensity to teach educators the how-tos instead of offering a theoretical framework that can provide clear-cut principles and even directions. According to them, needful is truly a learner-centred instruction (Cranton & Cohen, 2013). The humane-compassionate approach, grounded on cognitive constructivist and social constructivist principles as presented in this study, is a response to Cranton and Cohen and serves as a guide for institutions on crafting timely and relevant faculty training.

SUMMARY AND CONCLUSION

In the traditions of Piaget and Vygotsky, a balance between independent learning and supportive strategies characterised my pedagogical framework during the remote COVID-19 environment. Students, especially the more vulnerable ones, benefitted from a teaching approach that made learning not only bearable but motivating amid the threat of the virus. This approach includes adjusting deadlines, having a constant online presence and giving timely feedback even during weekends, creating a safe and positive environment, and boosting students' morale and confidence while optimising learning experience. Other constructivist strategies include keeping an open mind and integrating students' input regarding the direction of the courses, checking the welfare of the learners on a regular basis and creating non-restrictive constructivist learning environments. Furthermore, regular synchronous meetings were conducted as students valued the virtual presence of their teacher. Fun and interactive learning often characterised synchronous meetings, and motivating students to succeed was a regular strategy. Teacher-student and student-student virtual interactions were also employed to mitigate social isolation. These forms of support reflect flexibility, sensitivity and empathy, mirroring aspects of social constructivism.

More than facilitating technical know-how and mastery of online tools, educators must embrace a pedagogical framework that is humane and compassionate based on Piaget's cognitive constructivist and Vygotsky's social constructivist orientations. Needed is a supportive system that, while emphasising individual construction of knowledge, also recognises the humanness of learners, taking into consideration their endless struggles in tackling academic life independently because of the complications wrought by prolonged distance learning. In precarious times like these, it is incumbent upon educators to employ constructivist approaches in higher education that effectively deliver and/or facilitate optimal learning and the development of critical skill sets.

Finally, the role of an instructor is changing. We have transcended from being mere sharers of knowledge and facilitators of skill acquisition to builders of individuals via compassionate methodologies inside or outside the virtual classroom. In a way, this is nothing new since educators are regarded as guardians in the context of learning, reflective of the *in loco parentis* concept with or without the health and education crisis. In short, let us be generous when motivating and building our students by consistently creating positive learning environments, as discussed in this chapter.

Rethinking our pedagogical strategies is a matter of urgency. Distance learners simply cannot handle the same amount of pre-pandemic course work as well as the same level of difficulty of tasks and assessments. A humane and compassionate approach, whether in an online or face-to-face context, is not only essential in education, but should be mandated without affecting educational quality. College students clamour for understanding, empathy and adequate scaffolding in a consistently positive learning environment, highlighting the centrality of supportive approaches and methodologies in a fully remote context. Students—susceptible to unpleasant circumstances wrought by the global health crisis—can and will thrive in challenging situations if pedagogy is grounded in empathy. This humane and compassionate pedagogical approach could assist tertiary education in playing a pivotal role in Southeast Asia's social and economic recovery.

REFERENCES

Academy of Prosocial Learning. (2016). *Cultivating compassion and empathy.* https://www.prosocialacademy.org

Aguilera-Hermida, A. P. (2020). College students' use and acceptance of emergency online learning due to COVID-19. *International Journal of Educational Research Open, 1*(100011).

Ahmad, C. N. C., Ching, W. C., Yahaya, A., & Abdullah, M. F. N. L. (2015). Relationship between constructivist learning environments and educational facility in science classrooms. *Procedia—Social and Behavioral Sciences, 191*, 1952–1957.

Al-Kumaim, N. H., Alhazmi, A. K., Mohammed, F., Gazem, N. A., Shabbir, M. S., & Fazea, Y. (2021). Exploring the impact of the COVID-19 pandemic on university students' learning life: An integrated conceptual motivational model for sustainable and healthy online learning. *Sustainability 2021, 13*(5), 1–20. https://doi.org/10.3390/su13052546

Ali, W. (2020). Online and remote learning in higher education institutes: A necessity in light of COVID-19 pandemic. *Higher Education Studies, 10*(3), 16–25. https://doi.org/10.5539/hes.v10n3p16

AlSaqqaf, A., & Ke, H. (2021). Investigating e-learning readiness during the COVID-19 pandemic among Malaysian ESL teachers: What are the limitations of current scales? *KnE Social Sciences, 5*(6), 41–46. https://doi.org/10.18502/kss.v5i6.9176

Bagayas, S. (2020). *Students of top 4 PH schools urge CHED to suspend online classes.* Rappler. https://www.rappler.com/nation/255852-students-top-schools-philippines-call-ched-suspend-online-classes-coronavirus-outbreak/#:~:text=Student%20governments%20of%20the%20Ateneo,in%20the%20middle%20of%20an

Battelle for Kids. (2019). *Framework for 21st century learning definitions.* Partnership for 21st Century Learning.

Bélanger, P. (2011). Three main learning theories. In P. Bélanger (Ed.), *Theories in adult learning and education* (1st ed., pp. 17–34). JSTOR. https://doi.org/10.2307/j.ctvbkjx77.6

Binkley, M., Erstad, O., Herman, J., Raizen, S., Ripley, M., Miller-Ricci, M., & Rumble, M. (2012). Defining twenty-first century skills. In P. Griffin, B. McGaw, & E. Care (Eds.), *Assessment and teaching of 21st century skills.* Springer.

Blazar, D., & Kraft, M. A. (2017). Teacher and teaching effects on students' attitudes and behaviors. *Educational Evaluation and Policy Analysis, 39*(1), 146–170. http://www.jstor.org/stable/44984574

Brown, L. (2014). Constructivist learning environments and defining the online learning community. *i-manager's Journal on School Educational Technology, 9*(4), 1–6.

Burnett, C. (2000). Humane education. *Animals Today, 8,* 18–20.

Butina, M. (2015). A narrative approach to qualitative inquiry. *Summer Clinical Laboratory Science, 28*(3), 190–196.

Chambers, V., Roberto, M., & Zencak, J. (2021, May 13). *Lessons learned from assessing students in a pandemic: It's ok to be more compassionate.* Harvard Business Publishing Education. https://hbsp.harvard.edu/inspiring-minds/lessons-learned-from-assessing-students-in-a-pandemic

Chaturvedi, K., Vishwakarma, D. K., & Singh, N. (2021). COVID-19 and its impact on education, social life and mental health of students: A survey. *Children and Youth Services Review, 121*(105866), pp. 1–6. https://doi.org/10.1016/j.childyouth.2020.105866

Cranton, P., & Cohen, L. R. (2013). Learning through teaching: A narrative analysis. In V. Wang (Ed.), *The handbook of research on teaching and learning in K-20 education* (pp. 17–32). IGI Global. https://doi.org/10.4018/978-1-4666-4249-2.ch002

Danker, B. (2015). Using flipped classroom approach to explore deep learning in large classrooms. *The IAFOR Journal of Education, 3*(1), 171–186. https://iafor.org/journal/iafor-journal-of-education/volume-3-issue-1/article-10

Dennis, K., Bunkowski, L., & Eskey, M. (2007). The little engine that could—how to start the motor? Motivating the online student the shifting focus of compassionate education. *Student Motivation, 2*, 37–49.

Dessauvagie, A. S., Dang, H., Nguyen, T. A. T., & Groren, G. (2021). Mental health of university students in Southeastern Asia: A systematic review. *Asia Pacific Journal of Public Health, 34*(2–3), 172–181. https://doi.org/10.1177/10105395211055545

Deubel, P. (2003). Learning from reflections—Issues in building quality online courses. *Online Journal of Distance Learning Administration, 6.* http://www.westga.edu/~distance/ojdla/fall63/deubel63.htm

Dutton, J. E., & Worline, M. C. (2020). *Educators, it's time to put on your compassion hats: 4 ways to incorporate care and support into your online curriculum.* Harvard Business Publishing Education.

Dutton, J. E., & Wrzesniewski, A. (2020, May 12). *What job crafting looks like.* Harvard Business Review. https://hbr.org/2020/03/what-job-crafting-looks-like?ab=hero-subleft-3

Ferguson, L. M., Yonge, O., & Myrick, F. (2004). Students' involvement in faculty research: Ethical and methodological issues. *International Journal of Qualitative Methods, 3*(4), 56–68.

Filho, W. L., Wall, T., Rayman-Bacchus, L., Mifsud, M., Pritchard, D. J., Lovren, V. O., Farinha, C., Petrovic, D. S., & Balogun, A. (2021). Impacts of COVID-19 and social isolation on academic staff and students at universities: A cross-sectional study. *BMC Public Health, 21*(1213), 1–19. https://doi.org/10.1186/s12889-021-11040-z

Fosnot, C. T. (1996). Constructivism: A psychological theory of learning. In C. T. Fosnot (Ed.), *In Constructivism: Theory, perspectives and practice* (pp. 8–33). Teachers College Press.

Fosnot, C. T. (2005). *Constructivism: Theory, perspectives, and practice* (2nd ed.). Teachers College Press.

Freberg, L., & Angelo, N. B. (2021, August. 18). *Undergraduates need extra support this year—Here's how to help.* Harvard Business School Publishing Education. https://hbsp.harvard.edu/inspiring-minds/undergraduates-need-extra-support-this-year-heres-how-to-help

Gherghes, V., Stoian, C. E., Farcasiu, M. A., & Stanici, M. (2021). E-learning vs face-to-face learning: Analyzing students' preferences and behaviors. *Sustainability 2021, 13*(4381), 1–15. https://doi.org/10.3390/su13084381

Hamdan, A. (2012). Autoethnography as a genre of qualitative research: A journey inside out. *International Journal of Qualitative Methods, 11*(5), 585–606. https://doi.org/10.1177/160940691201100505

Honebein, P. C. (1996). Seven goals for the design of constructivist learning environments. In B. G. Wilson (Ed.), *Constructivist learning environments: Case studies in instructional design* (pp. 11–24). Educational Technology Publications.

Institute for Humane Education. (2021). *Why humane education?* https://humaneeducation.org/why-humane-education

Izhar, N. A., Al-Dheleai, Y. M., & Ishak, N. A. (2021). Education continuation strategies during COVID-19 in Malaysia. *International Journal of Academic Research in Business and Social Sciences, 11*(4), 1423–1436.

Joaquin, J. J. B., Biana, H. T., & Dacela, M. A. (2020). The Philippine higher education sector in the time of COVID-19. *Frontiers in Education, 22*(5), 1–6. https://doi.org/10.3389/feduc.2020.576371

Kozulin, A., Gindis, B., & Miller, S. M. (Eds.). (2003). *Vygotsky's educational theory in cultural context.* Cambridge University Press.

Kwong, A. S. F., Pearson, R. M., Adams, M. J., Northstone, K., Tilling, K., Smith, D., Fawns-Ritchie, C., Bould, H., Warne, N., Zammit, S., Gunnell, D. J., Moran, P. A., Micali, N., Reichenberg, A., Hickman, M., Rai, D., Haworth, S., Campbell, A., Altschul, D., Flaig, R., McIntosh, A. M., Lawlor, D. A., Porteous, D., & Timpson, N. J. (2021). Mental health before and during the COVID-19 pandemic in two longitudinal UK population cohorts. *The British Journal of Psychiatry, 218*(6), 334–343. https://doi.org/10.1192/bjp.2020.242

Lane, C. (2021, March 27). *Measures taken by UK universities against COVID-19.* QS Top Universities. https://www.topuniversities.com/student-info/health-support/measures-taken-uk-universities-against-covid-19

Lave, J., & Wenger, E. (1991). *Situated learning: Legitimate peripheral participation.* Cambridge University Press.

Lian, T. C., & Geok, L. S. (2009). Perceived social support, coping capability and gender differences among young adults. *Sunway Academic Journal, 6,* 75–88.

Ludwig, S. (2002). *Pragmatist realism: The cognitive paradigm in American realist texts.* University of Wisconsin Press.

McLeod, S. (2019). *Constructivism as a theory for teaching and learning.* Simply Psychology. https://www.simplypsychology.org/constructivism.html

Mind (2021). *Student mental health during coronavirus.* https://www.mind.org.uk/information-support/coronavirus/student-mental-health-during-coronavirus

Mohd Kassim, M. A., Pang, N. T. P., & James, S. (2020). COVID-19 pandemic—A review and assessing higher education institution undergraduate student's mental health status. *Borneo Epidemiology Journal, 1*(2), 96–103.

O'Connor, R. C., Wetherall, K., Cleare, S., McClelland, H., Melson, A. J., Niedzwiedz, C., O'Carroll, R. E., O'Connor, D., Platt, S., Scowcroft, E., Watson, B., Zortea, T. C., Ferguson, E., & Robb, K. (2021). Mental health and well-being during the COVID-19 pandemic: Longitudinal analyses of adults in the UK COVID-19 mental health & wellbeing study. *The British Journal of Psychiatry, 218*(6), 326–333. https://doi.org/10.1192/bjp.2020.212

Organisation for Economic Cooperation and Development (OECD). (2021a). *The state of school education: One year into the COVID pandemic.* OECD Publishing. https://doi.org/10.1787/201dde84-en

Organisation for Economic Cooperation and Development (OECD). (2021b). *The state of higher education: One year into the COVID-19 pandemic.* OECD Publishing. https://doi.org/10.1787/83c41957-en

Pearson. (2020). *9 strategies for effective online teaching.* https://www.pearson.com/ped-blogs/blogs/2020/03/9-strategies-for-effective-online-teaching.html

Rao, X. (2018). *University English for academic purposes in China: A phenomenological interview study.* Springer. https://doi.org/10.1007/978-981-13-0647-1

Richardson, V. (2003). Constructivist pedagogy. *Teachers College Record, 105*(9), 1623–1640.

Santos, R. I. (2020a). *Reflective teaching notes* (Emails). PDF. University of Asia and the Pacific.

Santos, R. I. (2020b). *Reflective teaching notes* (First-semester course evaluations). PDF. University of Asia and the Pacific.

Santos, R. I. (2021a). *Reflective teaching notes* (Second-semester course evaluations). PDF. University of Asia and the Pacific.

Santos, R. I. (2021b). *Reflective teaching notes* (Pedagogical strategies and canvas entries). PDF. University of Asia and the Pacific.

Santos, R. I. (2021c). *Reflective teaching notes* (Design portfolio feedback). PDF. University of Asia and the Pacific.

Savage, M. J., James, R., Magistro, D., Donaldson, J., Healy, L. C., Nevill, M., & Hennis, P. J. (2020). Mental health and movement behaviour during the COVID-19 pandemic in UK university students: Prospective cohort study. *Mental Health and Physical Activity, 19*(100357), pp. 1–6.

Scott, D. (2021). Philosophies of learning. In *On learning: A general theory of objects and object-relations* (pp. 159–172). UCL Press. https://doi.org/10.2307/j.ctv1b0fvk2.17

Selvanathan, M., Mohamed Hussin, N. A., & Nor Azazi, N. A. (2020). Students learning experiences during COVID-19: Work from home period in Malaysian higher learning institutions. *Teaching Public Administration, 41*(1), 13–22. https://doi.org/10.1177/0144739420977900

Sharp, C., Nelson, J., Lucas, M., Julius, J., McCrone, T., & Sims, D. (2020). *Schools' responses to COVID-19: The challenges facing schools and pupils in September 2020.* National Foundation for Educational Research.

Tan, J. P. L., Choo, S. S. L., Kang, T., & Liem, G. A. D. (2017). Educating for twenty-first century competencies and future-ready learners: Research perspectives from Singapore. *Asia Pacific Journal of Education, 37*(4), 425–436. http://doi.org/10.1080/02188791.2017.1405475

Tan, V. (2020, January 09). In focus: Prolonged school closure in Malaysia due to COVID-19 shakes up learning experience. *Channel News Asia.* https://www.channelnewsasia.com/asia/in-focus-malaysia-covid-19-school-closure-2020-parents-students-397026

Taştan, S. B., Davoudi, S. M. M., Masalimova, A. R., Bersanov, A. S., Kurbanov, R. A., Boiarchuk, A. V., & Pavlushin, A. A. (2017). The impacts of teacher's efficacy and motivation on student's academic achievement in science education among secondary and high school students. *EURASIA Journal of Mathematics, Science and Technology Education, 14*(6), 2353–2366. https://doi.org/10.29333/ejmste/89579

Tee, M. L., Tee, C. A., Anlacan, J. P., Aligam, K. J. G., Reyes, P. W.C., Kuruchittham, V., & Ho, R. C. (2020). Psychological impact of COVID-19 pandemic in the Philippines. *Journal of Affective Disorders, 277,* 379–391. https://doi.org/10.1016/j.jad.2020.08.043

Thandevaraj, E. J., Gani, N. A. N., & Nasir, M. K. M. (2021). A review of psychological impact on students online learning during COVID-19 in Malaysia. *Creative Education, 12*(6), 1296–1306. https://doi.org/10.4236/ce.2021.126097

The Hope Center for College, Community, and Justice. (2021, March 31). *#Real college 2021: Basic needs insecurity during the ongoing pandemic.* Temple University Libraries. https://scholarshare.temple.edu/handle/20.500.12613/6953

The University of Manchester. (n.d.). *Taking care of your wellbeing.* MyManchester Student Support. https://www.studentsupport.manchester.ac.uk/taking-care

Tichavsky, L. P., Hunt, A. N., Driscoll, A., & Jicha, K. (2015). "It's just nice having a real teacher": Student perceptions of online versus face-to-face instruction. *International Journal for the Scholarship of Teaching and Learning, 9*(2), 1–8. https://doi.org/10.20429/ijsotl.2015.090202

United Nations Educational, Scientific and Cultural Organisation (UNESCO). (2021). *COVID-19: Reopening and reimagining universities, survey on higher education through the UNESCO National Commissions.* UNESDOC Digital Library. https://unesdoc.unesco.org/ark:/48223/pf0000378174

University of Illinois. (2021). *Instructional strategies for online courses.* https://www.uis.edu/ion/resources/tutorials/pedagogy/instructional-strategies-for-online-courses

University of Oxford. (2021). *Welfare and support.* University of Oxford Student Life. https://www.ox.ac.uk/admissions/graduate/student-life/support-and-welfare

Unti, B., & DeRosa, B. (2003). Humane education: Past, present, and future. In D. J. Salem & A. N. Rowan (Eds.), *The state of the animals II: 2003* (pp. 27–50). Humane Society Press.

Valdez, M. (2021). *Year 1: Summary of feedback session* (2nd semester, term 1, academic Year 2020–2021) [PowerPoint Slides]. University of Asia and the Pacific.

Wang, C., Tee, M., Roy, A. E., Fardin, M. A., Srichokchatchawan, W., Habib, H. A., BachTran, B. X.T., Hussain, S., Hoang, M.T., Le, X.T., Ma, W., Pam, H. Q., Shirazi, M., Taneepanichskul, N., Tan, Y., Tee, C., Xu, L., Xu, Z., Vu, G. T., Zhou, D., Koh, B. J., Mcintyre, R. S., Ho, C., Ho, R. C., & Kuruchittham, V. J. (2021). The impact of COVID-19 pandemic on physical and mental health of Asians: A study of seven middle-income countries in Asia. *PLoS ONE, 16*(2), e0246824, 1–20. https://doi.org/10.1371/journal.pone.0246824

Wong, L. P., Alias, H., Md Fuzi, A. A., Omar, I. S., Mohamad Nor, A., Tan, M. P., Baranovich, D. L., Saari, C. Z., Hamzah, S. H., Cheong, K. W., Poon, C. H., Ramoo, V., Che, C. C., Myint, K., Zainuddin, S., & Chung, I. (2021). Escalating progression of mental health disorders during the COVID-19 pandemic: Evidence from a nationwide survey. *PLoS ONE, 16*(3), e0248916, 1–14.

Yilmaz, K. (2008). Constructivism: Its theoretical underpinnings, variations, and implications for classroom instruction. *Educational Horizons, 86*(3), 161–172.

Appendices

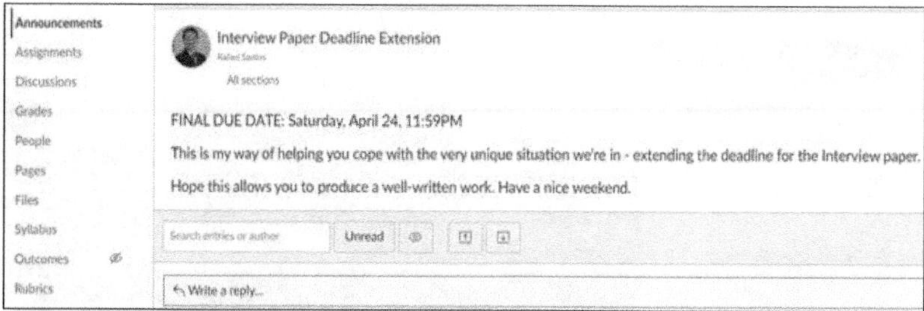

Appendix A Deadline adjustment
Source: Screenshot by author

Appendix B Active solicitation of feedback
Source: Screenshot by author

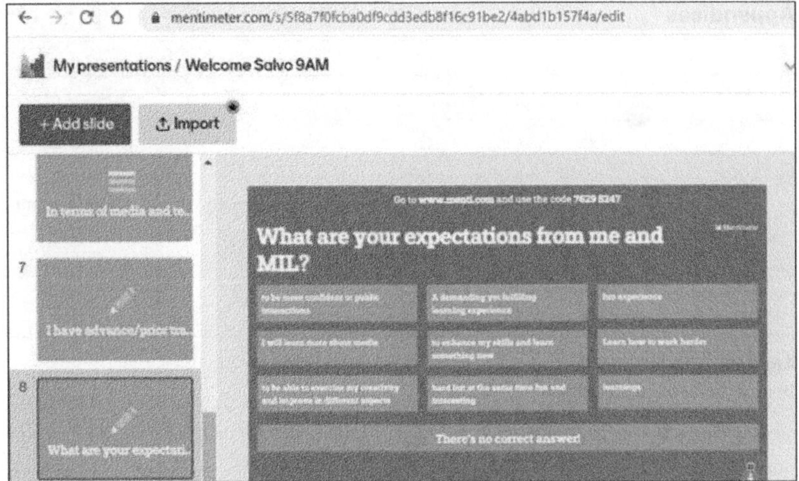

Appendix C Getting feedback through the Mentimeter application
Source: Screenshot by author

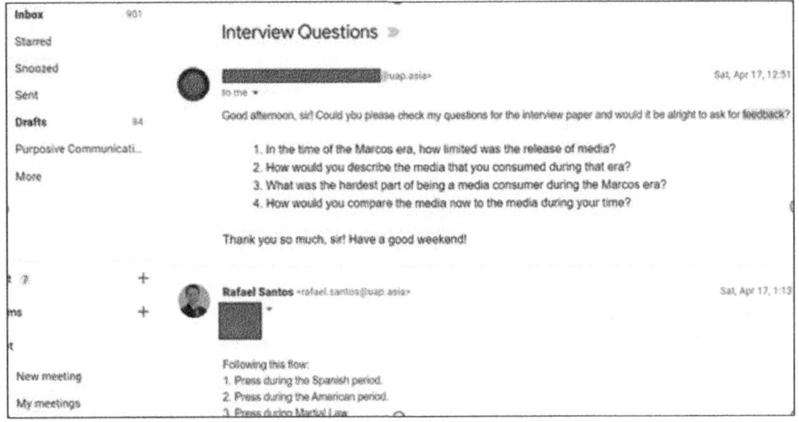

Appendix D Interaction via email
Source: Screenshot by author

Chapter 8

Rethinking Malaysian Universities' Business Models: Building Sustainable Business School Graduates

Benedict Valentine Arulanandam,* Glenda Crosling,‡ Siti Norbaya Azizan‡ & Graeme Atherton¤

ABSTRACT

In preparing business graduates for the business world, it is incumbent on schools of business within universities to adjust their educational offerings, aligning them with the ever-changing business landscape, especially in terms of technologically based inputs. Such an approach also indicates the sustainability of business academic programmes, supporting United Nations Sustainable Development Goal (SDG) 4 of quality education and Target 4.7, whereby learners develop knowledge and skills for sustainable development, including global citizenship. This chapter explores and reports on current business school programmes in some representative private universities in Malaysia in terms of the degree of inclusion of information technology (IT) and meta-dimensional analytical skills and technological capacities. A thorough audit of information on online websites for university business programmes about their technological-based inputs has been undertaken, supported by a small-scale case study of the views of business academic staff members in several private Malaysian universities and one Australian university. Thus, multiple-case mixed design research was used, involving content analysis. The finding is that there is a low level of inclusion of IT

* Sunway College, Malaysia
‡ Sunway University, Malaysia
¤ University of West London, United Kingdom

and meta-dimensional analysis skills and capacities in the curricula of the business programmes in this study, even though IT and data analytics elements are considerably well incorporated in the universities' promotions of relevant business programmes. By extension, it can be stated that there is a need to review curricula to support the development of students' meta-analysis skills and technological adaptation to meet market demand. The study in this chapter provides insight into the issues and direction for larger-scale future studies.

Keywords Business programme, business school, COVID-19, online learning, sustainable goal 4

INTRODUCTION

While changes due to digitalisation and Industrial Revolution 4.0 (IR 4.0) have been taking place over recent decades, the Coronavirus Disease 2019 (COVID-19) pandemic has precipitated sudden changes in all sectors of the global economy. This change affects mega- as well as micro-organisations. Every piece of the fabric of the business model is challenged. As a consequence, organisations such as universities are rethinking their business models, especially in the area of curriculum design, to produce work-ready and technology-savvy graduates to meet the technologically changed needs of organisations. While this has for some time been the call for business schools globally, the reality is that, by the time graduates have completed their undergraduate studies, their relevance for employment is compromised by outdated information in the light of technology-robust business processes, a chasm which is often too wide to be scaled.

While universities and their schools of business reacted promptly at the beginning of the pandemic by switching to "emergency remote learning" (Hodges et al., 2020; Krishnamurthy, 2020), many remained at the level of transferring on-campus learning into remote form. This was done without revisiting their curricula to enhance the inclusion of meta-dimensional analytics, including artificial intelligence (AI). As industries evolve on an unprecedented scale, business graduates must be equipped with new competencies (Rejikumar et al., 2019). Dynamic and innovative business graduates will be instrumental in enhancing productivity and solving problems in the context of the 21st century (Mian et al., 2020). Moreover, according to the Association to Advance Collegiate Schools of Business (2019), business graduates need to be co-creators of knowledge in order to bridge the chasm between classroom exposure and business practice so as to have a positive impact on society. This underpins SDG 4, which highlights the need for quality education that not only leads to inclusive and equitable education but, along with lifelong learning, includes the capacity for graduates to continue to contribute to society by way of constantly evolving skills.

Over recent years, and especially during the COVID-19 pandemic, companies have holistically used data analytics, AI, cloud computing and algorithms to assist in decision-making and steer their respective entities to a competitive advantage (Wilder & Ozgur, 2015). Hence, in the process of transforming, these building blocks further catapult businesses into a position of leverage. Following this, business graduates should be thoroughly prepared to contribute in this manner for the success of organisations. That is, business schools need to shift from an experimental position and embrace the critical needs of businesses today (Topi, 2016). An experimental position is a stop-gap measure and does not focus on the transformation of the ecosystem, but rather addresses the current need only. For example, as soon as COVID-19 was declared a pandemic, higher education institutions (HEIs) began placing all course content onto Moodle or Blackboard, and teaching took place only through these platforms, without reviewing curricula to include the aforestated skills. Empirical studies, such as that of Mikalef et al. (2018), have stressed that technical and analytical skills are crucial in business programmes. Studies by Gupta and George (2016), Vidgen et al. (2017), and Wamba et al. (2017) echo the same need, pointing out that businesses require such technical skills. Nevertheless, some business schools are not strongly incorporating these skills into their curricula, stating a lack of skilled academics able to drive it.

The Malaysian government has been motivating HEIs to embrace meta-dimensional analytics and technology and incorporate these into their curricula to produce graduates with skills relevant to industry. The Malaysian Ministry of Higher Education (MOHE), in their Education Blueprint (Higher Education), stressed 10 shifts to enhance the contribution of Malaysian higher education (Ministry of Higher Education, 2013). Of these, Shift No.

2 (Talent Excellence) and Shift No. 7 (Innovation Ecosystem) are relevant to this challenge and include the need to produce graduates equipped with technological and analytical skills as required by industries. In addition, the Malaysia Digital Economy Blueprint (2019) launched in October 2019 echoes the call to nurture a future-ready workforce as a building block for the Shared Prosperity Vision 2030, the 2023 Agenda for Sustainable Development, and the Twelfth Malaysia Plan. The Blueprint is based on six thrusts, one of which is to "Build Agile and Competent Digital Talent" (Thrust No. 4).

In this study, the degree of focus on meta-dimensional analytics and technology embedded in the curricula of undergraduate business programmes in private universities in Malaysia is explored, supporting the government's call to include such skills in business programmes. Comments from business school academic staff members in Malaysia and Australia that are relevant to the issues are included to further elaborate on the web-based findings. The study thus provides some insight into whether Malaysian graduates have had exposure to the latest data-driven approaches to equip them in participating in the future-ready workforce, as outlined by MOHE's Education Blueprint and the Malaysia Digital Economy Blueprint. This study is practical and indeed crucial at this time.

In discussing the study, this chapter provides information about university business programme curricula that will help reposition Malaysian universities to a world-class standard, catalysing growth and sustainability.

LITERATURE REVIEW

Transformation of university

The recent report of the global accounting company KPMG entitled *The Future of Higher Education in a Disruptive World* (KPMG, 2020) makes the point that while challenges in education are not new, the current pandemic has placed stress on all institutions of higher learning. The report also identifies that this disruption has simultaneously brought unprecedented opportunities for universities to redevelop, redesign and remobilise strategies, coupled with the demographic changes in student populations. As such, the current Gen-Z students entering higher education are IT savvy and have unique learning behaviours which tilt them towards online learning (Anastopoulou et al., 2012). Hence, traditional universities are being shaken in a way they have not experienced before. It thus seems to be an excellent opportunity for business schools, in particular, to make changes while the situation is in flux rather than waiting for the post-pandemic period. The possibility for universities to revert to a fully pre-COVID-19 position is very low, and it may be argued that business schools, in particular, will need a more refined business model that considers preparing business students with up-to-date skills to meet the demands of the business world.

Krishnamurthy (2020), in comments on business studies' curricula, points out that as the landscape of tertiary education becomes agile, students will be able to obtain knowledge and skills from a broader range of institutions and sharpen their skills at their own pace. For example, it is seen that universities will have no choice but to embrace diversity and inclusivity should they embark upon a transformation of their ecosystem, as digital transformation reaches all social strata and embraces the SDGs of diversity and inclusivity. Digital transformation addresses the fulfilment of SDG 4 for quality education, supporting business needs for graduates' skills and preparing graduates for global citizenship as per SDG 4 Target 4.7. In addition, Letheren et al. (2020) have argued that students will need to be able to solve problems or challenges via ethical inquiry and use AI in order to arrive at more accurate solutions.

As per the Triphasic Model seen in Figure 8.1, a transformational ecosystem for academic programmes needs to be derived for a transformational impact, with Instructional Continuity focusing on the continuation of support via IT as occurred in the initial stages of the pandemic. At this first stage, as per Figure 8.1, universities upgrade their IT hardware and software and mobilise training for staff members to handle this form of delivery. The second stage concerns sound Instructional Design, building on the student experience

Figure 8.1 The Triphasic Model
Source: Adapted from Krishnamurthy (2020)

and the needs of students and digital learning methodologies and tools supporting the digital learning environment. Finally, in the third phase, the use of AI-enabled Innovation occurs where there is seamless interaction between students and the system. As such, learning becomes interactive, and the teachers or lecturers are mere facilitators of students' learning. Here, students can space their learning and proceed at their own speed with ease.

Transformation of global business

Krishnamurthy's (2020) highly relevant view discussed earlier is that global business will consider health issues in a more serious manner, as this pandemic has brought about global shock waves. Furthermore, studies by Dingel and Neiman (2020) indicate that telework or work-from-home will be widespread, reducing physical interaction and lessening the operational overhead burden. Businesses will reassess their supply chain and operation processes, which will include many IT elements. Online business and borderless transactions will constantly increase with alternative investment opportunities (Krishnamurthy, 2020).

Transformation of students

As mentioned earlier, Gen-Z students are more inclined to be technology savvy than previous generations, and their receptiveness to technology and meta-dimensional analytics is positive. As Luthra and Mackenzie (2020) and Trust and Whalen (2020) point out, while there is greater confidence in online delivery in business operations, the view is that academic business programmes' content should encompass technology components to represent quality and adaptability. Such inclusion in the curricula of business studies will shape students' cognitive preparedness to embrace the demands of the job market.

Financial limitations

As business schools address the challenges to enhance their business programmes, it cannot be denied that investment into infrastructure and content development is required, which comes with financial implications. As the pandemic continues, business schools in Malaysia and many parts of the globe face financial constraints. However, the need for financial investment in university education cannot be ignored. Business schools must restrategise to source funding to revamp their curricula to incorporate IT and analytics into their programmes. On the other hand, if a lack of finances is put forward to avoid this, the opportunity for future-ready graduates will be further delayed, impacting the progress of the nation.

Curricula review

Members of the future workforce need to be well-equipped with knowledge of technology in order to remain relevant to the business world. According to McKinsey and Company (2017), approximately 375 million workers globally will be required to learn new skills and even transition to a new vocation. Furthermore, Waddack and Lozano (2015) concur that business schools are not producing business-necessary graduates, as curricula are not reviewed to include the current demands of the commercial world. It thus seems that much of the content of undergraduate programmes is relatively outdated. There is a clear chasm between business needs for quality graduates and the skills and capacities of graduates from business schools (Federal Council of Administration, 2014; Wagner, 2010).

Ecosystem within business schools

An ecosystem in any business or organisation is essential to facilitate seamless operations and smooth transactions; hence, a rich network system is crucial (Deloitte, 2015; Harvard Business Review, 2016; Kortelainen & Järvi, 2014). Establishing an ecosystem is vital for business schools, as it blends all components or divisions to provide efficient educational delivery for the students. Therefore, such infrastructure is necessary for the curriculum design to encapsulate the latest developments within the business community, ensuring students are well-equipped to face the employment market. According to studies by Wadee and Padayachee (2017), business schools are not ready to embrace ecosystem-based challenges due to much confusion and deeply rooted notions in traditional methodologies.

With an ecosystem, innovative capabilities will be unleashed for the purpose of value creation. Hence, graduates will be positioned to function in business communities as catalysts for value creation (Bischoff et al., 2018; Velu et al., 2013). Letaifa et al. (2013) and Göthlich (2003) have stressed that an effective ecosystem would mean seamless collaboration between members to produce positive results. In addition, Tapscott and Williams (2008) highlight four important principles for effective collaboration in an ecosystem: (1) sharing, (2) global mindset, (3) honesty, and (4) scrutiny. These attributes are vital for the development of the 21st-century workforce.

Information technology infrastructure

IT infrastructure is the backbone of an efficient ecosystem. Krishnamurthy (2020) notes that while COVID-19 provided a golden opportunity for business schools to leapfrog into the next phase of IT infrastructure, many still operate with the notion of positioning themselves back into the pre-COVID-19 environment. It seems they are merely scratching the surface when it comes to technologies within the schools. Financial constraints and future revenue unpredictability could be the stumbling blocks to improving IT infrastructure in these business schools.

METHODOLOGY

In this study, the authors conducted multiple-case, qualitative research using the mixed design approach through content analysis, which "comprises a searching-out of underlying themes in the materials being analysed" (Bryman, 2004, p.392). Secondary data were collected from the synopses of the business programmes offered on the universities' official websites and from the IT-related and data-analytical subjects in each academic year for all business undergraduate programmes in each private university studied. Relevant literature and pertinent comments from the business school academic staff members from several private universities in Malaysia and one university in Australia were used to support the web-based data and draw findings based on the research objective.

In exploring the inclusion of IT and meta-dimensional analysis skills and capacities in business programmes, four private universities in Malaysia (named University A, University B, University C and University D, for purposes of anonymity) were chosen as the study sample, as their offerings of business programmes at the undergraduate level represented range. The study of the web-based information provided a general overview of the business degrees in these universities in terms of whether the degrees had professional accreditation by the relevant accounting body, including internship placements and final year dissertations/projects, as well as pre-requisite mathematics entrance scores. These data are included in the universities' programme pages as part of digital marketing, providing a view of the nature of the learning experience. Also often included are testimonials of the study programmes, especially for prospective students, coupled with the degree of industry acceptance (HEM Education Marketing Solutions, 2021).

The curricula of the business programmes in these universities were then studied in terms of the number of IT and data-related subjects offered, as indicated by the subject titles. The representation of the degree of such subjects in relation to the overall content of the programmes was determined.

The synopsis of each business degree provided on the web was also explored in terms of focus on IT and data-analytical approaches. Words such as "big data processing", "business analytics", "financial technology and innovation" and "e-marketing" included in the synopsis were deemed to indicate the incorporation of analytical and IT skills as part of students' learning outcomes.

The collected data were organised and analysed through Microsoft Office Excel software to generate descriptive findings in the form of frequency and percentages. In addition, relevant keywords and indicators from the programmes' synopses were tabulated for further data analysis.

The theoretical framework for the study, as seen in Figure 8.2, has been adapted from Krishnamurthy's (2020) framework in Figure 8.1 to understand the transformation of online learning and the technology-led remaking of business schools. The adaptation for this study was the inclusion of the elements for syllabus review and the ecosystem within business schools. Hence, for the purpose of business school transformation, this study addresses the components of IT and meta-dimensional analytics in the syllabi of business schools and the incorporation of IT to enhance the ecosystem in order to produce future-ready graduates.

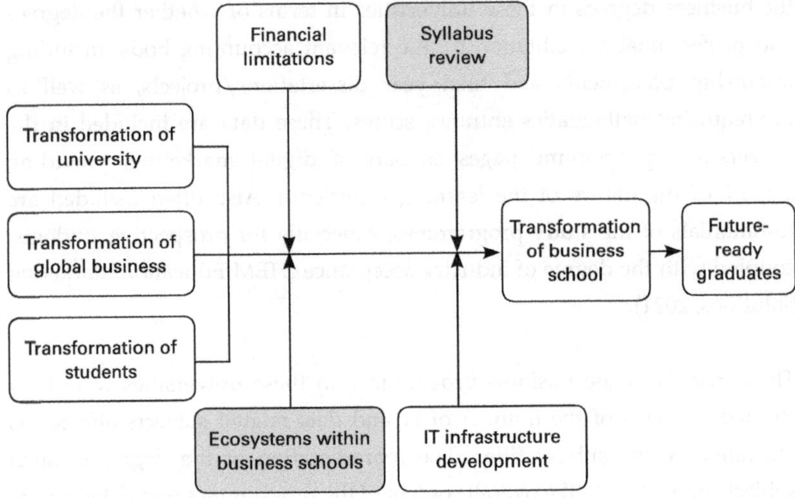

Figure 8.2 Theoretical framework: Transformation of business schools
Source: Adapted from Krishnamurthy (2020)

Finally, from the small-scale case study undertaken, comments of academic staff members in open-ended survey questions were reviewed and included to add to the findings from the web-based data.

ANALYSIS AND DISCUSSIONS

Web-based data

Table 8.1 provides an overview of the undergraduate programmes offered by the business schools in the four private universities in Malaysia. University D, which offers the highest number of undergraduate business degree programmes, has over 50% of their programmes with professional accreditation. All business programmes in University A and most in University D offer internship or industrial placement in the undergraduate programmes. All programmes in University D and most in University B have subjects with dissertation or final project requirements. As for the mathematics pre-requisite, all universities have less than 50% of their programmes requiring students to obtain credit in the subject at *Sijil Pelajaran Malaysia*[1] level or

1 Malaysian Certificate of Education at fifth-form secondary school or Year 10.

equivalent. These percentage values reflect the level of emphasis by the business schools, in various aspects determining the quality of their business programme curricula in terms of positioning the universities at a world-class standard. For instance, with over 50% professionally accredited business degree programmes, University D indicates a considerably good level of commitment to upholding industry standards, superior professionalism and continued learning (MBO Partners, 2021) by producing professionally recognised business graduates at a global quality level.

Table 8.1 Summarised information on undergraduate business programmes in the four private universities

No.	Information on Undergraduate Business Programmes	Details			
		Uni A	Uni B	Uni C	Uni D
1	Number of programmes offered	11	13	8	19
2	Number of programmes with professional accreditation	5	0	5	12
3	Number of programmes with internship/industrial placement	11	8	7	17
4	Number of programmes with dissertation/final project	6	11	5	19
5	Pre-requisite of credit in mathematics at *Sijil Pelajaran Malaysia* level or equivalent	5	7	3	8

Web-based analysis of the subjects offered by the universities in the range of business programmes provided data on the degree of inclusion of IT and meta-dimensional analysis skills and capacities. Table 8.2 shows the number of IT-related and data-analytical subjects. Looking at the overall percentage values by university, it can be observed that each university provides less than 20% of IT-related and data-analytical subjects for business undergraduate programmes from the first year until the third year. The highest percentage was recorded by University B, which offers 18% of the subjects in all three academic years, followed by University A (17%) and University C (11%). Considering its highest number of programmes offered (as seen in Table 8.1), University D seems to provide the least number of subjects related to IT and data analytics, with only 4% of the total number of subjects throughout the three academic years. These percentage values indicate the low level of inclusion of IT and meta-dimensional analysis skills and capacities in business programmes offered by the private universities.

Table 8.2 The incorporation of subjects related to information technology (IT) and data analytics in the four private universities' business programmes

No.	Uni.	Number of Subjects by Year							
		Year 1		Year 2		Year 3		Overall (by university)	
		Total related subjects (all)	% by all subjects	Total related subjects (all)	% by all subjects	Total related subjects(all)	% by all subjects	Total related subjects(all)	% by all subjects
1	Uni A	9 (57)	16%	6 (46)	13%	15 (76)	20%	30 (179)	17%
2	Uni B	9 (68)	13%	21 (78)	27%	9 (72)	13%	39 (218)	18%
3	Uni C	3 (49)	6%	6 (55)	11%	7 (45)	16%	16 (149)	11%
4	Uni D	3 (136)	2%	7 (150)	5%	8 (150)	5%	18 (436)	4%
	Overall (by year)	24 (310)	8%	40 (329)	12%	39 (343)	11%	103 (982)	11%

Meanwhile, on a yearly basis, it is also critical to note that there is no significant trend in the total number of related subjects in all universities. While University C shows an increasing percentage from Year 1 to Year 3, none of the universities highly emphasise the incorporation of such subjects in their final year. The highest percentage in Year 3 is recorded by University A, which offers 20% of IT-related and data-analytical subjects for final-year students. This finding shows a lack of consistency in the degree of inclusion of IT and meta-dimensional analysis skills and capacities throughout the study years in the four universities. The consistency of course content coverage and delivery can ensure consistent student learning experiences and outcomes, thus significantly improving course coherence and quality control (The National Center for Academic Transformation, 2014).

Table 8.3 summarises keywords used in the short description or synopsis of the business programmes, indicating the elements incorporated or implemented in the undergraduate business programmes in the case of private universities. Text content in synopses on websites is part of online advertising used to sell certain products. It includes any information that represents the media, such as books and websites, and captures the attention of readers or visitors (Cactus Communications, 2021). For quality purposes, text content is required to be accurate. Nowadays, digital marketing has an increasingly critical role in the higher education sector, not only for its marketing but also for its entire ecosystem. Most academic institutions worldwide now use digital marketing technologies to connect and engage with prospective students, as well as for pedagogical purposes (Jain, 2019).

Table 8.3 Assessment of the business programmes' synopses in official websites

No.	Indicator/ aspect	Keywords/elements	Included in the synopsis			
			Uni A	Uni B	Uni C	Uni D
1	Global	Globally recognised/ accreditation	/			
		Global marketplace		/		/
		International linkage		/		
		International perspective/ global mindset	/	/	/	/
2	Infrastructure	Practical/hands-on experience/project-based	/	/	/	/
		Labs/workshops	/			/
		Software (IT/statistical)	/	/		
		Technological tools	/	/		/
3	Ecosystem	Real-world/stimulating learning environment	/	/	/	/
		Industrial players	/	/	/	/
		Customers/stakeholders	/		/	/
		Human resources/ management		/	/	
		Big data processing	/			
		Teaching practices			/	/
		Internship	/	/	/	/

Table 8.3 Assessment of the business programmes' synopses in official websites (cont'd)

No.	Indicator/ aspect	Keywords/elements	Included in the synopsis			
			Uni A	**Uni B**	**Uni C**	**Uni D**
4	University level	Sustainability elements	/			/
		Interdisciplinary	/		/	
		Engagement with industries	/	/	/	/
		National priority areas/ policies	/			
		Community service			/	
5	Business school level	Industry relevant	/	/	/	/
		Business analytics	/			
		Integrated/blended curriculum		/	/	/
		Training and skill development	/	/		
		Student coaching/ teamwork			/	
6	Student level	Career prospect	/	/	/	/
		Thinking skills (critical, creative)	/	/	/	/
		Analytical/mathematical/ statistical skills	/	/	/	/
		Technical/IT skills	/	/	/	/
		Problem-solving skills		/		/
		Soft skills	/	/	/	/
		Theory and practical knowledge	/	/	/	/
		Professional qualification	/			/

In this study, the analysis of the study programmes' synopses does not reflect real or actual promotional and marketing practices and implementation by each university; rather, it is mainly based on the programmes' synopses provided on the universities' official websites. Thus, analysis was undertaken to assess whether the digital marketing efforts by the business schools reflect the actual incorporation of IT-related and data-analytical elements in the business programme curricula.

As the analysis indicates, the programme synopses were classified into six aspects or indicators, namely global, infrastructure, ecosystem, university level, business school level, and student level. These six indicators were developed based on the study's theoretical framework adapted from Krishnamurthy (2020), as shown in Figure 8.1 earlier. Each indicator comprises several keywords or elements identified from the programmes' synopses in the business schools' official websites.

Providing some insight into the study's issues, comments of academic staff members support the views expressed in the literature and indicate an awareness of the need for business school curricula to further address the needs of the workplace. All academic staff members indicated that it is vital to include meta-analysis and technical adaptation into business school curricula to remain relevant in a business world that moves to a data-driven model. Several academic staff members indicated they do not see that the skills in the business programmes match the business demands for graduates. However, one academic staff member commented that the skills do match, indicating that the programme at their university includes a one-year industry placement which leads to graduate employment. All staff members indicated that the curricula should be reviewed to reflect the changing business environment, with the review period being put forward ranging from every five years to every semester.

Based on the data given in Table 8.3, the main findings are as follows:

(1) **Overall, the majority of the elements in each indicator are covered in the business programme synopses.** At least one keyword in each indicator is observed in all universities, and more than 50% of total observations were recorded for each indicator. The indicator mostly highlighted in the business programme synopses is the student-level aspect, whereby all universities list various learning outcomes students can obtain from their studies.

(2) **The incorporation of IT and data-analytical elements, both theories and practical, are generally stated in most of the programme synopses.** Three of the four universities mention integrated or blended curricula. At the student level, learning outcomes related to IT and data analytics, such as technical, data-analytical and IT skills, are mentioned for the relevant programmes in all four universities. Both practical and theoretical knowledge for the students is covered in the programme synopses of all universities.

(3) **From the global aspect, all universities include an international perspective or a global mindset in the synopses of their business programmes.** However, other elements describing the global aspect are not specifically highlighted in the synopses of most programmes: two universities mention the global marketplace, and only one university mentions globally recognised accreditation and international linkage, respectively.

(4) **In terms of infrastructure, all universities provide practical and hands-on elements, and some indicate the availability of necessary infrastructure.** These include IT and statistical software, labs and other technological tools. For instance, in University A, labs are provided as a space for students to venture into innovations and build businesses. Powerful software and expansive data for business analytics are also available at the university.

(5) **In terms of ecosystem, all universities mention real-world and stimulating learning environments, industrial players and internships in the programmes' synopses.** Three universities include terms related to customers. Only a few universities include terms related to teaching practices and human resource management.

(6) **At the university level, all universities disclose their engagement with industries in the business programmes, especially related to internship and industrial training.** Only two universities (University A and University C) mention an interdisciplinary approach in their business programmes. This is an interesting finding, as today's business graduates need a more integrated learning approach (Bajada & Trayler, 2013). The inclusion of this aspect in promoting the study programmes can indicate a transformation of a traditional business curriculum through an interdisciplinary approach. In addition, there is clearly a lack of emphasis on sustainability; only University A mentions the term "sustainability" among other core elements in the global business environment in describing the career prospects arising from the study programmes. According to Sharma (2021), SDG integration into the business curriculum must be an institutional priority. Thus, disclosing such an aspect in the programme synopsis may reflect the business school's commitment towards the goal. Furthermore, only University A mentions developing

business graduates' training and skills in long-term national priority areas. Such an aspect would indicate the consistency between institutional and national policies in promoting business degree programmes.

(7) **At the business-school level, most business programmes in all the universities are industry-relevant and have integrated or blended curricula.** Not all business schools in the universities incorporate business analytics, training and skill development, student coaching and teamwork in their programmes' synopsis.

(8) **At the student level, all universities clearly mention the graduates' career prospects upon completing the business programmes.** The necessary skills to be obtained by students throughout the study years are clearly stated, such as creative thinking, critical thinking, problem solving, and other relevant technical and soft skills. However, not all universities explain the professional qualifications to be obtained by the students.

The analyses above reveal that the inclusion of IT and meta-dimensional analysis skills and capacities in business programmes offered by the four private universities in Malaysia is currently still at a low level (i.e. less than 20% of the overall total). Although the analysis of the programme synopses indicates the necessary level of infrastructure, ecosystem and learning outcomes of the business schools in the universities, these do not seem to be reflected in the business programme curricula, as the percentages indicate. As per Ernst and Young's report (2018), it is important to incorporate approximately 56% of the curriculum with technology-related modules in the degree programme to enable students to fit into the business landscape. While the Ernst and Young's report was for the Australian environment, it is an important indication of the needs of 21st-century businesses. Prior studies by Rienties and Townsend (2012) have highlighted that technology and pedagogy must be equally balanced for universities to produce rich learning experiences for a new generation of business students. This is also in line with MOHE's Shift No.1, which aims to produce holistic and balanced graduates for the workforce. Furthermore, several studies have identified that among the common problems faced by business undergraduates in Malaysia include gaps in employability skills (Suppramaniam et al., 2019), insufficient technical knowledge, poor communication skills, a lack of tech-savvy skills and a lack of industrial exposure (Heang et al., 2019). Therefore, in line with these issues, our study findings provide evidence stressing the importance for Malaysian universities to revamp their business programmes by infusing more IT and meta-dimensional analysis skills and capacities into the curriculum in order to be relevant to the business environment.

In his study, Wymbs (2016) proposes five ways to infuse data analytics into the undergraduate business curriculum:

(1) Develop a new interdisciplinary course.
(2) Align the business course with the needs of practice.
(3) Capture the union of disciplines.
(4) Use real-world projects.
(5) Strengthen faculty members' expertise.

In line with the above, our study similarly highlights that Malaysian universities need to consider addressing the gaps in practical curriculum components like real-time projects, industrial training, community-based activities, as well as training and skill development in enhancing the integration of IT and data-analytical elements into business programmes. Furthermore, as the findings show, there is still a limited sophisticated and interdisciplinary approach to developing more hybrid business programmes that could transform the traditional business degree offerings in Malaysia.

Case study data

In addition to the above, the survey gathered the perspectives of academic staff members about the inclusion of IT and meta-dimensional analysis skills and capacities in business programmes. The responses are shown in Table 8.4.

An analysis of the survey results in Table 8.4 indicates the following:

(1) The frequency of business curriculum review varies across universities: at several universities, this frequently occurs (every year or semester), and in several others, it is infrequent. As noted by the respondents, some reasons for the lack of review are the high turnover rate of academic staff members and the relevance of the curriculum. At the same time, changing needs and technologies support frequent curriculum reviews.

Table 8.4 The academic staff members' responses: IT and meta-dimensional analysis skills and capacities in business programmes

No.	Question	Responses
1	How often does your business school review the curriculum of its business programmes to keep up to date with the changing business environment?	R[2]1: "Not too sure, perhaps every five years" R2: "Every few years" R3: "Hardly" R4: "Once a semester" R5: "Annually"
2	Pertaining to Question 1, what are the reasons a curriculum review is/is not undertaken?	R1: "Depends on market needs" R2: "High turnover of academic heads and lecturers" R3: "Still perceived as relevant" R4: "To keep up with employment needs and changing technologies at most workplaces" R5: "Not applicable"
3	In your opinion, are the skills and knowledge of your students adequate to match the demands of the business world when they graduate?	R1: "No" R2: "Not really" R3: "Lacking" R4: "Yes" R5: "Yes, my programme includes a one-year placement. Most of them, if not all, land a job offer immediately after they graduate."
4	Does the curriculum content of your business programme/s match the explanation on the university/school website for the programme and its outcomes? Please can you explain why, or why not, this is so?	R1: "Partially yes, what is claimed is being taught" R2: "Yes, the curriculum content in the programmes is identical to that shown on the website" R3: "Yes" R4: "Yes" R5: "Yes"
5	In your opinion, are the business programmes in your business school sustainable in that they prepare your students for the evolving requirements in businesses?	R1: "No" R2: "Not really, need further alignment with market trend and demand" R3: "Partially" R4: "Yes" R5: "Yes"
6	Do you think the current curriculum of business courses allows your students to develop skills and knowledge in meta-dimensional analysis and technological adaptation? Kindly explain.	R1: "No" R2: "No" R3: "Insufficient" R4: "Yes, MQA framework covers this" R5: "Yes, we have modules where students have the opportunity to learn and use current and emerging technologies"
7	Do you think it is necessary for university students to be equipped with data-driven approaches to support their participation in the future-ready workforce? Kindly explain.	R1: "Yes, it the most vital skill" R2: "Yes definitely, the business world is moving towards a data-driven mode" R3: "Yes, to remain relevant and employable" R4: "Yes" R5: "Yes"

[2] R refers to the survey respondents, numbered consecutively.

(2) Several respondents pointed out that students' skills and knowledge in meeting the demands of the business world are inadequate, and existing business curricula are not adequate to develop students' skills and knowledge in meta-dimensional analysis and technological adaptation.

(3) The curriculum content of the business programmes is in line with the universities' official website information.

(4) In terms of sustainability, the universities' business programmes may need further improvement in preparing students for the evolving business world.

(5) All the respondents agreed that business graduates need to be well-equipped with the necessary data-driven approaches to bring to their future jobs in business.

Overall, the survey provided insights from the academic staff members' perspective on the importance of meta-analysis and technical adaptation into business school curricula. At present, inadequacy in graduates' technological adaptation and meta-analysis skills and knowledge remains a vital issue in preparing graduates for the constantly changing business environment. Employers and business educators emphasise both soft and hard skills in bridging the gap between business students' skills or competencies and those required in the job market (Alshare & Sewailem, 2018). In addition, the most desirable skills for business graduates nowadays include data analytics, modelling, problem solving and written communication, and several software skills like SQL, Python and Java (Stanton & Stanton, 2020) and other technical skills such as statistics and programming (Verma et al., 2019).

CONCLUSION

Undeniably, IT has become a vital and integral part of business operations. Globally, prospective employers are increasingly searching for business graduates with the necessary analytical and technological skills to support their capacity for value creation and knowledge to thrive in today's globalised economy. Thus, it is imperative for universities to be able to produce industry-relevant and technology-savvy business graduates in response to this need.

Based on the analyses reported in this study, it can be concluded that there remains a low level of inclusion of IT and meta-dimensional analysis skills and capacities in business programmes in the four Malaysian private universities. While IT and data analytics elements are considerably well incorporated in the universities' promotion of related business programmes, such incorporation is not fully reflected in the curriculum; that is, based on the number of related subjects throughout the academic years. Furthermore, the academic staff members' comments in this study also indicate the need to address business graduates' technological adaptation and meta-dimensional skills and knowledge. This is supported by the quality and frequency of curricula review to tailor graduate employability to match the changing demands of the business world.

At the national level, it can be stated that more effort is needed from higher education providers and policymakers to revamp business programmes in universities through the infusion of IT and data analytics towards addressing the rapid changes in the global market. While this study contributes to the issue, future work can be undertaken to provide further findings on incorporating IT and meta-dimensional analytics in the business programmes' curriculum. One way is by considering six essential conditions to gauge universities' efforts and progress towards IT integration: (1) vision, (2) practice, (3) proficiency, (4) equity, (5) access, and (6) systems (United Nations Educational, Scientific and Cultural Organisation, 2005).

This study was of a representative sample and not of all private and public universities in Malaysia. The data derived was complemented with a qualitative view of the topic by the small-scale survey respondents. However, the study provides a view to underpin future research for a broader picture of the issue. In summary, this study indicates the reality of nurturing a future-ready workforce in Malaysian private universities for the benefit of local businesses.

REFERENCES

Alshare, K., & Sewailem, M. F. (2018). A gap analysis of business students' skills in the 21st century: A case study of Qatar. *Academy of Educational Leadership Journal, 22*(1), 1–22.

Anastopoulou, S., Sharples, M., Ainsworth, S., Crook, C., O'Malley, C., & Wright, M. (2012). Creating personal meaning through technology-supported science learning across formal and informal settings. *International Journal of Science Education, 34* (2), 251–273.

Association to Advance Collegiate Schools of Business. (2019). *A new collective vision for business education.* https://www.aacsb.edu/vision

Bajada, C., & Trayler, R. (2013). Interdisciplinary business education: Curriculum through collaboration. *Education + Training, 55*(4–5), 385–402.

Bischoff, K., Volkmann, C. K., & Audretsch, D. B. (2018). Stakeholder collaboration in entrepreneurship education: An analysis of the entrepreneurial ecosystems of European higher educational institutions. *The Journal of Technology Transfer, 43*(1), 20–46.

Bryman, A. (2004). *Social research methods* (2nd ed.). Oxford University Press.

Cactus Communications. (2021). *The five "S" of blurb writing—5 awesome tips.* Editage. https://www.editage.com/info/book-editing-services/articles/the-five-S-of-blurb-writing-check-these-5-awesome_tips.html

Deloitte. (2015). *Business ecosystems come of age.* Deloitte University Press.

Dingel, J. I., & Neiman, B. (2020). How many jobs can be done at home? *NBER Working Paper,* No. 26948, *Journal of Public Economics, 189,* 1–8. https://www.nber.org/papers/w26948.pdf

Ernst & Young. (2018). Australian Government: Australian Trade and Investment Commission. *Why Australia: Benchmark report 2018.*

Federal Council of Administration. (2014). Letter n° 109/2014/CFA/CFP, 2014.

Göthlich, S. E. (2003). *From loosely coupled systems to collaborative business ecosystems* (No. 573). Manuskripte aus den Instituten für Betriebswirtschaftslehre der Universität Kiel No. 573, Kiel, Germany.

Gupta, M., & George, J. F. (2016). Toward the development of a big data analytics capability. *Information & Management, 53*(8), 1049–1064.

Harvard Business Review. (2016). *The ecosystem equation: Collaboration in the connected economy.* Harvard Business School Publishing.

Heang, L. T., Ching, L. C., Mee, L. Y., & Huei, C. T. (2019). University education and employment challenges: An evaluation of fresh accounting graduates in Malaysia. *International Journal of Academic Research in Business and Social Sciences, 9*(9), 1061–1076.

HEM Education Marketing Solutions. (2021). *8 essential marketing steps of launching a new college program.* https://www.higher-education-marketing.com/blog/marketing-college-program

Hodges, C., Moore, S., Lockee, B., Trust, T., & Bond, A. (2020). The difference between emergency remote teaching and online learning. *Educause.* https://er.educause.edu/articles/2020/3/the-difference-between-emergency-remote-teaching-and-online-learning

Jain, R. (2019). *Digital marketing in higher education: Importance, benefits and impact.* https://www.asmaindia.in/blog/digital-marketing-higher-education importance-benefits-impact

Kortelainen, S., & Järvi, K. (2014, June 8–11). Ecosystems: Systematic literature review and framework development. *Innovation for Sustainable Economy & Society* [Conference presentation]. XXV ISPIM Conference, Dublin, Ireland.

KPMG. (2020). *The future of higher education in a disruptive world.* KPMG International.

Krishnamurthy, S. (2020). The future of business education: A commentary in the shadow of the COVID-19 pandemic. *Journal of Business Research, 117,* 1–5.

Letaifa, S. B., Gratacap, A., & Isckia, T. (2013). *Understanding business ecosystems: How firms succeed in the new world of convergence?* De Boeck Superieur.

Letheren, L., Russell-Bennett, R., & Whittaker, L. (2020). Black, white or grey magic? Our future with artificial intelligence. *Journal of Marketing Management, 36*(3–4), 216–232.

Luthra, P., & Mackenzie, S. (2020). *4 ways COVID-19 education future generations.* World Economic Forum. https://www.weforum.org/agenda/2020/03/4-ways-covid-19-education-future-generations

Malaysia Digital Economy Blueprint. (2019). Economic Planning Unit, Prime Minister's Department. https://www.ekonomi.gov.my/sites/default/files/2021-02/malaysia-digital-economy-blueprint.pdf

MBO Partners. (2021). *Professional certifications: 5 benefits you won't regret.* https://www.mbopartners.com/blog/how-manage-small-business/five-benefits-of-professional-certification

McKinsey & Company. (2017). *Jobs lost, jobs gained: Workforce transitions in a time of automation.* https://www.mckinsey.com/~/media/BAB489A30B724BECB5DEDC41E9BB9FAC.ashx

Mian, S. H., Salah, B., Ameen, W., Moiduddin, K., & Alkhalefah, H. (2020). Adapting universities for sustainability education in Industry 4.0: Channel of challenges and opportunities. *Sustainability, 12,* 11–31.

Mikalef, P., Giannakos, M. N., Pappas, I. O., & Krogstie, J. (2018). The human side of big data: Understanding the skills of the data scientist in education and industry. In *2018 IEEE Global Engineering Education Conference* (EDUCON) (pp. 503–512).

Ministry of Higher Education. (2013). *Malaysian education blueprint 2015–2025 (higher education).*

Rejikumar, G., Raja Sreedharan V., Arunprasad, P., Persis, J., & Sreeraj, K. M. (2019). Industry 4.0: Key findings and analysis from the literature arena. *Benchmarking: An International Journal, 26*(8), 2514–2542. https://doi.org/10.1108/BIJ-09-2018-0281

Rienties, B., & Townsend, D. (2012). Integrating ICT in business education: Using TPACK to reflect on two course redesigns. In P. Van den Bossche, W. Gijselaers, & R. G. Milter (Eds.), *Learning at the crossroads of theory and practice* (pp. 141–156). Springer.

Sharma, P. (2021). Business education must be driven by sustainable development goals. *The Star.* https://www.thestar.com.my/news/education/2021/04/11/business-education-must-be-driven-by-sustainable-development-goals

Stanton, W. W., & Stanton, A. D. A. (2020). Helping business students acquire the skills needed for a career in analytics: A comprehensive industry assessment of entry-level requirements. *Decision Sciences Journal of Innovative Education, 18*(1), 138–165.

Suppramaniam, S., Siew, P. H. K., & Ainara, G. (2019). An employability assessment of fresh business graduates in Kuala Lumpur from the perspective of employers. *International Journal of Recent Technology and Engineering, 7*(5S), 307–317.

Tapscott, D., & Williams, A. D. (2008). *Wikinomics: How mass collaboration changes everything.* Penguin.

The National Center for Academic Transformation. (2014). *How to redesign a college course using NCAT's methodology.* https://www.thencat.org/Guides/AllDisciplines/How%20to%20Redesign%20A%20College%20Course.pdf

Topi, H. (2016). Advancing data science education through a transdisciplinary education conversation. *Opinion: IS Education, 7*(1), 26–27. https://doi.org/10.1145/2875438

Trust, T., & Whalen, J. (2020). Should teachers be trained in emergency remote teaching? Lessons learned from the COVID-19 pandemic. *Journal of Technology and Teacher Education, 28*(2), 189–199.

United Nations Educational, Scientific and Cultural Organisation. (2005). *Integrating ICTs into the curriculum: Analytical catalogue of key publications.* UNESCO Asia and Pacific Regional Bureau for Education. https://files.eric.ed.gov/fulltext/ED496228.pdf

Velu, C., Barrett, M., Kohli, R. A., & Salge, T. O. (2013). *Thriving in open innovation ecosystems: Toward a collaborative market orientation.* University of Cambridge.

Verma, A., Yurov, K. M., Lane, P. L., & Yurova, Y. V. (2019). An investigation of skill requirements for business and data analytics positions: A content analysis of job advertisements. *Journal of Education for Business, 94*(4), 243–250.

Vidgen, R., Shaw, S., & Grant, D. B. (2017). Management challenges in creating value from business analytics. *European Journal of Operational Research, 261*(2), 626–639.

Waddack, S., & Lozano, J. M. (2015). Developing more holistic management education: Lessons learned from two programs. *Academy of Management Learning & Education, 12,* 285–294.

Wadee, A. A., & Padayachee, A. (2017). Higher education: Catalysts for the development of an entrepreneurial ecosystem, or ... are we the weakest link? *Science, Technology and Society, 22*(2), 284–309.

Wagner, T. (2010). *The global achievement gap: Why even our best schools don't teach the new survival skills our children need and what we can do about it.* Basic Books.

Wamba, S. F., Gunasekaran, A., Akter, S., Ren, S. J. F., Dubey, R., & Childe, S. J. (2017). Big data analytics and firm performance: Effects of dynamic capabilities. *Journal of Business Research, 70,* 356–365.

Wilder, C. R., & Ozgur, C. O. (2015). Business analytics curriculum for undergraduate majors. *INFORMS Transactions on Education, 15*(2), 180–187.

Wymbs, C. (2016). Managing the innovation process: Infusing data analytics into the undergraduate business curriculum (lessons learned and next steps). *Journal of Information Systems Education, 27*(1), 61–74.

Chapter 9

Smart Education for Smart Cities: Cloud-Based EEG Solution for Mental Health and Cognitive Skills Assessment for Higher Education in the ASEAN Region

Nicolas Hamelin* & Wendy Ong‡

ABSTRACT

With a combined population of around 540 million and to respond to the challenges posed by rapid urbanisation and digitalisation, the Association of Southeast Asian Nations (ASEAN) region has embarked on an ambitious smart city development programme. In this context, Southeast Asian higher education plays a vital role in establishing and strengthening the region's global standing. To some extent, ASEAN higher education has gradually improved access to education, quality and relevance. Yet, as the region's success depends on new knowledge, innovation and the introduction of new and advanced production methods, higher education institutions (HEIs) need quality control and standardisation. Hence, assessing students' skills and mental health status becomes a necessity. This chapter explores the utilisation of portable electroencephalogram (EEG) systems to provide affordable and reliable skills and mental health appraisals of ASEAN's culturally and economically diverse student population. A cloud-based EEG portable system is proposed as an affordable solution for educators and students to detect potential mental health issues and assess the cognitive

* SPJAIN Neuroscience Lab, Australia & The American University in Cairo, Egypt

‡ Brunel University London, United Kingdom

and emotional skills necessary to build a workforce of future managers and leaders across the ASEAN region.

Keywords ASEAN, EEG, higher education, human resource, mental health, skills assessment

INTRODUCTION

Higher education: A smart city challenge

With ASEAN's growing population, smart cities have been on many ASEAN countries' developmental framework agenda. Some major challenges of smart cities are human resources (HR) and education. At the heart of smart cities are better-educated individuals and highly skilled workers. Smart cities appeal to innovative and creative managers and leaders and, along with dynamic workers, create an ever-virtuous cycle of growth. Urban transformations command a high level of organisation and a significant percentage of skilled individuals to manage complex economic, social and technological structures. Smart education to train future leaders, decision makers, managers or technical personnel is a necessary building block for any smart city. In 2015, ASEAN announced that capital investments and skilled labour could move freely between Brunei, Cambodia, Indonesia, Laos, Malaysia, Myanmar, Thailand, the Philippines, Singapore and Vietnam. In the education sector, the goal was to increase coordination and standardisation (Moussa et al., 2022). However, standardisation has been a constant source of tension between various ASEAN partners; while some countries have strict examination rules, others have less stringent regulations. University professors often report they are not allowed to fail students who have disbursed sizeable sums for education, with Welch (2020) reporting considerable corruption in the higher education sector. This has detrimental societal and economic effects—it increases hiring costs, negatively impacts graduate wages, and reduces economic returns and competitiveness (Yuan & Ishak, 2022). Hence, HR rarely relies on university grades to evaluate a candidate for employment; instead, it uses ad-hoc specialised tests.

One of the most employed psychometric tests for HR is the Caliper Profile test. The Caliper test is "an objective assessment that accurately measures an individual's personality characteristics and individual motivations to predict on-the-job behaviours and potential" (Caliper Corporation, 2022, para. 1). Another prominent test is the Myer-Briggs Type Indicator, with 89 Fortune 100 companies using the indicator to screen prospective employees. However, the reliability of these tests is questionable. For example, there is no agreement on how to gauge work-related stress due to the various ranges of stress dynamics (Shin, 2013). Leadership training results in many measurement instruments (Zaccaro & Banks, 2001). However, the definition of leadership itself varies greatly (Kan, 2002). For example, the Multifactor Leadership Questionnaire, which measures transformational leadership, transactional leadership, passive/avoidant behaviours and leadership outcomes, is readily available online with companies offering training. For example, JobTestPrep provides information about the test to help prepare a candidate for examination. Much research has shown that personality tests are poor predictors of future job performance (Meijer, 2020; Moore, 2017; Morgeson et al., 2007). On the other hand, EEG tests provide an unbiased measure of neural activities and a robust assessment of a person's emotional and cognitive ability, as EEG signals are highly representative of cognitive and emotional processing (Dvorak et al., 2018; Mikolajczak et al., 2010; Santesso et al., 2006). For example, various EEG studies have shown that stress levels can be measured with an accuracy of 96% (Jun & Smitha, 2016; Subhani et al., 2017).

Early detection of mental health issues

Mental health literacy in the ASEAN region has traditionally been poor. Communities have a negative attitude towards mental illness and very few students seek formal help and professional treatment (Fairuziana et al., 2020). Accordingly, resources allocated to mental health are limited and universities rarely provide counselling services to their students (Dessauvagie et al., 2021). Pengpid and Peltzer (2018) have found that 11.5% of university students across ASEAN countries were potentially at risk of eating disorders associated with psychological factors such as depression. While less than 10% of Indonesian, Thai and Vietnamese students were affected, this number increased to 20.6% in Malaysia and Myanmar. Another study of university students in Cambodia, Laos, Malaysia, Myanmar, Thailand and Vietnam using a systematic database search (Dessauvagie et al., 2021) has found occurrences of mental health problems among university students to be alarmingly high; 29.4% of students suffered from depression, 42.4% suffered from anxiety, 16.4% suffered from stress, 13.9% reported disordered eating, while suicidality was reported in 7% to 8% of students.

Unresolved mental health issues are costly for nations. For instance, the Royal Australian and New Zealand College of Psychiatrists has found that the cost of severe mental illness in Australia was $56.7 billion per year in 2014 (Cook, 2019). Mental health issues account for 30% of diseases worldwide, with an estimated cost of $2.5 trillion in 2010 and is expected to reach $6 trillion by 2030 (Marquez & Saxena, 2016). Yet, most mental health issues are left undetected, primarily due to a lack of mental health professionals and services early on. It has been suggested that wearables and mobile apps are a potential low-cost solution to detect and address mental health issues early (Dewa et al., 2019). Societal expectations and increasingly complex student profiles create unprecedented stress levels for educators and learning support staff members. With diminishing gains through educational interventions, educators are searching elsewhere, having explored brain-based strategies over the last few decades.

This chapter examines the feasibility of a low-cost, practical and versatile cognitive skills and mental health assessment tool for tertiary institutions in the ASEAN region. The tool has the potential to be used by HR departments in staff employment processes and, importantly, with at-risk students in higher education for the benefit of the future workforce in smart cities. The general principle of the tool in terms of developing higher education students' emotional intelligence and critical and creative thinking can also be integrated into the curriculum and in the teaching and learning approaches of academic programmes.

Significance and objectives of the study

Higher education in the ASEAN region faces two important challenges. The first challenge questions how ASEAN higher education can achieve the quality control and standardisation needed for its ambitious smart cities' development goals. The second challenge revolves around the limited resources available for the early detection of mental health issues affecting a large percentage of the student population. This study investigates the use of a practical, affordable and portable cloud-based system for mental health and skills assessment for students in higher education in the ASEAN region.

LITERATURE REVIEW

Portable electroencephalogram (EEG) system as a solution to assess potential mental health issues and cognitive skills

Most countries' mental health support services are underfunded and overwhelmed (Bannister, 2021). The recent Coronavirus Disease 2019 (COVID-19) pandemic has rendered the situation even more concerning (Sharma et al., 2020), with children often being left behind (Racine et al., 2020). Figueroa and Aguilera (2020) posit that a technological revolution is needed to "[scale] up the delivery of confidential mental health services to patients across a wide range of platforms, from elemental health to mobile interventions such as apps and text messaging" (p. 1). This research shows how readily the EEG systems can detect mental health issues early and avoid overburdening mental health services. In particular, the use of portable EEG headsets to assess mental health issues has been gaining popularity (Saeedi et al., 2021; Seal et al., 2021).

EEG detection framework

The cloud-based software provides a novel technique to scientifically measure cognitive intelligence, emotional intelligence and intuitive skills, and perform the measurements and computation by the implemented software residence on the cloud. The system is based on using an EEG helmet to measure coherence scores, frontal asymmetry indices and cognitive load. Coherence and frontal asymmetry are standard metrics in social cognitive neuroscience. Coherence is a measure of interconnectedness in different areas of the brain. High coherence in the right hemisphere is linked to greater emotional balance and understanding of one's own emotions and those of others (Huang, 2021). It also reflects a greater cognitive understanding of the bigger picture. The frontal alpha asymmetry index is defined as the difference between right and left alpha activity over the frontal regions of the brain. People with an increased left-frontal alpha have been found to process information positively, while right-lateralisation indicates a more negative processing mode. The frontal asymmetry score measures the motivation towards (approach) or away from (avoidance) something or someone. Greater left-side prefrontal cortex activity is associated with approach-related and goal-directed action planning, while the right suggests avoidance-related emotions (Salminen et al., 2021; Zhang et al., 2020).

Data are acquired locally with the help of a 14-electrode EEG helmet and a computer. Data are transferred from the EEG helmet to the computer via low-energy Bluetooth. The data are then uploaded to a server (cloud computer), where they are analysed and processed using a proprietary algorithm. Emotional intelligence and cognitive skills are also determined from the data. EEG data analysis under calibrated stimuli or tasks allows the measurement of traits based on a specific test. For example, Amsterdam Dynamic Facial Expression Set–Bath Intensity Variations are used as a task while EEG data are recorded (Moshirian Farahi et al., 2019). Respondents are subjected to specific stimuli and EEG data are recorded, processed and analysed. A 14-electrode Emotiv-X EEG headset provides access to professional-grade brain data with an easy-to-use design. The data are transferred wirelessly and an algorithm computes the respondents' information uptake ability, emotional skill, cognitive load levels, attention, memory, emotion regulation and engagement. The system is cloud-based and can be accessed from any computer with any operating system (Figure 9.1). Machine learning will be gradually implemented as the database increases to position respondents' scores to profile individual mental health status precisely (Ieracitano, 2020).

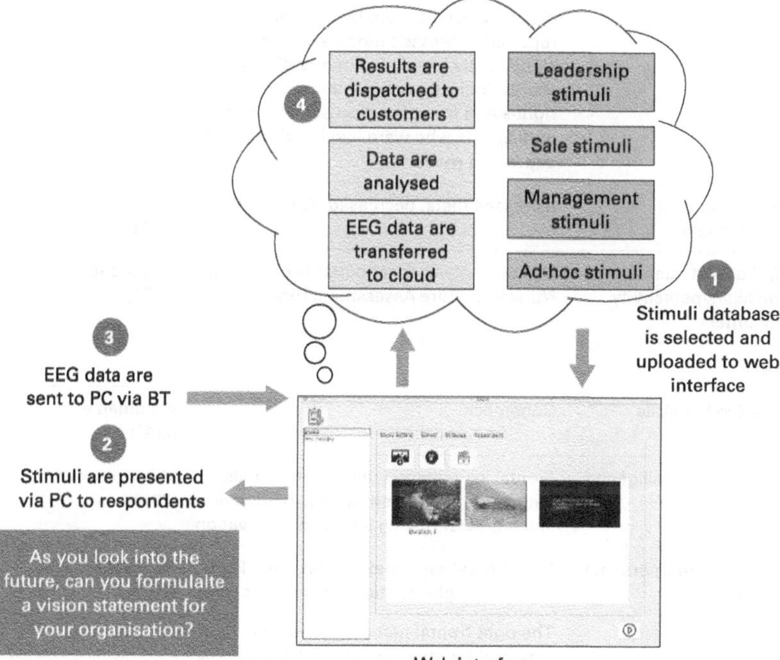

Figure 9.1 Schematic of a cloud-based mental health and human resources (HR) measurement system

EEG data analysis for mental health detection and human resource skills

Analysis of EEG data under calibrated stimuli permits the measurement of specific mental health issues such as neuroticism, depression, stress level, anxiety and autistic disorders. Respondents were subjected to specific stimuli and EEG data were recorded, processed and analysed. Table 9.1 shows the relationship between mental health issues and the relevant research with

Table 9.1 Mental health and HR measurement skills based on electroencephalogram (EEG)

Mental Health Issue	Measure	Reference
Stress	Coherence	Gaylord et al. (1989)
Autistic spectrum disorder	Reduced alpha power	Coben et al. (2013)
Neuroticism	Significant and positive correlation between neuroticism and mid-frontal asymmetry (F3–F4) and the lateral-frontal (F7–F8)	Moshirian et al. (2019)
Depression and anxiety	Link between resting frontal EEG asymmetry and depression and anxiety Participants who were high in self-reported depressed mood exhibited significantly lower asymmetry difference scores, indicative of greater relative right-sided frontal cortical activity than participants who were low in self-reported depressed mood	Thibodeau et al. (2006)
Mild cognitive impairment	Increased theta, decreased alpha power	Jelic & Kowalski (2009)
Childhood attention-deficit/hyperactivity disorder	Use of single-channel portable EEG using Nursing Culture Assessment Tool	Johnstone et al. (2021)
HR		
Leadership skills	Coherence	Waldman et al. (2011)
Emotional intelligence	Frontal asymmetry (alpha), individuals with higher trait of emotional intelligence show greater resting left frontal activation	Mikolajczak et al. (2010)
Effective interpersonal skills	High frontal asymmetry index (F4 > F3) = Increased right-frontal asymmetry (alpha) The right frontal part of the brain is essential for effective interpersonal communication and social relationships	Bonnstetter et al. (2015)

EEG data. Table 9.1 also links the EEG data to human characteristics of interest to HR in an educational context. It is proposed that this process also has the potential for use with students in higher education. The first column in Table 9.1 states the mental health issue, the second column refers to the corresponding EEG measurements to detect the associated condition, while the third column lists the related references.

Applications of the system for higher education setting

Cognitive and behavioural profiles of students in higher education have become increasingly complex and resistant to educational interventions supported by adaptations and modifications. This phenomenon has impeded beneficial outcomes to teaching and learning, while significantly increasing educators' stress. Furthermore, changing demographics, new and increasing demands on a university's time and expertise, a shortage of specialist availability and financial resources to fund programming, in conjunction with the ever-increasingly complex student profiles documented by educational ministries, have been confirmed by administrators worldwide as barriers to educational gains for growing numbers of vulnerable students. The advanced, portable EEG technology has not historically been available for educational contexts. Owing to technological advances, portable EEG devices are now widely available and implemented in various medical, business and educational settings (Babiker et al., 2016; Williams et al., 2020). The new wearable, non-invasive EEG headset offers the possibility of easily measuring university students' cognitive and emotional skills and adapting the teaching material or methodology and potential mental health issues affecting students. In this capacity, the proposal is revolutionary in programme design and assessment methodology.

METHODOLOGY

Stimuli presentation and EEG measurement

The system is based on presenting the respondents with calibrated emotional stimuli. Those stimuli are selected from the International Affective Picture System (IAPS) and the International Affective Digitised Sound System (IADS) database. IAPS and IADS are emotional, visual and acoustic stimuli, respectively. Both coherence score and frontal asymmetry score are measured while respondents are submitted to either or both IAPS and IADS stimuli. While the stimuli are presented, a 14-electrode EEG headset measures the coherence ratio between three electrodes located on the brain's right frontal regions: Fp2, F4, and F7 (using the International 10/20 Electrode System). Once measured, a coherence score is calculated for the beta frequency (20–30Hz). Coherence and frontal asymmetry values are calculated from these data.

Similarly, a 14-electrode EEG headset measures the frontal asymmetry ratio while the stimuli are presented. As mentioned earlier, the frontal alpha asymmetry index is the difference between right and left alpha activity over frontal regions of the brain (Asymmetry Index = ln, alpha power right F4/ alpha power left F3). Specifically, FAA using electrodes F4/F3 and F8/F7 is measured using the international 10/20 Electrode System in the 8–12 Hz alpha frequency band. For cognitive skills measurement, the negative asymmetry index corresponds to respondents with a dominant left hemisphere (i.e. the focus is mainly logical and rational thinking), indicating that the respondents may make good planners. Positive asymmetry index corresponds to staff with dominant right hemispheres (i.e. the focus is primarily imagination, creativity, visual imagery and emotional response), which indicates that they may make good managers or leaders. The degree of emotional intelligence can be determined using frontal asymmetry measures. In this case, a positive frontal asymmetry index is linked to higher activity in the right frontal part of the brain, essential for effective interpersonal communication and social relationships. In inspirational leadership, especially the espousal of socialised visionary communication, greater left-sided prefrontal cortex activity appears to be associated with approach-related and goal-directed action planning, while the right suggests avoidance-related emotions (Waldman et al., 2011).

Experimental design

Twenty respondents were submitted to eight emotional and cognitive stimuli to test the proposed system. The participants were all Master of Business Administration (MBA) students in their final year, with an equal proportion of male and female students. Ten students were from India, three from Vietnam, five from Indonesia and two from the Philippines. All respondents had three to five years of work experience in large corporations prior to enrolling in the MBA programme. The emotional stimuli were chosen from the IAPS database, while the respondents' cognitive capacity was assessed via a Stroop test. The Stroop Color and Word test assesses a person's aptitude to regulate cognitive interference generated by a stimulus, while simultaneously processing another stimulus (Jensen, 1965). In a Stroop test experiment, respondents must say the colour of the word, not what the word says. The Stroop test has been extensively used to measure frontal lobe execution and the distinctive cognitive functions these brain regions facilitate (Demakis, 2004).

Finally, to measure leadership skills, the respondents were asked to orally answer two questions based on the research by Waldman et al. (2011) about the future of their organisations: "Can you please describe your current plans for your organisation, as well as plans for yourself in the future?" and "As you look to the future, can you formulate a vision statement for your organisation?" Respondents could answer these questions with a personalised or socialised vision. Respondents with socialised visions were found to have a higher coherence score than those with a more personalised response (Waldman et al., 2011). Business leaders with a socialised vision of leadership have a higher degree of care and compassion, focusing on the greater good of the community and on uprooting societal problems. On the contrary, business leaders with a personalised vision of leadership show a low degree of care and compassion, and focus on both personal and shareholder motivations; they tend to act in self-interest and exploit and disregard others (Hamelin et al., 2018; Nielsen et al., 2010; Pless et al., 2021).

Higher education students must integrate a socialised vision of leadership in their learning. The 2008 financial crisis made tertiary institutions question what knowledge is and how knowledge is taught. Before the crisis, profit was often prioritised above all other dimensions (Wang et al., 2011). In the aftermath of the crisis, HEIs were made to re-evaluate their teaching of leadership and ethics. Yet, recent research has shown that very little progress has been made in modernising teaching curricula; the financial crisis came and went, but faculties were reluctant to question their curricula and teaching methods (Hainline et al., 2010). Most importantly, the increasing cost of education, the harsh competitive landscape and students' financial success are often used as the only measure of quality in education. This perpetuates a system encouraging corporate greed and social inequality, which originated the 2008 financial crisis (Friedland & Jain, 2022).

RESULTS AND DISCUSSIONS

Data from EEG coherence offers robust assessments of the working synchronisation level between various brain regions (Thatcher et al., 1986). Coherence corresponds to the percentage of the variance between regions of the brain. A high percentage (> 90%) suggests reasonably strong synchronicity between brain sites, whereas a lower percentage (around 10%) points to relatively poor synchronicity between different regions (Balthazard et al., 2012).

Using the results from Respondent A and Respondent B in Table 9.2 as typical of the overall study cohort of 20 respondents, they clearly show that Respondent A has a better coherence score and can better synchronise emotions and decision-making. Respondent B has a lower coherence score and a higher frontal asymmetry score, which implies the person is more emotional and more likely to have effective interpersonal communication and good social relationship skills. In the same vein, Respondent A's frontal asymmetry score is lower than Respondent B's, implying goal-directed action planning. As stated previously, the data and analysis of Respondent A and Respondent B are presented as typical results: both Respondent A and Respondent B are Asian males in the same age range (20–25 years old) with similar years of work experience in large corporations. The same experiment was conducted with 20 respondents from an MBA cohort, and similar coherence scores were recorded. We found two distinct groupings: one clustering around 85% and another around 32%. Hence, such a wearable, non-invasive EEG headset is potentially a practical way to measure university students' cognitive and emotional skills.

Table 9.2 EEG analysis results for coherence and frontal asymmetry responses to calibrated stimuli

Stimulus	Respondent A	Respondent B
Neutral 	Coherence value: 66.37% Frontal asymmetry for pair 1: 1.40	Coherence value: 40.07% Frontal asymmetry for pair 1: 3.22
Stroop test 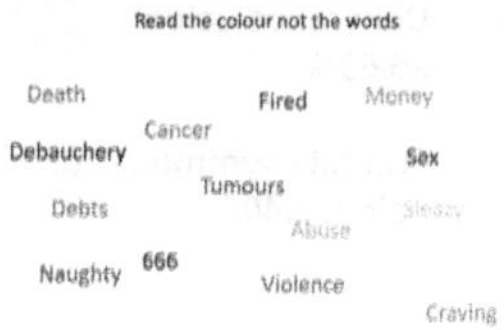 Read the colour not the words Death Fired Money Cancer Debauchery Sex Tumours Debts Abuse Sleazy Naughty 666 Violence Craving	Coherence value: 95.38% Frontal asymmetry for pair 1: 0.93	Coherence value: 76.86% Frontal asymmetry for pair 1: 0.60
Negative (fear) 	Coherence value: 58.67% Frontal asymmetry for pair 1: 0.70	Coherence value: 50.66% Frontal asymmetry for pair 1: 2.62
Negative (fear) 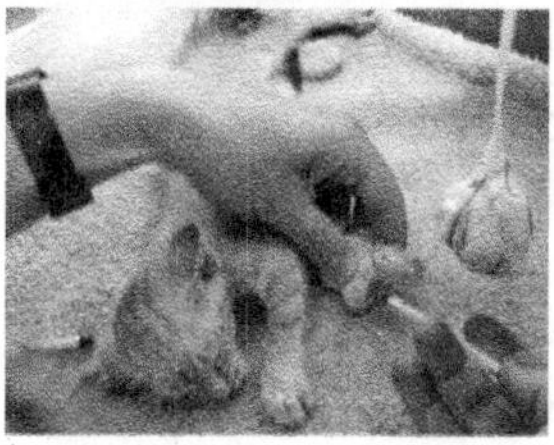	Coherence value: 98.01% Frontal asymmetry for pair 1: 0.88	Coherence value: 11.42% Frontal asymmetry for pair 1: 2.18

Table 9.2 EEG analysis results for coherence and frontal asymmetry responses to calibrated stimuli (cont'd)

Stimulus	Respondent A	Respondent B
Negative (fear)	Coherence value: 43.85% Frontal asymmetry for pair 1: 0.76	Coherence value: 22.93% Frontal asymmetry for pair 1: 3.45
Positive (excitement)	Coherence value: 64.57% Frontal asymmetry for pair 1: 1.00	Coherence value: 26.63% Frontal asymmetry for pair 1: 2.40
Can you please describe your plans for your organisation as well as your plans for yourself in the future?	Coherence value: 80.65% Frontal asymmetry for pair 1: 0.66	Coherence value: 52.89% Frontal asymmetry for pair 1: 1.38
As you look to the future, can you formulate a vision statement for your organisation?	Coherence value: 89.60% Frontal asymmetry for pair 1: 0.79	Coherence value: 28.71% Frontal asymmetry for pair 1: 2.25

Source: Marchewka et al. (2014)

CONCLUSION, LIMITATIONS AND FUTURE WORK

The development of smart cities in ASEAN depends on the effective training and utilisation of students and the workforce. The system and method presented in this chapter propose a novel technique to scientifically, safely and non-invasively assess cognitive and emotional intelligence in these populations more accurately than existing options. Teaching and learning delivery in tertiary education can be tailored around students' specific cognitive and emotional intelligence profiles. These results may even give rise to new pedagogical approaches with ecological validity, which can be applied to students outside the ASEAN region. The proposed system may help in the early detection of mental health conditions in at-risk students, benefitting all stakeholders and reducing costs to society. From an HR perspective, the system can better identify applicants with particular personality and cognitive traits, matching them with suitable roles and better utilising the workforce that smart cities rely on. The system's simplicity also allows for scalability, which will be crucial for acquiring enough data to train users to implement the model. The first measurements show that differences in cognitive and emotional ability can be recorded; further tests will focus on implementing machine learning to increase measurement accuracy and compare these measurements with other standard psychometric tests such as the Multifactor Leadership Questionnaire (Rowold, 2005).

Emotional intelligence in education has long been promoted as a solution that benefits students and societies (Devis-Rozental, 2018; Machera & Machera, 2017). It is proposed that using such a system as discussed in this chapter during a three- or four-year tertiary education curriculum will help shift faculties and institutions away from traditional teaching methodologies and create curricula that enhance emotional intelligence, critical and creative thinking—attributes at the heart of ASEAN's future smart cities.

REFERENCES

Babiker, A., Faye, I., & Malik, A. (2016, August). Investigation of situational interest effects on learning using physiological sensors: Preliminary result. *2016 6th International Conference on Intelligent and Advanced Systems (ICIAS)*, 1–5.

Balthazard, P. A., Waldman, D. A., Thatcher, R. W., & Hannah, S. T. (2012). Differentiating transformational and non-transformational leaders on the basis of neurological imaging. *The Leadership Quarterly, 23*(2), 244–258.

Bannister, R. (2021). Underfunded mental healthcare in the NHS: The cycle of preventable distress continues. *BMJ, 375*, n2706. https://doi.org/10.1136/bmj.n2706

Bonnstetter, R. J., Hebets, D., & Wigton, N. L. (2015). Frontal gamma asymmetry in response to soft skills stimuli: A pilot study. *NeuroRegulation, 2*(2), 70–85.

Caliper Corporation. (2022) *Hire and develop talent with more precision*. https://calipercorp.com/caliper-profile/#:~:text=The%20Caliper%20Profile%20is%20an,the%2Djob%20behaviors%20and%20potential

Coben, R., Chabot, R. J., & Hirshberg, L. (2013). EEG analyses in the assessment of autistic disorders. In M. F. Casanova, A. S. El-Baz, & J. Suri (Eds.), *Imaging the brain in autism* (pp. 349–370). Springer.

Cook, L. (2019). *Mental health in Australia: A quick guide*. Parliament of Australia.

Demakis, G. J. (2004). Frontal lobe damage and tests of executive processing: A meta-analysis of the category test, Stroop test, and trail-making test. *Journal of Clinical and Experimental Neuropsychology, 26*(3), 441–450.

Dessauvagie, A. S., Dang, H. M., Nguyen,T. A. T., & Groen, G. (2021). Mental health of university students in Southeastern Asia: A systematic review. *Asia Pacific Journal of Public Health, 34*(2-3), 172–181.

Devis-Rozental, C. (2018). *Developing socio-emotional intelligence in higher education scholars*. Springer International Publishing.

Dewa, L. H., Lavelle, M., Pickles, K., Kalorkoti, C., Jaques, J., Pappa, S., & Aylin, P. (2019). Young adults' perceptions of using wearables, social media and other technologies to detect worsening mental health: A qualitative study. *PloS One, 14*(9), 1–14.

Dvorak, D., Shang, A., Abdel-Baki, S., Suzuki, W., & Fenton, A. A. (2018). Cognitive behavior classification from scalp EEG signals. *IEEE Transactions on Neural Systems and Rehabilitation Engineering, 26*(4), 729–739.

Fairuziana, Mawarpury, M., Lay, A. E., Fitriani, Y., & Fitria, Y. (2020). Mental health literacy in South East Asia in a cultural context: A systematic review. *Proceedings of the 3rd International Conference on Psychology in Health, Educational, Social, and Organizational Settings (ICP-HESOS 2018)*, 516–524. https://www.scitepress.org/Papers/2018/85915/85915.pdf

Figueroa, C. A., & Aguilera, A. (2020). The need for a mental health technology revolution in the COVID-19 pandemic. *Frontiers in Psychiatry, 11*(523), 1–5.

Friedland, J., & Jain, T. (2022). Reframing the purpose of business education: Crowding-in a culture of moral self-awareness. *Journal of Management Inquiry, 31*(1), 15–29.

Gaylord, C., Orme-Johnson, D., &Travis, F. (1989).The effects of the transcendental mediation technique and progressive muscle relaxation on EEG coherence, stress reactivity, and mental health in black adults. *The International Journal of Neuroscience, 46*(1–2), 77–86.

Hamelin, N., Nasiri, N., Rezaei, S., & El Haddou-Yousefi, Y. (2018). Comparing work-related values of US, Canadian, Chinese, Iranian, and Moroccan Business Students: Multi-theory perspective. *Asian Journal of Business Research, 8*(1), 1–17.

Hainline, L., Gaines, M. S., Feather, C. L., Padilla, E., &Terry, E. J. (2010). Changing students, faculty, and institutions in the twenty-first century. *Peer Review, 12*(3), 7–11.

Huang, C. (2021). Recognition of psychological emotion by EEG features. *Network Modeling Analysis in Health Informatics and Bioinformatics, 10*(12), 1–11.

Ieracitano, C., Mammone, N., Hussain, A., & Morabito, F. C. (2020). A novel multi-modal machine learning based approach for automatic classification of EEG recordings in dementia. *Neural Networks, 123*, 176–190.

Jelic, V., & Kowalski, J. (2009). Evidence-based evaluation of diagnostic accuracy of resting EEG in dementia and mild cognitive impairment. *Clinical EEG and Neuroscience, 40*(2), 129–142.

Jensen, A. R. (1965). Scoring the Stroop test. *Acta Psychologica, 24*(5), 398–408.

Johnstone, S. J., Parrish, L., Jiang, H., Zhang, D. W., Williams, V., & Li, S. (2021). Aiding diagnosis of childhood attention-deficit/hyperactivity disorder of the inattentive presentation: Discriminant function analysis of multi-domain measures including EEG. *Biological Psychology, 161*(108080).

Jun, G., & Smitha, K. G. (2016). EEG based stress level identification. *2016 IEEE International Conference on Systems, Man, and Cybernetics (SMC)*, 3270–3274.

Kan, M. (2002). Reinterpreting the multifactor leadership questionnaire. In K. W. Parry & J. R. Meindl (Eds.), *Grounding leadership theory and research: Issues, perspectives, and methods* (pp. 159–173). Information Age Publishing Inc.

Machera, R. P., & Machera, P. C. (2017). Emotional intelligence (EI): A therapy for higher education students. *Universal Journal of Educational Research, 5*(3), 461–471.

Marchewka, A., Żurawski, Ł., Jednoróg, K., & Grabowska, A. (2014). The Nencki Affective Picture System (NAPS): Introduction to a novel, standardized, wide-range, high-quality, realistic picture database. *Behavior Research Methods, 46*, 596–610.

Marquez, P. V., & Saxena, S. (2016). Making mental health a global priority. *Cerebrum: The Dana Forum on Brain Science*, cer-10-16.

Meijer, J. (2020). Learning potential, personality characteristics and test performance. In J. H. M. Hamers, A. J. J. M. Rujissenaars, & K. Sijtsma (Eds.), *Learning potential assessment* (pp. 341–362). Taylor & Francis.

Mikolajczak, M., Bodarwé, K., Laloyaux, O., Hansenne, M., & Nelis, D. (2010). Association between frontal EEG asymmetries and emotional intelligence among adults. *Personality and Individual Differences, 48*(2), 177–181.

Moore, D. A. (2017). How to improve the accuracy and reduce the cost of personnel selection. *California Management Review, 60*(1), 8–17.

Morgeson, F. P., Campion, M. A., Dipboye, R. L., Hollenbeck, J. R., Murphy, K., & Schmitt, N. (2007). Reconsidering the use of personality tests in personnel selection contexts. *Personnel Psychology, 60*(3), 683–729.

Moshirian Farahi, S. M., Asghari Ebrahimabad, M. J., Gorji, A., Bigdeli, I., & Moshirian Farahi, S. M. M. (2019). Neuroticism and frontal EEG asymmetry correlated with dynamic facial emotional processing in adolescents. *Frontiers in Psychology, 10*(175).

Moussa, M., Doumani, T., McMurray, A., Muenjohn, N., & Deng, L. (2022). Shifting frameworks in a university in the ASEAN economic community: Challenges and recommendations in post-COVID-19. In *Cross-Cultural Performance Management* (pp. 237–260). Palgrave Macmillan.

Nielsen, R., Marrone, J. A., & Slay, H. S. (2010). A new look at humility: Exploring the humility concept and its role in socialized charismatic leadership. *Journal of Leadership & Organizational Studies, 17*(1), 33–43.

Pengpid, S., & Peltzer, K. (2018). Risk of disordered eating attitudes and its relation to mental health among university students in ASEAN. *Eating and Weight Disorders—Studies on Anorexia, Bulimia and Obesity, 23*(3), 349–355.

Pless, N. M., Murphy, M., Maak, T., & Sengupta, A. (2021). Societal challenges and business leadership for social innovation. *Society and Business Review, 16*(4), 535–561.

Racine, N., Korczak, D. J., & Madigan, S. (2020). Evidence suggests children are being left behind in COVID-19 mental health research. *European Child & Adolescent Psychiatry, 31*(9), 1479–1480.

Rowold, J. (2005). *Multifactor leadership questionnaire: Psychometric properties of the German translation by Jens Rowold.* Mind Garden.

Saeedi, A., Saeedi, M., Maghsoudi, A., & Shalbaf, A. (2021). Major depressive disorder diagnosis based on effective connectivity in EEG signals: A convolutional neural network and long short-term memory approach. *Cognitive Neurodynamics, 15*(2), 239–252.

Salminen, M., Hamari, J., & Ravaja, N. (2021). Empathising with the end user: Effect of empathy and emotional intelligence on ideation. *Creativity Research Journal, 33*(2), 191–201.

Santesso, D. L., Reker, D. L., Schmidt, L. A., & Segalowitz, S. J. (2006). Frontal electroencephalogram activation asymmetry, emotional intelligence, and externalising behaviors in 10-year-old children. *Child Psychiatry and Human Development, 36*(3), 311–328.

Seal, A., Bajpai, R., Agnihotri, J., Yazidi, A., Herrera-Viedma, E., & Krejcar, O. (2021). DeprNet: A deep convolution neural network framework for detecting depression using EEG. *IEEE Transactions on Instrumentation and Measurement, 70,* 1–13.

Sharma, V., Ortiz, M. R., & Sharma, N. (2020). Risk and protective factors for adolescent and young adult mental health within the context of COVID-19: A perspective from Nepal. *The Journal of Adolescent Health, 67*(1), 135–137.

Shin, H. C. (2013). Measuring stress with questionnaires. *Journal of the Korean Medical Association, 56*(6), 485–495.

Subhani, A. R., Mumtaz, W., Mohamed Saad, M. N., Kamel, N., & Malik, A. S. (2017). Machine learning framework for the detection of mental stress at multiple levels. *IEEE Access, 5,* 13545–13556.

Thatcher, R. W., Krause, P. J., & Hrybyk, M. (1986). Corticocortical association fibers and EEG coherence: A two compartmental model. *Electroencephalography and Clinical Neurophysiology, 64*(2), 123–143.

Thibodeau, R., Jorgensen, R. S., & Kim, S. (2006). Depression, anxiety, and resting frontal EEG asymmetry: A meta-analytic review. *Journal of Abnormal Psychology, 115*(4), 715–729.

Waldman, D. A., Balthazard, P. A., & Peterson, S. J. (2011). Leadership and neuroscience: Can we revolutionise the way that inspirational leaders are identified and developed? *Academy of Management Perspectives, 25*(1), 60–74.

Wang, L., Malhotra, D., & Murnighan, J. K. (2011). Economics education and greed. *Academy of Management Learning & Education, 10*(4), 643–660.

Welch, A. (2020). Of worms and woodpeckers: Governance & corruption in East and Southeast Asian higher education. *Studies in Higher Education, 45*(10), 2073–2081.

Williams, N., McArthur, G., & Badcock, N. A. (2020). *10 Years of EPOC: A scoping review of Emotiv's portable EEG device*. BioRxiv.

Yuan, T. K., & Ishak, S. (2022). Relationship between corruption, governance, and economic growth in ASEAN. In S. A. Abdul Karim (Ed.), *Shifting economic, financial and banking paradigm* (pp. 119–130). Springer.

Zaccaro, S. J., & Banks, D. J. (2001). Leadership, vision, and organisational effectiveness. In S. J. Zaccaro & R. J. Klimoski (Eds.), *The nature of organisational leadership: Understanding the performance imperatives confronting today's leaders* (pp. 181–218). Jossey-Bass.

Zhang, J., Hua, Y., Xiu, L., Oei, T. P., & Hu, P. (2020). Resting state frontal alpha asymmetry predicts emotion regulation difficulties in impulse control. *Personality and Individual Differences, 159*(9), 109870–109877.

Chapter 10

Future-Ready Graduates: Work-Study Programme in Singapore

Razwana Begum Abdul Rahim*

ABSTRACT

This chapter discusses the development of the work-study degree (WSDeg) in Singapore, with a focus on strengthening the framework to meet the demand for a resilient workforce. The WSDeg is part of a suite of work-study programmes (WSPs) offered by Singapore-based institutes of higher learning (IHLs). Recognising the need for graduates to have core skills to succeed in the workforce, this initiative was launched in 2015 by the Ministry of Education (MOE) and SkillsFuture Singapore. The WSDeg has progressively gained in popularity, but adapting an on-the-job (OTJ) training model to fit into the traditional university curriculum is a challenge. In the context of Singapore, learning has always been conventional, with emphasis on academic achievements. Differing slightly, the WSDeg introduces a work-based learning approach to develop students' employability skills and personal qualities. To engage students in workplace learning, support from employers is critical. Considering the volatility of the working world, employers often require workers with experience and may not prioritise support for the WSDeg. This chapter explores the intricacies of the development and promotion of this initiative. By meticulously mapping the different components of the WSDeg with the traditional components of the undergraduate programme, this chapter identifies areas that can be further strengthened and provides suggestions to effectively develop students to be future ready.

* Singapore University of Social Sciences, Singapore

Keywords COVID-19, future-ready workforce, institute of higher education, work-study programme, Singapore

INTRODUCTION

Singapore is one of Asia's top success stories. Within four decades following independence in 1965, the small state has transformed itself into a global hub of trade, finance, transportation and education (Abeysinghe, 2015). Indeed, education has played a critical role in this transformation, considering Singapore has no natural resources (Aoki, 2015). The strength of the transformation is further underlined in the context where, at the point of independence, the country was in chaos, with tensions between the diverse groups of people in Singapore leading to racial and religious violence (Lim et al., 2014). Looking further back into its history, Singapore was developed by migrants from different parts of the world. Singapore was also colonised by the British and invaded by the Japanese. The country shared a close relationship with Malaysia, and the subsequent separation from the latter further aggravated the rift between the different groups of people, posing a real threat to the safety and security of Singapore (Cheng, 2001).

Education policies, alongside social and economic policies under the leadership of the first Prime Minister of Singapore, the late Lee Kuan Yew, represented a series of pragmatic policies that did not disparage any racial, cultural or minority groups. Strategic decisions were made to unite the population with a common language, thus English became Singapore's working language. To support unification and prevent racial tensions, Malay, Mandarin and Tamil, alongside English, were proclaimed in the Constitution of the Republic of Singapore as official languages of the nation, allowing the Malay, Chinese and Indian communities to retain the use of their mother tongue (May, 2006). The policy advanced Singapore's unique identity as a multilingual society (Goh & Gopinathan, 2008). Importantly, for the discussion in this chapter, the education policy also allowed for the provision of universal primary and secondary education without discrimination.

With the above overview, this chapter discusses the educational background that led to the development of the WSDeg in Singapore. The government's policies highlight the value of developing people through education and the need to review the education system to meet the demands of employers. The discussion looks into policies targeted at WSPs in countries like Germany and Thailand to identify practices that can further strengthen the educational framework in the development of future-ready graduates.

BACKGROUND OF THE WORK-STUDY DEGREE (WSDEG) IN HIGHER EDUCATION IN SINGAPORE

The following review of the development of education policy and approaches in Singapore places into context the rise of the WSDeg in Singapore as a means to develop future-ready graduates.

As highlighted by Goh and Gopinathan (2008), the initial survival-driven education policy following independence created the pathway to economic growth and development. The educational framework concentrated on the development of people—Singapore's greatest asset. By increasing the capacity and capability of the people, Singapore was able to overcome the challenges in its development as a nation. Over time, Singapore became attractive to investors and companies in the manufacturing and electrical sectors, establishing factories that required human resources. With that, the focus of the education policy shifted towards being efficiency driven.

The New Education System was introduced in 1979 to ensure opportunities for all. The curriculum focused on the development of students according to their learning pace and ability, with greater emphasis on bilingualism, moral education, civics, science, mathematics and technical education. By providing targeted assessment, more students progressed to vocational institutions, polytechnics and universities. Again, the emphasis was on future development and the role of people in it. That is, with an educated workforce, the labour demands were met and Singapore's economy continued to expand (Gopinathan, 2007).

The meticulously planned and prescribed educational framework provided positive outcomes for students, with most of them being able to secure employment. However, this regime was observed to be overly paternalistic, creating a spoon-feeding culture with an over-reliance on leaders for direction

(Goh & Gopinathan, 2008). Teaching became more about transmitting information, and teachers were focused on testing students using mainly summative assessments that resulted in rote learning (Gopinathan, 1997; Ng, 2010). Rote learning is described as learning without thinking (Freire, 1972), and this contrasts with the need in the country for graduates who could operate more proactively rather than passively as a result of such a learning routine. The over-emphasis on examination and grading pressured teachers to teach and complete the syllabus within the stipulated duration. In all, the rigid curriculum and limited autonomy made it harder for teachers to nurture students to think out of the box, as required for future development in Singapore within the knowledge-based globalised world.

In response to these issues, education moved towards an ability-driven policy in the late 1990s. The change was critical, considering Singapore relies on its people to ensure its future. There was a relentless pursuit towards developing a knowledge-based economy. To drive this message, the then-Prime Minister Goh Chok Tong introduced the Thinking Schools, Learning Nation (TSLN) vision in 1997. The objective was to promote a lifelong passion for learning. To achieve this vision, schools in Singapore worked towards teaching critical thinking, information technology skills and citizenship education (Koh, 2004). With the shift towards holistic education, the government gradually reduced the emphasis on examinations, providing students with more choices in their studies (Heng, 2012). The TSLN considered all students' skills and talents to be equally valuable and nurtured—whether in academics, arts, sports or community endeavours.

The progressive development in educational policies placed Singapore in the top category in the provision of education globally (Tan, 2018). Among Asian countries, Singapore stands out for its stellar academic performance in international assessments. Singaporeans have consistently outperformed students from other countries, doing well in the global assessment for reading, mathematics and science (Tan, 2018).The focus on education has led to positive outcomes. However, to continue the development and sustainability of Singapore, education policies cannot remain stagnant. Despite the initial focus on performance and top positions at international examinations, Singapore is moving towards balancing both education and practical experiences. This requires changes to the higher education system in the country, as discussed next in this chapter.

HIGHER EDUCATION IN SINGAPORE

The ability-driven policy directs students to different paths. Upon completion of their secondary education, students are given the option to pursue technical and vocational studies at institutes of technical education or polytechnics. They can also take the academic route by completing their education at junior colleges. Those who do well continue to complete their undergraduate degree, and this space has become competitive. Singapore has six autonomous universities (AUs), with the National University of Singapore (NUS) and Nanyang Technological University (NTU) ranked in the top 20 in Asia. The other universities, namely Singapore Management University, Singapore University of Social Sciences (SUSS), Singapore University of Technology and Design, and Singapore Institute of Technology (SIT), have their own niche branding.

With the introduction of the Global Schoolhouse policy in 2002, students can complete their undergraduate studies with foreign universities and institutions in Singapore (Waring, 2014). This policy attracted more than 300 private educational institutions (PEIs). PEIs provide an alternate route for students to gain an undergraduate degree. The larger PEIs in Singapore, namely the Singapore Institute of Management Global Education, Kaplan, PSB Academy and Management Development Institute of Singapore, attract students with their diverse range of studies. James Cook University from Australia has its subsidiary in Singapore, attracting students not only from Singapore but also from the region. With their differentiated admission criteria and teaching pace, PEIs continue to do well in Singapore. Some degrees can be completed faster, sometimes in a year, compared with three to four years in an AU. PEIs also offer flexible learning options, allowing students to work and study at the same time.

The heavy emphasis on the role of education in human power development led to one negative consequence—an oversupply of university graduates. Obtaining a degree may not necessarily secure a job or a better one, especially if the degree is irrelevant to the position. The market has begun differentiating between degrees that carry their full worth in knowledge and skills and those that are essentially paper qualifications (Ng, 2015). As a result, university graduates sometimes work in low-paying or low-skill jobs, for which they are either overeducated or underemployed according to their educational qualifications. Employers are unable to locate local graduates with technical and soft skills to fill the gaps in the work requirements (Lai, 2020). Thus, it has become clear that employers prefer graduates with more experience, vital skill sets and relevant OTJ training such as internships, attachments and industrial projects, since real-world experience develops employable skills (Mokhtar, 2017).

The requirements from employers have thus pushed the government towards cultivating partnerships and collaboration between industry players and educational institutions (Lai, 2020). For instance, workplace training was introduced into degree curricula to help raise local graduates' employability. The SkillsFuture Council was formed to spearhead the development of an integrated system of education, training and career progression for Singaporeans. The mandate is to strengthen the linkages between education and training institutions and industry needs.

WORK-STUDY PROGRAMMES (WSPS) IN SINGAPORE

Within the development of education in Singapore and the key role of human personnel in it, WSPs in Singapore can be traced back to the 1960s when the government decided to set up two polytechnics to support adult learning. The concept evolved into lifelong learning in the 1980s, when dedicated institutions were set up to promote this form of learning. Over time, the terms used to describe these initiatives changed. However, the objectives remain the same. The schemes and programmes aim to support adult learners, encouraging them to upgrade themselves. In the context of young school leavers taking on an undergraduate programme, the purpose is to guide them in acquiring relevant work-specific skills (Lester & Costley, 2010).

This approach culminated in 2015 with the launch of WSPs for IHLs in the form of the SkillsFuture Earn and Learn Programme (ELP). Since then, demand from individuals and employers has been strong, and in 2017, a new work-study modality called the WSDeg was introduced. This model offers students the opportunity to acquire relevant skills and experience in certain fields. The WSDeg is similar to the cooperative education programme that focuses on integrating classroom learning with a structured OTJ training.

Companies and universities co-design and co-deliver curricula that closely interconnect theory and practice. Assessment of the students in the workplace is done collaboratively as well. To support educational institutions with this new modality of learning, the National Centre for Workplace Learning (NACE) was formed in 2018. Institutions can tap into experts from NACE and adapt the rubrics to certify new OTJ blueprints from ELP-participating companies (National Centre for Workplace Learning, 2022).

The WSDeg programme is currently offered across four AUs—NUS, NTU, SUSS and SIT—in the areas of information technology, business, engineering and science. The programme can be completed between three to four years and is offered to both full-time and part-time students. The application process varies between the AUs. For instance, at NTU, students are only invited to participate in the WSDeg in their second year, but at SIT, students can apply for the programme soon after enrolment. Employees from participating sponsor companies are also encouraged to apply, and they may approach their employer for a letter of recommendation to join the programme. However, the employees still need to fulfil the AUs' admission criteria. The WSDeg is generally delivered in two modes. The first is via the Term-In/Term-Out (TI/TO) model, where students alternate between spending one to two terms (or trimesters) in university and at the workplace. The second is through the Work-Day/Study-Day (WD/SD) model, where students alternate between working for a few days of the week in the partner company and studying for the remaining days of the week (Ministry of Education [MOE], 2020a).

As of 2019, approximately 350 students have successfully enrolled in a WSDeg (MOE, 2020a). The partner companies are chosen for their capacity and dedication to implementing quality OTJ training and meaningful career development opportunities for fresh graduates. Partners come from diverse sectors, multinational corporations (MNCs) and small and medium-sized enterprises (SMEs). The job placements are directly related to the field of study.

The WSDeg is an attractive option for both students and employers. While students gain experience, upgrade their skills and improve their employability, partner companies can use the WSDeg to adopt a structured approach to developing a talent pipeline. They can identify, recruit and groom suitable talent, and also assess the student's academic progression. By working personally with students in developing their specialised career trajectory, partner companies enable immediate assimilation of the employees and improve retention. Students may receive a stipend or allowance as part of this programme, or other forms of financial incentives such as scholarships and sponsorship packages. These sponsorship packages vary between partner companies, and they may also offer sign-on bonuses should the students continue to work with the company upon graduation. Any possible bond requirements in return for sponsorships may differ across partner companies, and penalties for contract termination are unique to the respective sponsorship contractual agreements (MOE, 2020a).

The WSDeg stands out among existing WSPs as it provides a higher level of collaboration between industries and universities. From 2017, the number of programmes has increased from 10 to 30 in 2019, mainly in the areas of data science, engineering and hospitality. Singapore is eager to build a work-study modality of learning that facilitates stronger linkages between the curriculum taught in school and the needs of the workplace. The government expects WSPs as a whole to benefit 12% of each age cohort by 2025. There are challenges, however, in the joint development and co-delivery of the curricula. The combination of institution-based learning and structured OTJ training requires changes to the traditional perspective of education, where educators are at the core of the system, taking the lead and being the gatekeepers of knowledge. The shift towards progressive education in the context of WSPs requires students to take on an active role and for the industry to co-develop, support and assess the learning journey of the students. This is a move away from the assessment-focused approach (MOE, 2020a).

Such a learning trajectory requires students to be active in demonstrating their knowledge and understanding. Students need to consider the potential benefits and view their attachment as more than a temporary experimental assignment. They are not just helping in the context of a typical internship stint; they spend more time with their employer in WSPs and should view their tasks seriously and recognise that they contribute to their potential future employers. They should take ownership and not expect indulgence from their supervisors, and relinquish the spoon-feeding culture and be enthusiastic about the training (Goh & Gopinathan, 2008). The aim is to develop students to acquire work-related skills, specifically applying theories and concepts to work within a stipulated industry. The students need to learn how to integrate knowledge into real-world applications (MOE, 2022).

Changes also need to take place in IHLs so that students are better prepared to adapt to the working world. The curricula need to develop traits such as resiliency, flexibility, communication, teamwork and critical thinking in students. The lesson plans should include activities where such traits can be assessed. Students should be aware that such traits are valuable in the work environment and will enhance their future employability outcomes. By sharing the details with the students, the activities will be taken seriously and students will be open to exploring, learning and not being afraid to fail. They will willingly participate in such experiential-based learning without expecting academic staff to guide them with a step-by-step manual (McRae et al., 2020).

To ensure successful outcomes, academic staff need to be aligned with such teaching methodology. The activities designed need to be relevant to the industry, and this requires the academic staff to monitor and keep track of the changes in the industry. They need to bridge the gap between theory and practice by being aware of the trends in the environment, including the latest developments in the industry. They need to take on a proactive role and be flexible in the delivery of knowledge.

The aspiration for the nation and its people to adopt lifelong learning mantras, policies and processes should also consider environmental factors, such as economic recessions or pandemics, that can disrupt the delivery of WSPs. It is more challenging for industry partners to focus on such programmes in a crisis. Providing opportunities for students requires effort and time. There are also other factors for consideration, such as the Coronavirus Disease 2019 or COVID-19 pandemic, where public health safety became a priority. To meet the health security requirements, organisations changed their way of working. Many interns who joined during the pandemic did so virtually and were inducted online. The pandemic also made it more difficult for organisations to engage interns, considering the lack of business. For instance, it is more challenging for some industries such as hospitality and tourism to be part of such programmes. Considering the fast-changing landscape and the foundation of WSPs that requires student engagement, it is imperative to design alternative ways to assess students' learning outcomes.

SINGAPORE'S WSDEG IN A GLOBAL CONTEXT: WSPS IN GERMANY AND THAILAND

Many countries have established WSPs, and the models adopted by Germany and Thailand are reviewed in this chapter to provide greater insights into what works for WSPs. Germany is renowned for its successful implementation of WSPs (Baethge & Wolter, 2015), while Thailand provides a Southeast Asian perspective on WSPs. The framework derived from these can be adapted across all WSPs, including those in Singapore, in the development of a future-ready workforce.

Germany, just like Singapore, started integrating both theory and practice into a cooperative education to address the shortage of skilled workers. Germany wanted to shift from the overly subscribed traditional university system that produced graduates who could demonstrate extensive academic experience but with little to no knowledge application experience in the real world. WSPs provide an opportunity for students to apply theories learnt at the university into practice. By doing so, students are able to adopt practical skills to complete a task. On the other hand, WSPs that are not planned well may demoralise students from being part of a profession.

Unlike Singapore, where WSDeg programmes are offered by academically oriented AUs, the German higher education system divides the universities based on this programme (Schindler & Reimer, 2011). The Duale Hochschule Baden-Württemberg (DHBW), known in English as Baden-Württemberg Cooperative State University, was the first German higher education institution to blend OTJ training and undergraduate academia (Reinhard et al., 2016). Established in 1974, this model is based on work-integrated learning that combines practical OTJ training with an undergraduate university qualification (Reinhard & Gerloff, 2020). This effort was spearheaded by the state government and three major employers in the state of Baden-Württemberg—Daimler-Benz, Bosch and SEL.

The success of the DHBW is founded on its opening of nine prominent locations and three branch campuses and collaborations with more than 10,000 sponsoring companies, where students are employed and reimbursed for the duration of their studies. Such hybrid institutions are known as the university of cooperative education (*Berufsakademie*) and are perceived as semi-tertiary institutions. The universities of cooperative education provide programmes in engineering, technology, business studies and social work. Another category known as universities of administration (*Verwaltungshochschulen*) provides training of civil servants for public administration and police functions. Both institutions are situated in between tertiary and non-tertiary education and collectively account for approximately 3% of the total student body in higher education.

German working adults are welcomed into these semi-tertiary institutions (Dobbelstein & Taylor, 2004). Particularly, the sponsoring company can select the students (then employees) and place them into the work-integrated learning programme upon meeting the minimum entry criteria. Unlike Singapore's WSDeg, where the university recruits students and source partner companies, in Germany it is the sponsoring company that recruits the students (Reinhard et al., 2016). Semi-tertiary institutions, especially universities of cooperative education, are very selective in terms of students' academic performance since sponsoring training organisations commit significant investments in the selected students (Schindler & Reimer, 2011). Hence, German students must possess a contract of employment and a university entrance qualification before commencement (Reinhard & Gerloff, 2020). Students are employed by the same sponsoring company throughout their studies.

In both semi-tertiary institutions, during the three-year programme, German students spend almost equal time at school and the sponsoring training organisation (Schindler & Reimer, 2011). They have to sign a contract with a specific employer in charge of the in-firm aspect of the dual training. The contract is a standard document provided by the DHBW (Reinhard et al., 2016). Similar to Singapore's stipend requirement, the most distinctive feature of German semi-tertiary institutions is the monthly salary provided to the student. For universities of cooperative education, the sponsoring organisation is usually a private firm, but for universities of administration, it will be the state or public administration. Since Singapore does not distinguish between the WSDeg programmes, all MNCs, SMEs and government ministries can partake as a partner company. Notably, unlike Singapore where students may have to adapt to both TI/TO or WD/SD schedules, Germany adopts only the TI/TO model where students alternate semesters between work and study (Reinhard et al., 2016). Furthermore, the DHBW works closely with its sponsoring companies such that concepts students learn in one semester can be immediately applied in the following semester (Engel-Hills et al., 2010).

In terms of labour market rewards, a graduate employment rate of 90% is achieved (Reinhard & Gerloff, 2020). One study by Hillmert and Kröhnert (2003) has found that for universities of cooperative education, graduates lag behind the more established academic universities. On the other hand, graduates from universities of administration are classified into the same salary grade in the public sector. Overall, however, the transition from school to employment is smooth for these graduates of semi-tertiary institutions since the sponsoring organisation remains interested in retaining them.

An Asian perspective is taken from the cooperative education found in Thailand. In 1993, Suranaree University of Technology (SUT) was the first university in Thailand to integrate mandatory cooperative education into its curricula (Reinhard et al., 2016). It offers degrees in social technology, engineering, agricultural technology, science and medicine (Coll et al., 2003). In addition, SUT worked together with private and public organisations in the design of its curricula. Walailak University is another institution that emphasises the importance of industry in education. In 2013, Walailak Management School's tourism and hospitality industry programme incorporated work-based learning projects into its curriculum, where sponsoring industry companies, such as resorts, hotels and tour companies, collaborate with the university's academic staff to impart the latest industry-relevant skills and experience in the tourism industry.

The Thai cooperative education system is divided into nine regional Cooperative Education Networks, which work with the institutions and industries in their respective regions to enhance the profile of cooperative education as a best practice model (Reinhard et al., 2016). This has progressively contributed to the active cooperation of over 13,000 sponsoring companies. Additionally, students can freely design their career paths and select their preferred available placements, allowing them to receive work experience in different sponsoring companies, similar to Singapore's WSDeg but varying from Germany's DHBW.

In SUT, students have a mandatory requirement to minimally spend 16 weeks at a sponsoring company during the third term of their third year of study or during any term in their fourth study year (Reinhard et al., 2016). SUT encourages students eager to gain more work experience to take on additional work terms up to three trimesters (48 weeks) to meet their graduation requirements (Sirijeerachai, 2009). The work terms are full-time, with distinct goals, and are remunerated. As for Walailak University, students in their second year will have a partly practical and partly academic (WD/SD) schedule (Pinpetch & Baum, 2009). In their third and fourth year, there will be three paid cooperative education trimesters where students work full time at their sponsoring companies (TI/TO). Additionally, work-based learning projects will be assigned during the third year.

At SUT, the level of remuneration will meet the minimum wage with variations based on the type and size of the sponsoring company (Reinhard et al., 2016). Since students hold temporary job positions, their remuneration is referred to as compensation and not salary. However, sponsoring companies are required to provide health and accident insurance for their employed students. If the student undertakes a period of work experience without regular remuneration, the sponsoring company has to provide supplementary benefits, including accommodation, food and transportation. On the other hand, at Walailak University, the sponsoring companies are mostly private companies (almost 90%), where students receive a daily allowance or a monthly salary as remuneration. In addition, hotels and resorts that serve as sponsoring companies typically provide students with accommodation, meals and transportation. However, some sponsoring companies such as government organisations and small tourism companies do not have the budget for cooperative education programmes and thus cannot offer students any remuneration (Reinhard et al., 2016).

Walailak University's cooperative education has improved students' employability, as prime sponsoring companies eagerly hire students (Reinhard et al., 2016). For example, some companies even make job offers on the students' first day of their last trimester in cooperative education. This means students can secure a job before graduation. Additionally, a majority of the sponsoring companies are keen to offer supervisory positions to students, allowing students to catapult into a middle-management level position. On the other hand, SUT graduates have historically suffered from low employment rates.

The success of WSPs in Germany, Thailand and Singapore can be attributed to three factors. The first is the targeted policies and support from the government in the development of the programmes. The employers' concern over graduates' inability to apply theory into practice was taken seriously and led to the innovative move to merge academic understanding with real-world experiences. All three countries considered education as critical, and it was necessary to continuously reinvent the education system to sustain progression. With support from the MOE and dedicated involvement from Workforce Singapore and SkillsFuture Singapore, Singaporeans of all ages are able to make informed learning and career choices. The services offered are geared towards Singapore's lifelong learning philosophy and are aligned with the development of a future-ready workforce—one that is able to learn, unlearn and relearn continuously.

The second factor is the support from employers and their willingness to take on an active role in developing the curriculum and programme. All three countries initiated WSPs based on the needs and requirements of employers. Germany developed a dedicated dual-track system specifically for WSPs. Thailand adopted similar strategies, working closely with organisations from the tourism industry to promote tourism studies. The employers not only provide work attachments, but also co-create the syllabus, course content and assessments. In Singapore, the AUs manage the WSDeg and, by taking on a partnership role, they have been able to form alliances with some organisations. For instance, SUSS has successfully partnered with NTUC First Campus in developing programmes related to early childhood care and education, and with the Ministry of Home Affairs/Home Team Academy in the development of the undergraduate programme in public safety and security. The role played by the IHLs in the development of WSPs is critical for their sustainability. As highlighted by Dalrymple et al. (2014), collaboration between IHLs, industry and students is necessary for knowledge to be meaningful. By forming partnerships, students are likely to receive targeted education directly relevant to the industry and thus able to perform their duties effectively upon graduation.

The third factor is the demand from students and support from parents. Germany's industrial exposure can be traced back to early education, creating curiosity and interest in students. In Thailand, WSPs provide an alternate option for students, and the close association with certain industries such as tourism makes WSPs attractive to students. In Singapore, academic achievement is a priority and, considering Singapore has two high-ranked universities in Asia (NUS and NTU), students may not be keen to go the extra mile of working and studying at the same time. Younger students, fresh from polytechnics or junior colleges and with limited exposure and experience, are likely to embark on short-term work attachment courses instead of committing themselves to a WSP in a particular industry. Those who choose to embark on this learning journey are likely interested in pursuing a specific career and require certain qualifications to be eligible for accreditation within that industry (Ng et al., 2020).

In general, WSPs provide benefits to both students and employers. However, the programmes need to be designed in partnership with the industry. This requires effort from both IHLs and industry partners. Some industries—for instance, security-related industries with highly confidential data—may be unable to accommodate students or co-supervise them. In other contexts, employees in the industry may not be fully knowledgeable in assessing and monitoring students according to the learning outcomes. For IHLs, development and teaching need to change to adapt to the needs of students and industries. Industry collaborations require the academic staff members to be open and flexible in receiving and giving feedback. To increase students' enrolment in such programmes, there is a need to clearly articulate the value of WSPs to not just the students, but also teachers in secondary schools and junior colleges. Parents need to understand the benefits of such a programme and encourage their children to explore industry-related courses. The education system in Singapore provides much support to its students. Great amounts of resources are given to students, most of whom receive additional coaching in the form of tuition so they can achieve higher grades. This pursuit of excellence is remarkable. However, it may not necessarily prepare students to take on real-world challenges. With that consideration, WSPs aim to strengthen students' ability to perform at work by inculcating critical skills at the onset of their learning journey.

WORK IN THE FUTURE AND THE WSDEG IN SINGAPORE

Work is in a state of flux and changes are occurring at a rapid pace. Disruption, globalisation, demographic shifts and advances in technology drive transformation. The pandemic has accelerated the process of change, influencing shifts in what was considered work, its space and the methods to carry it out. At the onset of the pandemic, employers scrambled to continue operations and make work possible for employees. Technology supported the changes, but the great shift took place abruptly. Without preparation, some employees became lost and the quality of their work suffered. The pandemic pushed the workforce into an unorthodox space. The uncertainty, fear and limited engagement created tension and chaos. The constant changes in the environment, including the rules and regulations, aggravated workflow. Unprepared employees were unable to adapt; some had to quit while others carried on working, suffering from isolation and depression.

People are critical to an organisation and contribute directly to economic success. In making changes to work, employees' well-being and engagement with others should be considered. While employers can implement workforce investment strategies, change organisational structure and invest in talent growth, these measures will only result in the desired outcome if employees are committed to them and are willing to change. Without employees' support, any form of transformation is likely to fail. The unusual situation with the pandemic is not something that can be rehearsed or planned. However, the situation can be better managed if employers take the time to equip their employees with skills and support them by modelling desired behaviours.

The workplace is changing quickly, with new jobs being created and old ones being replaced due to emerging technology. For young people pursuing tertiary education, it is hard to keep up with workplace trends. The education sector should identify these changes and prepare students for the future of work. It is not just about preparing them to be savvy in the use of technology; it is also about developing their human skills to adapt, innovate and be in control of new technology. A future-ready workforce comprises humans and machines, and it is important for organisations to consider and review the purpose of all their roles in the automation process. Redefining the roles may require very different sets of skills and capabilities. Since the skills are constantly changing, involving employees at the onset of the transformation process is necessary.

Future-ready employees should be able to meet today's challenges and adapt to tomorrow's trials. They must be able to observe and understand the work pattern and the required changes. With that, making informed decisions and simplifying deviations from traditional work processes become easier. This requires employees to embrace the culture of constant learning and be part of the lifelong learning movement, while employers should integrate learning as part of work. In other words, learning never stops. Even if an employee is a graduate, they need to continue upgrading the skills required to meet changes in the work environment. The organisation's culture and employers play a major role in ensuring this learning process. The focus is not just about hiring the right individual with the right knowledge, but also on developing a workforce built on enduring capabilities. Such capabilities include imagination, empathy, curiosity, resilience, creativity, teamwork and critical thinking. With such skills, employees are able to learn, apply and adapt knowledge and skills to meet changes in the workplace.

Considering the evolving nature of work, Singapore's WSPs include specific skills as part of their framework. In August 2019, SkillsFuture Singapore embarked on a review of the General Skills Competencies (GSCs) and introduced the new Critical Core Skills (CCS). GSCs are common, transferable skills that enable individuals to be employable and employed, facilitate their career mobility, and enable the acquisition of technical skills and competencies relevant to specific job roles in the sector. GSCs were developed and introduced as part of the Singapore Skills Framework in May 2016. CCS comprises 16 competencies grouped into three clusters of skills that workplaces deem most essential. The first cluster focuses on critical thinking. The objective is to increase the cognitive ability of employees to think broadly and creatively, and for them to be able to see the connections and opportunities amid change. The second cluster focuses on interacting with others. This cluster aims to support employees with their engagement and interaction skills, learn from one another and come together to resolve an issue or seek solutions. The third cluster focuses on staying relevant, for employees to keep abreast with workplace changes and to be motivated to pursue the technical skills required to perform work effectively.

Most employers are aware of the need to invest in human capital and understand the significant return on investment in upskilling and reskilling employees. The upgrading of knowledge specific to the industry can help employees remain relevant and develop innovative practices to address changes. WSPs provide great opportunities for employees to explore the development of generic and industry-specific skills. In 2016, SkillsFuture Singapore launched the Skills Framework, which is part of the Industry Transformation Maps. This was co-created with employers, government, industry associations, unions and education institutions. The Framework provides key information on sectors, including the existing and emerging skills required for the occupation or job roles. Employers can easily tap into the list of training programmes and explore the various training options for their employees.

For IHLs, the skills competency framework and industrial transformation map play a major role in developing, delivering and assessing courses. Students are no longer assessed purely based on traditional written examinations. They are required to do presentations and take up courses that are experiential by nature. To increase students' ability to think critically, assessments are based on real-world challenges or issues. By working in groups, students learn the value of teamwork. They are also engaged with practitioners from the industry, allowing them to make informed decisions in selecting their career pathways.

The WSP is unique with its focus on theory and its application in the real workplace. The work attachment is developed with the employer, with the intention of introducing students to industry-specific knowledge and skills. By being part of this programme, employers can also assess the resilience of students in facing challenges. The ability to be agile and resilient in overcoming problems is a skill that can be inculcated as part of the WSP. Accountability and commitment are factors to be considered as well in the development of a future-ready workforce. With WSPs, students are working for employers over a period of time. During this period, employers can work towards forming close work relationships with students, developing their interest and commitment to be part of the workplace. For students, while they may possess some experience and have completed a short internship period in a specific sector, WSPs provide greater opportunities to explore and understand the culture of an organisation. The option of working while studying allows students to get to know the organisation, their peers and employer. By forming a close relationship at the outset, students are likely to remain committed and open to changes in the work environment. Considering the competitive job market and the challenges young graduates face when entering the workforce, WSPs can help students develop professional identities and critical networks while obtaining the practical skills and knowledge relevant to the industry.

CONCLUSION

This chapter maps out the educational landscape and the changes that led to the development of WSPs. Considering the benefits of WSPs and how they can support the development of a future-ready workforce, it is imperative to continuously promote the framework to employers and students. It is also necessary to conduct research studies, evaluate the impact of the programme, and highlight the successful outcomes of such programmes. By identifying the specific future-ready skills embedded in the programme, IHLs and industry partners can help students succeed in the workplace. In the context of the WSDeg, AUs should take on the leading role in developing academic-related courses with consideration of the ways to increase the resilience quotient for graduates to be future ready.

REFERENCES

Abeysinghe, T. (2015). Lessons of Singapore's development for other developing economies. *The Singapore Economic Review, 60*(3), 1–13. https://doi.org/10.1142/S0217590815500290

Aoki, N. (2015). Institutionalization of New Public Management: The case of Singapore's education system. *Public Management Review, 17*(2), 165–186. https://doi.org/10.1080/14719037.2013.792381

Baethge, M., & Wolter, A. (2015). The German skill formation model in transition. *Journal for Labour Market Research, 48*, 97–112.

Cheng, A. L. H. (2001). The past in the present: Memories of the 1964 "racial riots" in Singapore. *Asian Journal of Social Science, 29*(3), 431–455. https://doi.org/10.1163/156853101X00181

Coll, R. K., Pinyonatthagarn, D., & Pramoolsook, I. (2003). The internationalization of cooperative education: A Thailand perspective. *Asia-Pacific Journal of Cooperative Education, 4*(2), 1–6.

Dalrymple, R., Kemp, C., & Smith, P. (2014). Characterising work-based learning as a triadic learning endeavour. *Journal of Further and Higher Education, 38*(1), 75–89. https://doi.org/10.1080/0309877x.2012.699516

Dobbelstein, T., & Taylor, S. (2004). Analyzing the world of work's requirements with the aim of enthusing companies about cooperative education. *Asia-Pacific Journal of Cooperative Education, 5*(1), 1–6.

Engel-Hills, P., Garraway, J., Jacobs, C., Volbrecht, T., & Winberg, C. (2010). Working for a degree: Work-integrated learning in the higher education qualifications framework. *Kasigano Universities of Technology, 7*, 62–88.

Freire, P. (1972). *Pedagogy of the oppressed: Translated by Myra Bergman Ramos.* The Continuum International Publishing Group Inc.

Goh, C. B., & Gopinathan, S. (2008). Education in Singapore: Development since 1965. In B. Fredriksen & J. P. Tan (Eds.), *An African exploration of the East Asian education* (pp. 80–108). The World Bank.

Gopinathan, S. (1997). Educational development in Singapore: Connecting the national, regional and the global. *The Australian Educational Researcher, 24*(1), 1–12.

Gopinathan, S. (2007). Globalisation, the Singapore developmental state and education policy: A thesis revisited. *Globalisation, Societies and Education, 5*(1), 53–70.

Heng, S. K. (2012). *Keynote address by Mr Heng Swee Kiat, Minister for Education.* Ministry of Education Work Plan Seminar, Ngee Ann Polytechnic Convention Centre.

Hillmert, S., & Kröhnert, S. (2003). Differenzierung und Erfolg tertiärer Ausbildungen: Die Berufsakademie im Vergleich. *German Journal of Human Resource Management: Zeitschrift für Personalforschung, 17*(2), 195–214. https://doi.org/10.1177/239700220301700204

Koh, A. (2004). Singapore education in "New Times": Global/local imperatives. *Discourse: Studies in the Cultural Politics of Education, 25*(3), 335–349. https://doi.org/10.1080/0159630042000247917

Lai, L. (2020, October 24). *Bridging the skills gap: Is education the key?* The Business Times. https://www.businesstimes.com.sg/opinion-features/features/bridging-skills-gap-education-key

Leong, W. S., & Tan, K. (2014). What (more) can, and should, assessment do for learning? Observations from "successful learning context" in Singapore. *The Curriculum Journal, 25*(4), 593–619. https://doi.org/10.1080/09585176.2014.970207

Lester, S., & Costley, C. (2010). Work-based learning at higher education level: Value, practice and critique. *Studies in Higher Education, 35*(5), 561–575.

Lim, S., Yang, W. W., Leong, C-H., & Hong, J. (2014). Reconfiguring the Singapore identity space: Beyond racial harmony and survivalism. *International Journal of Intercultural Relations, 43,* 13–21. https://doi.org/10.1016/j.ijintrel.2014.08.011

Lim, S. M., Foo, Y. L., Yeo, M. F., Chan, C. Y. X., & Loh, H. T. (2020). Integrated work study program: Students' growth mindset and perception of change in work-related skills. *International Journal of Work-Integrated Learning, 21*(2), 103–115.

May, S. (2006). Language policy and minority rights. In T. Ricento (Ed.), An introduction to language policy (pp. 255–272). Blackwell Publishing.

McRae, N., Pretti, J., & Stevens, T. (2020). *Preparing for the future of work through work-integrated learning.* University of Waterloo. https://publications.uwaterloo.ca/future-of-work-through-work-integrated-learning/welcome

Messer, L. (2021). Building a resilient workforce for tomorrow by investing in the employees of today. *Journal of Securities Operations & Custody, 13*(4), 354–364.

Ministry of Education (MOE). (2020a, February 18). *Work-study components in undergraduate degree programmes.* Ministry of Education Singapore. https://www.moe.gov.sg/news/parliamentary-replies/20200218-work-study-components-in-undergraduate-degree-programmes

Ministry of Education (MOE). (2020b, January 6). *Singaporean graduates from autonomous universities and private universities in Singapore.* Ministry of Education Singapore. https://www.moe.gov.sg/news/parliamentary-replies/20200106-singaporean-graduates-from-autonomous-universities-and-private-universities-in-singapore

Mokhtar, F. (2017, February 24). UniSIM and SIT to offer work-study degree programmes. *TODAY*. https://www.todayonline.com/singapore/new-work-study-degree-programmes

National Centre of Excellence for Workplace Learning. (2021, March 20). *National workplace learning framework.* https: https://www.nace.edu.sg/framework/national-workplace-learning-framework

Ng, J., Yeo, M. F., & Foo, Y. L. (2020). The integrated work study programme at Singapore Institute of Technology: More than a traditional internship model. In S. M. Lim, Y. L. Foo, H. T. Loh, & X. Deng (Eds.), *Applied learning in higher education: Perspective, pedagogy, and practice* (pp. 17–26). Informing Science Press.

Ng, J. Y. (2015, May 23). As graduate numbers grow, a hard truth: Not all degrees are equal. *TODAY.* https://www.todayonline.com/singapore/big-read-graduate-numbers-grow-hard-truth-not-all-degrees-are-equal

Ng, P. T. (2007). Quality assurance in the Singapore education system in an era of diversity and innovation. *Educational Research for Policy and Practice, 6*, 235–247.

Ng, P. T. (2010). The evolution and nature of school accountability in the Singapore education system. *Educational Assessment, Evaluation and Accountability, 22*(4), 275–292.

Pinpetch, S., & Baum, T. (2009). Development of cooperative education in tourism and hospitality industry: Issues in the context of Thailand. *Thai Journal of Cooperative Education, 1*(2), 21–42.

Reinhard, K., & Gerloff, A. (2020). Internationalizing cooperative education: Implementing the German DHBW model in Thailand and China. *International Journal of Work-Integrated Learning, 21*(3), 289–301.

Reinhard, K., Pogrzeba, A., Townsend, R., & Pop, C. A. (2016). A comparative study of cooperative education and work-integrated learning in Germany, South Africa, and Namibia. *Asia-Pacific Journal of Cooperative Education, 17*(3), 249–263.

Schindler, S., & Reimer, D. (2011). Differentiation and social selectivity in German higher education. *Higher Education, 61*(3), 261–275.

Sirijeerachai, G. (2009). Managing SUT cooperative education: Can it be the best practice in Thailand? *Thai Journal of Cooperative Education, 1*(1), 39–55.

Tan, A. L. (2018). Journey of science teacher education in Singapore: Past, present and future. *Asia-Pacific Science Education, 4*(1), 1–16.

Waring, P. (2014). Singapore's global schoolhouse strategy: Retreat or recalibration? *Studies in Higher Education, 39*(5), 874–884.

Chapter 11

Improving Employability of Future Business Graduates in Malaysia Through Sustainable Private College-Industry Partnerships: A Phenomenological Study

Thiruchelvi K Murugiah*

ABSTRACT

Unemployment among business graduates in Malaysia is a growing concern and has further worsened due to the Coronavirus Disease 2019 (COVID-19) pandemic. Business graduates have often been perceived as unprepared for the future workplace. To address this issue, a phenomenological study was conducted in a local private college based on three research aims and objectives: (1) to investigate the causes of unemployment among business graduates, (2) to determine the values that bind shared value partnerships between a private college and industry partners, and (3) to propose a measurable approach to implement such sustainable shared value partnerships. The study involved nine participants: one administrator, two students, two lecturers, two former students, and two industry partners. An interpretive phenomenological approach and triangulation of data sources using NVivo 12 Plus software arrived at the essence of the phenomenon which typifies the research participants' experiences. The findings include: (1) the ad-hoc nature and lack of sustainable collaborations led to the industry's generally low opinion of business graduates, (2) the nature of skill needs

* Sunway University, Malaysia

is broadly generalised, and (3) the measuring of ad-hoc sustainable shared value partnerships is premature, as the focus of businesses is on profit. To assess sustainable shared value partnerships, organisational culture changes are required to improve performance and create sustainable values for stakeholders. The study suggests that the industry-college collaborations are in the initial stages of conceptualising sustainable shared value partnerships and that measurable collaborations through problem solving can improve the employment prospects of future business graduates in Malaysia.

Keywords Future business graduate employability, industry partners, private college, sustainable shared value partnerships

INTRODUCTION

The increase in graduate unemployment, especially among business graduates, has been an ongoing problem in Malaysia (Che Omar & Rajoo, 2016; Tan, 2021). According to a report, Malaysia's unemployment stood at 4.8% in the fourth quarter of 2020, totalling 772,900 people (+1.1% month-on-month) (Tan, 2021). The report claims that the number of jobs created has declined from 104,000 in 2019 to 73,000 in 2020. It is apparent that job dynamics were changing due to the pandemic, and businesses were required to adopt digitalisation through sustainable means or risk shutting down (Tan, 2021).

To prepare for the Industrial Revolution 4.0 (IR 4.0), education leaders have called on higher education institutions (HEIs) to engage with industry partners to ensure that the programmes offered align with rapidly changing work needs (Ministry of Higher Education [MOHE], 2021). Notably, the aim is to ensure that future graduates have the capabilities to meet the new qualification requirements relevant to the digital economy (Azman et al., 2020).

It is concerning that graduates in Malaysia are being perceived as not well prepared for work and that the existing education system has not provided the skills needed for IR 4.0 (Mustafa, 2019; Mottain, 2019; Tanius et al., 2018). There are also claims that the pedagogical approaches have remained traditional, with an emphasis on rote learning and summative assessments.

The argument is that such assessments emphasise memorisation and final examinations, which seem irrelevant in developing the skills needed for future work (Nordin & Norman, 2018).

Contrary to such claims, it needs to be noted that the Ministry of Education (MOE) has identified 10 major shifts in the Malaysian Education Blueprint 2015–2025 (Higher Education) to transform the nation into a digital economy. The vision and mission of the MOE are to ensure that every Malaysian has access to quality education. Furthermore, the emphasis has been to uphold the quality of the local education system to develop each citizen to their full potential for nation-building (MOHE, 2021). While the education system has been designed to encourage collaborations between academia and industry, there appears to be a gap in aligning education performance indicators to develop a quality workforce that can advance Malaysia as a global economic contender by 2025.

In support of the government's aspiration, the study in this chapter aims to identify the reasons for unemployment among business graduates in Malaysia. The phenomenological study undertaken in the business school of a private college provides insights into possible broader issues involving the local employment market, particularly for business graduates seeking work in the future digital economy.

LITERATURE REVIEW

This chapter first reviews relevant literature to contextualise the study presented. This is then followed by the study findings in relation to the research questions, their discussion and the arising conclusions.

Business graduate unemployment in Malaysia

The Department of Statistics Malaysia (2020) reports that the total number of jobs in the industry decreased by 236,000 year-on-year to 8.38 million in the second quarter of 2020. The report shows that the unemployment rate was 5.4% in May 2020 due to harsh economic conditions caused by the COVID-19 pandemic. The report also indicates that the overall economy was weak in generating new jobs and that the country was not making full use of its human capital. A survey by Khazanah Research Institute in 2018 has also found that unemployment in Malaysia was concentrated among the youth (Leo, 2019). The statistical report also reveals that 35% of unemployed graduates were from the fields of social sciences, business and law (Leo, 2019).

Based on reports in 2015 and 2019, the local industries' experiences of business graduates have remained unchanged. Business graduates have been claimed to be average, with 70% of employers being disappointed with the applicants' quality (Leo, 2019). However, the poor ratings are not attributed to academic qualifications but to the candidates' attitudes and communication skills during the job interview and at work. The business graduates seeking work have been found to lack English language proficiency and are unrealistic on salary, benefit expectations, job choice and company (Thomas, 2021).

For Malaysia to be a globally competitive nation, claims that business graduates do not meet work requirements in the industry need to be addressed. Concerns over the widening gap between industry expectations and business graduates' capabilities, and a lack of industry and academia collaborations should also be tackled (Leo, 2019; Maizatul, 2018; Mustafa, 2019). The concern is binding as the School-to-Work Transition of Young Malaysians survey conducted in 2018 by the Khazanah Research Institute claims that graduates were, in fact, well educated but remained unemployed due to job scarcity (Leo, 2019). The survey attributes misleading information about business graduates' employability to a lack of purposeful interactions between industry and HEIs. The survey further claims the need for collaborations between both sectors to expose young people to changes in the job market (Ministry of Human Resources [MOHR], 2021).

Higher education and industry collaborations

Notably, measurable shared value partnerships should be encouraged between HEIs and industry partners during the digital transformation in the local economy. Engagement between the two sectors will be mutually beneficial, as such collaborations will help minimise potential skill mismatches in future hiring processes. Nakagawa et al. (2017) suggest the need for a "trading zone" for university-industry engagements to improve the skills of future business graduates (p. 38). They state that implementing the trading zone will foster better-shared value collaborations between universities and industries through the exchange of academic theories, research findings, and practical expertise from the industry. According to the study, the agreed-upon trading zone would enable the transfer of values between both sectors and reduce the skill mismatch faced in the industries (Nakagawa et al., 2017).

Significance of 21st-century skills in Malaysia and globally

Many concerns have also been related to graduates' skill competencies and employability. Malaysia and the rest of the world recognise the significance of 21st-century skills for nation-building. In this regard, the MOE (2015) claims that preschool, primary, secondary, and higher education should share a common vision on ethics and spirituality, leadership skills, national identity, language proficiency, thinking skills and knowledge to reflect a balanced education. On the international scene, the Partnership for 21st-Century Learning (P21) framework has been used to ensure that students develop 21st-century skills through learning outcomes and support systems (Battelle for Kids, 2019).

Studies prior to the COVID-19 pandemic have suggested the need for collaboration between higher education and industrial sectors. Nakagawa et al. (2017), Murugiah (2017) and O'Connor et al. (2011), in referring to industry engagement, indicate that common ground is required for collaboration, mainly when pedagogies involve experiential learning. These studies highlight the need to develop collaborative opportunities through non-monetary, mutually beneficial problem-solving initiatives. Again, the call is for higher education and industry to create contemporary and mutually advantageous partnerships, including the transfer of knowledge and shared values, while also improving industry access to academic knowledge and tertiary student access to practical experience (Nakagawa et al., 2017).

Reframing Malaysian higher education

The notion of reframing Malaysian higher education through the 10 shifts in the Malaysian Education Blueprint 2015–2025 (Higher Education) encourages HEIs to adopt new learning and teaching technologies to drive the nation's education mandate for a highly skilled local workforce. This transformation would need to begin by transforming traditional class lectures and making changes to assessments to reflect the needs of the future workforce (MOHE, 2018). This approach to new curriculum design and resultant policies encourages engaging and purposeful collaborations between academia and industry, enabling both sectors to work closely and engage as education partners. This call aligns with the nation's goal to produce a competent workforce facing global challenges and to transform the nation into a digital economy (Maizatul, 2018; MOHE, 2018).

The reforms also call for teaching and learning to engage students in new open learning spaces, with redesigned pedagogies focusing on heutagogy (self-directed learning), paragogy (peer-oriented learning) and cybergogy (virtual-based learning) (MOHE, 2018). However, cultivating this shift in mindset has been slow because developing such collaborations takes time and may not be immediately aligned with existing business goals. Furthermore, the COVID-19 pandemic has shown that sustainable shared value collaborations between HEIs and industry are becoming necessary to bridge the workforce skills gap in nation-building (Thomas, 2021).

Instilling measured shared valued partnerships requires a shift from the typical business focus on profitability to value creation and inclusive collaboration. In the interim, it has been suggested that to build sustainable shared value partnerships between higher education and industry, the focus should be on delivering tangible social benefits (Mustafa, 2019; Shared Value Initiative, 2019).

Resistance to change

Katz and Kahn (1978) suggest adopting an open system model to manage resistance to change. According to them, the model will involve identifying environmental elements that have the potential to affect the system and the resources required to enable the process of transformation to be exported back to the environment that is based on problem solving as a community. This is so that organisations can co-exist in an ecosystem with a continuous flow of information between stakeholders (Katz & Kahn, 1978).

Aligned with the Malaysian education aspiration, the study in this chapter aims to identify the reasons for unemployment, particularly among business graduates in Malaysia. The phenomenological study was undertaken in the business school of a private college to provide insights into possible bigger issues involving the local employment market, particularly for business graduates seeking work in the digital economy.

To address resistance to change, students will ideally adopt self-determined learning attributes as they engage with industry and society as undergraduates (MOHR, 2021). Such initiatives will be beneficial as students realise that to be gainfully employed in the future, they will need to self-assess their lifelong learning attributes (Blaschke, 2012; Mohamad, 2018).

PROBLEM STATEMENT

The COVID-19 pandemic and current recessionary economic conditions in Malaysia have accelerated concerns over business graduates' growing unemployment and the quality of higher education, as industries have claimed that graduates lack workplace knowledge, skills and appropriate attitude (Leo, 2019; Maizatul, 2018; Mustafa, 2019). Without understanding the causal reasons, the problem will continue to persist. Solutions can be identified from current stakeholders' experiences to enable sustainable shared value partnership collaborations that will lead to future business graduates being gainfully employed in IR 4.0 (Bakar et al., 2015; Selamat et al., 2017).

As a business lecturer, I embarked on this study within the scope of my workplace to understand ways to improve the employability of future business graduates, based on existing collaborations between the business school and industry partners. The study is relevant because factors for improvement need to be identified as the local economy transitions. Also of interest, as a HEI, it is our responsibility to develop our business course learning engagements with local industry partners in a sustainable manner to improve future employment possibilities (Shared Value Initiative, 2019).

Within the study, there is a need to identify why collaborations with industry have been unsuccessful in addressing unemployment among business graduates. Employers have continued to assert that there is a mismatch between what businesses require and the skills graduates show (Thomas, 2021). With the pandemic, it has also been found that the nation is facing structural unemployment, as evident in the lack of job creation and opportunities (Thomas, 2021). Proactive solutions are required to help minimise the gap in hiring future business graduates.

As an institution of higher education, there is also a need to determine the values recognised by our industry partners underpinning the employment of business graduates, while also improving the employability prospects of future graduates. Measurable approaches should be explored inclusively by implementing sustainable shared value partnerships between HEIs and industry partners to ensure that business graduates are gainfully employed in the digital economy.

Therefore, the research questions (RQ) to be addressed in the study are as follows:

(1) RQ 1: Why are many business graduates unemployed?
(2) RQ 2: What are the values needed for collaboration between the private college and industry to improve the employability and enterprise prospects of future business graduates?
(3) RQ 3: What measurable sustainable shared value partnerships can the private college and industry jointly adopt to improve employability and enterprise prospects of future business graduates?

WORK TRANSFORMATION IN INDUSTRIAL REVOLUTION 4.0

IR 4.0 involves a significant shift from a manufacturing-based economy to a knowledge-based one, which will demand the creation of jobs that are not yet available (Reif, 2018). The global digital shift will change current work needs and result in thousands of job losses worldwide as artificial intelligence, robotics and other innovative technologies replace routine jobs (Selamat et al., 2017). To avoid future unemployment crises amongst graduates in the digital economy, HEIs and industries have been advised to proactively collaborate to develop relevant skills for jobs not yet in demand (Rajaendram, 2018).

Changes in work in the future are unavoidable. While it was common in the past to prepare a learner for a single career, such as accountancy or engineering, studies have shown that the future workforce would expect to transition through several careers in their lifespan (Reif, 2018; Soffel, 2016). To address the anticipated changes to future employment, the Malaysian education system should acquaint students with the shifts occurring in various industries. Such learning experiences will assist future graduates in incorporating skills through work-related learning opportunities. Therefore, HEIs should also consider developing pre-emptive pedagogies for future graduates to remain globally competitive and adaptable to digital transformation (MOHE, 2018).

It is Malaysia's aspiration that its people can compete among the best in the world. To achieve this significant goal, the nation will be required to produce a skilled workforce to match the needs of IR 4.0 (Soffel, 2016). Further, Azmi et al. (2018) anticipate that IR 4.0 will widen the skills gap because technological transformation will create new jobs that demand new skills. The study also suggests that HEIs consider engaging with industry partners in their programme offerings to reduce future skills gaps (Azmi et al., 2018).

SHARED VALUE PARTNERSHIPS: TEACHING AND LEARNING

Tan (2021) claims that the Malaysian government faces intense challenges in implementing education reforms because Malaysian culture prioritises examinations and rote learning. It is asserted that the Malaysian public does not recognise the need for holistic values such as critical thinking, problem solving and creativity. This report puts forward the need for initiatives to gain the trust and support of Malaysians to facilitate the country's education quality transformation, and to focus on the skill mismatch between higher education and industry to change the overall experience of Malaysians (Tan, 2021).

In the book *Thank You for Being Late*, Friedman (2017) points out that students should be taught the workings of the world and shown how to construct frameworks for seeing the world in parallel to the growth of existing digital technology infrastructures. He also suggests that new jobs need to be transformed into work, requiring the continuous flow of lifelong learning.

Other studies prior to the COVID-19 pandemic have also suggested the necessity of collaborations between higher education and industrial sectors (Murugiah, 2017; Nakagawa et al., 2017; O'Connor et al., 2011). Notably, shared values to access between industry and academic knowledge and between tertiary students and practical experience should not be seen as a social responsibility or philanthropy but as a new way for businesses to achieve economic success (Porter & Kramer, 2011).

SHARED VALUE PARTNERSHIPS: HIGHER EDUCATION AND INDUSTRY

Shared value partnerships operate in accordance with the United Nations Sustainable Development Goals (SDGs), especially Goal 4 of quality education, which requires education to be inclusive and equitable while promoting lifelong learning. Goal 4 encourages collaborative endeavours to achieve learning goals and assessments that measure the effectiveness of collaborative efforts. Past studies have shown that education reforms in the future era of technological and digital advancement will require humanising education (Abdul Razak, 2018; Katz & Kahn, 1978). Such foresight into the current digital transformation remains relevant, as it has become apparent that there is a need to provide students with social and emotional learning to support the development of IR 4.0 employment skills.

MEASURING APPROACH IN SHARED VALUE PARTNERSHIPS

Measuring shared value partnerships will require a shift from the typical business focus on profitability to value creation. To build sustainable shared value partnerships between higher education and industry, the focus should be on delivering tangible social benefits that result in profitable businesses. However, the idea of integrated shared value strategy and measurement remains in preliminary stages. It is therefore suggested that in the interim, inclusive sustainable business strategies should focus on achieving both economic and social values in competitive businesses (Nakagawa et al., 2017; Porter & Kramer, 2011).

Past research also indicates that it is possible for two complementary problems to be identified between an industry practitioner and a student—access to academic knowledge and practical experience. By sharing theoretical insights and, in return, gaining experiential knowledge from industry players, students can learn from genuine business situations.

The collaborative drive to sustainable shared value partnerships should focus on business and social outcomes based on problem solving in knowledge exchanges. The aim is to develop genuine sustainable shared value partnerships, with symbiotic interactions improving the credibility between both sectors. The inclusive social value benefit will result from partnerships that are innovative in solving problems collectively (MOE, 2015).

ADDRESSING CHALLENGES TO SHARED VALUE PARTNERSHIPS IN EDUCATION

The way forward for HEIs is to consider innovative ways of including industries in anticipating the future of work in IR 4.0. As a point of reference, a sustainable shared value partnership can follow the following process (Nakagawa et al., 2017; Porter & Kramer, 2011):

(1) Step 1: Identify social issues.
(2) Step 2: Make a business case with relevant activities.
(3) Step 3: Track progress.
(4) Step 4: Assess change and use insights to identify new values.

SKILL NEEDS AND THE DIGITAL ECONOMY

Penjana HRDF, under the Ministry of Finance (MOF) and the MOHR Malaysia, has released an economic recovery plan to provide training incentive programmes in response to the high number of job losses due to the COVID-19 pandemic (MOHR, 2021). The objective is to reskill the local workforce and help small- and medium-sized enterprises (SMEs) in digitalisation (MOHR, 2021). However, the notion that there will be enough work opportunities available for everyone after graduation continues to be an uncertain assumption (Leo, 2019; Thomas, 2021). Notably, there are many changes to work needs, and it has been observed that work involving routine tasks and offshore work is gradually declining (MOHR, 2021). Thus, as the nation deals with digital transformation in the economy, stakeholders will also seek new hires with relevant skills. To manage the gap in skills expectations between HEIs and industry, it is recommended that the gap be addressed through properly situated collaborations. Validation from participating stakeholders will help overcome future scepticism about the quality of future business graduates and create better job matches for the purpose of nation-building.

CONCEPTUAL FRAMEWORK

The conceptual framework shown in Figure 11.1 illustrates an ideal ecosystem that will enable a continuous sustainable partnership between key stakeholders. Ideally, HEIs and industry collaborations will lead to changes in education needs that prepare students and educators for the ever-changing evolution in learning, space and technology (Nordin & Norman, 2018).

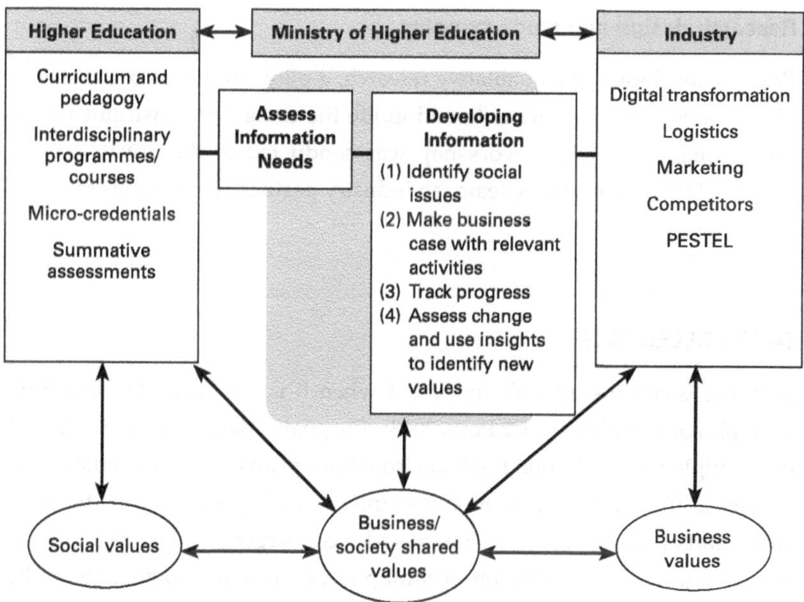

Figure 11.1 Conceptual framework: Sustainable shared value partnership between higher education and industry partners

Note: The conceptual framework encourages the inclusion of symbiotic, sustainable shared value partnerships founded on creating business opportunities, improving corporate assets and addressing social needs.

METHODOLOGY

This qualitative research used a phenomenological approach to understand individuals' common or shared experiences (Creswell & Poth, 2018; Denzin & Lincoln, 2011). The study used a social constructivism standpoint, often described as interpretivism. The research participants at the private Malaysian college were invited to the study because of their keen interest in understanding the world they lived and worked in. In this study, the inquirers (participants and researcher) inductively developed a pattern of meaning (Burr, 2015; Creswell & Poth, 2018; Denzin & Lincoln, 2011). In practice, the research questions were designed to give participants the flexibility to construct their meaning of the situation, which is an important aspect of a phenomenological study. This social constructivist research addressed the processes of interaction among the individual participants to establish a clear problem-solving foundation to address the skill needs of future business graduates in Malaysia through sustainable private college and industry partnerships.

Research design and study samples

Prior to developing the qualitative research, a pilot study was conducted in a private college to gather data and guide the design and instrumentation for the main research. A workshop was conducted in the private college with the business academic team, an industry partner and students from the business school.

DATA COLLECTION

A theme is considered well supported when it is reinforced by data from multiple sources (Creswell & Poth, 2018). The goal of data triangulation based on multiple data collection methods from both primary and secondary data sources in this study (interview transcripts, workshop survey from the pilot study, and document analysis) was to seek a convergence of results following initial reviews. The evaluation of multiple resources would strengthen the research and provide a more definitive conclusion (Creswell & Poth, 2018).

Secondary data sources

Pilot study: Business school workshop

To determine the scope and research design of the main study, a pilot study in the form of a business school workshop was conducted in a private college. The workshop was held in a specifically organised session with the approval of the college principal. The participants involved existing business students, their lecturers, and an industry partner with his team. In the workshop, students were introduced to the industry partner's product offerings and to the way the company grew their business both online and physically in several states. Upon completion of the three-hour workshop, all participants were provided with survey feedback forms. The survey questions, which the college principal approved, provided open-ended questions to gain participants' insights about their workshop experiences. The survey results also helped determine the viability and scope of the main research design. The data collected from the survey results were then imported into the NVivo 12 Plus software to generate 30 codes and 85 references.

Document analysis

The documents reviewed in the study included both online and offline research journals and research publications. A sample of the literature review sources was placed under the "LR Sources" file classification in the NVivo 12 Plus software to illustrate the number of codes and references attributed to each LR source.

Primary data sources

This phenomenological study sample size included one administrator, two business students (final year), two business graduates (former students), two business lecturers (with a minimum of five years of work experience), and two industry partners from the product and service industry. The qualitative interpretive framework was used in the study to draw on social constructivism: (1) to seek an understanding of the world they live and work in, and (2) to identify the existing axiological beliefs (role of values), where individual values are honoured and negotiated.

In-depth interviews with private college participants

The objective of the interviews was to derive insights from the participants about their views on the skills needed to prepare for future work. The participant interview protocol and consent forms were provided. The interview questions were formed based on research questions that guided the study, to understand lived experiences with regard to the rising graduate unemployment in the country. The interview questions were further reviewed and validated by an appointed external expert reviewer. Each participant's interview transcript was transcribed and imported into the NVivo 12 Plus software. The data collection time frame involved interviewing participants within a 14-week semester. The interview sessions unavoidably coincided with the movement control order[1] from mid-March 2020 to July 2020. Due to the unprecedented COVID-19 pandemic, all participants were called on to reorganise the interview sessions to be conducted online. All interview participants agreed to one or two recorded sessions using Zoom within the agreed time frame at their convenience. Permission was sought from the interview participants, and the interview protocol was edited, signed and adhered to in order to protect the ethical and validation considerations within the study.

Interview data collection process

The data collection process for each interview participant is provided in Figure 11.2.

The protocol for the phenomenological study involved the reduction of themes to textural description (what occurred) and structural description (how it occurred) to arrive at the essence and meaning of the experience (Chopra et al., 2017). The research audit trail was used as a guide for the reading and memoing of emergent ideas and to document the reduction process, as shown in Figure 11.3.

1 Travel restrictions implemented by the Malaysian government in response to the Coronavirus Disease 2019 pandemic to prevent its further outbreak.

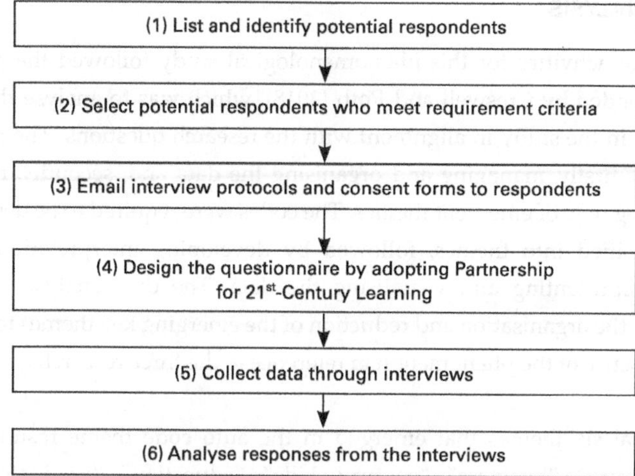

Figure 11.2 Flowchart for the data collection process for each interview participant
Source: Creswell & Poth (2018)

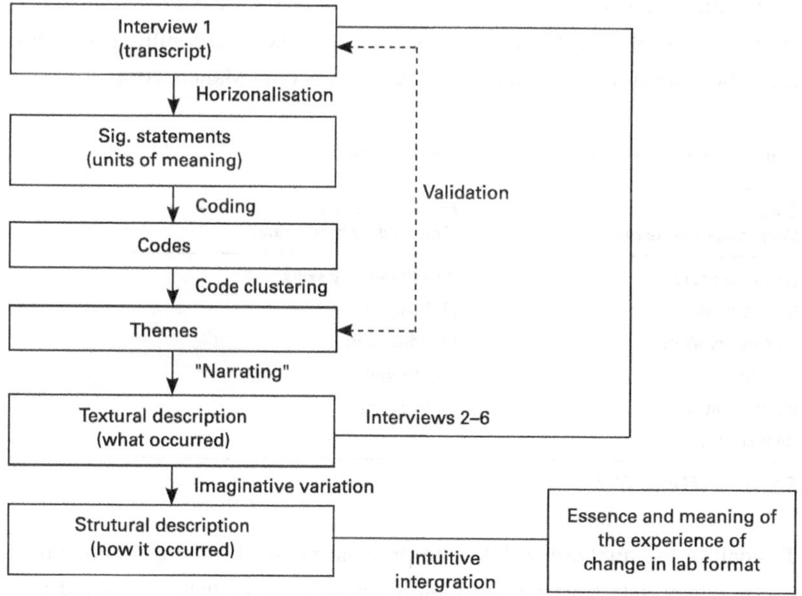

Figure 11.3 Reduction of themes to textural and structural descriptions
Source: Chopra et al. (2017)

DATA ANALYSIS

The spiral activities for this phenomenological study followed the process recommended by Creswell and Poth (2018), which was to analyse the data collected in the study in alignment with the research questions. The process involved, firstly, managing and organising the data and, secondly, reading and taking note of emergent themes. The codes were required to be described and classified into themes, followed by developing interpretations and, finally, representing and visualising the data. The data analysis process involved the organisation and reduction of the emerging key themes to arrive at the essence of the phenomenon in reference to the three research questions.

The initial six themes that emerged in the auto code theme results were "21st century", "business", "century skills", "education", "graduates" and "learning", as shown in Figure 11.4.

To gain deeper insights from the primary and secondary data sources collected, all three data sources were triangulated using QSR NVivo 12 Plus @qualitative analysis software (Abd Gani et al., 2020). Five key themes emerged from the triangulation, as shown in Table 11.1, resulting from the thematic analysis conducted on the data sources (van Manen, 2014).

Table 11.1 Reduction of six themes to five key themes

Six themes (Auto code theme results)	**Five key themes (Reduced by bracketing)**
(1) 21st century	(1) 21st-century skills
(2) business	(2) business
(3) century skills	(3) education
(4) education	(4) graduates
(5) graduates	(5) learning
(6) learning	

Source: van Manen (2014)

To analyse the qualitative data, the process involved moving in analytical circles where data from text and audio-visual material were converted into respective narratives that represented the interview participants.

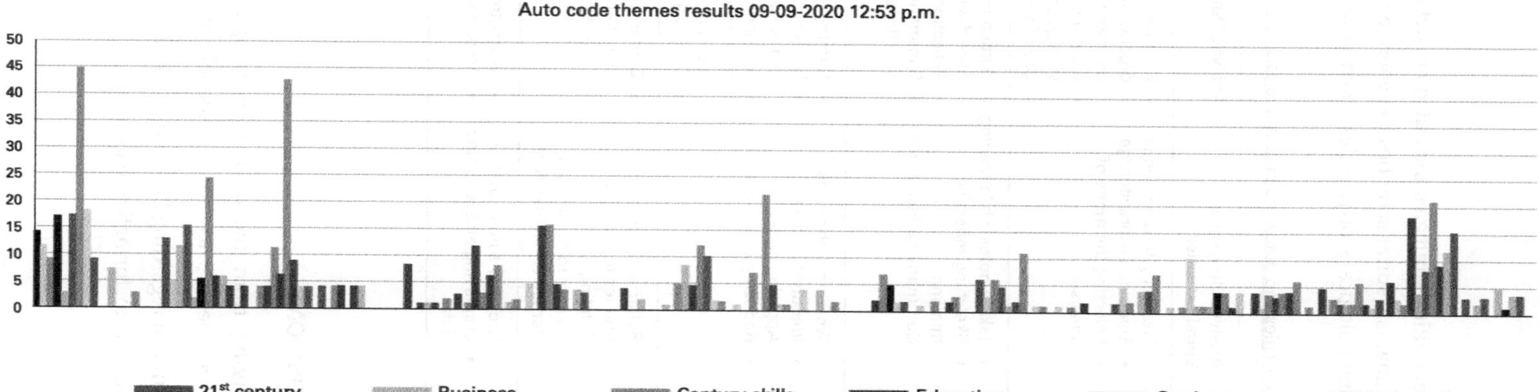

Figure 11.4 Auto code theme results identify the themes based on the sentence structure and content analysis
Source: Creswell & Poth (2018)

The data analysis spiral activities, strategies and outcomes detail the analytical strategy using the data analysis spiral activities to generate specific analytic outcomes for the phenomenological study, as described in Table 11.2.

Table 11.2 Spiral activities, strategies and outcomes of data analysis

Data Analysis	Analytic Strategies Spiral Activities	Analytic Outcomes
Managing and organising data	• Preparing files and units • Ensuring secure storage • Selecting the mode of analysis	• File naming and database organising of files, text units and recordings • Creation of a long-term file storage plan • Use of software
Reading and memoing emergent ideas (an audit trail being a validating strategy to document the thinking process)	• Taking notes while reading • Sketching reflective thinking • Summarising field notes	• Written memos leading to code development • Reflections over time • Summaries or probing questions
Describing and classifying codes into themes	• Working with words • Identifying codes • Applying codes • Reducing codes to themes	• Naming of initial codes • Listing of code categories and descriptions • Assignment of codes to units of text and recordings • Coding finalisation
Developing and accessing interpretations	• Relating categories/ themes to one another • Relating categories and themes to the analytic framework in literature	• Contextual understanding and diagrams • Theories and propositions
Representing and visualising data	• Creating a point of view • Displaying and reporting data	• Matrix trees or models • Accounts of the findings

Source: Creswell & Poth (2018)

FINDINGS AND DISCUSSIONS

The key themes emerging from the data analysis spiral activities are represented as Theme 1 to Theme 5, as shown in the following text:

(1) **Theme 1**: Skills mismatch regarding 21st-century skills.

(2) **Theme 2**: For business: Transformation required.

(3) **Theme 3**: For education: Development of sustainable shared value partnerships required.
(4) **Theme 4**: For graduates: Stakeholder gap issues exist.
(5) **Theme 5**: For learning: Academic insights are required.

The key themes are aligned with the three research questions to provide the accounts of the results, as shown in Tables 11.3, 11.4 and 11.5.

Table 11.3 RQ1: Reasons for unemployment among business graduates

Main Related Themes	Sub-themes	Results
Theme 1: Skills mismatch regarding 21st-century skills **Theme 4:** For graduates: Stakeholder gap issues exist	• Education for employment • Stakeholder perception of students	• Differing skill needs/ expectations between education and industries • Limited collaboration opportunities to collectively address the existing skills gap and unemployment issues among future business graduates

Table 11.4 RQ2: Values needed for collaboration between private college and industry

Main Related Themes	Sub-themes	Results
Theme 2: For business: Transformation required **Theme 3:** For education: Development of sustainable shared value partnerships required **Theme 5:** For learning: Academic insights are required	• Management perspectives • Creation of unexpected connections • Problem solving	• The need for transformation within business organisations that enables a work culture focused on problem solving and sustainable values • The call to promote an organisation-wide awareness and adoption of sustainable shared value partnerships focused on problem solving • To enable mutually valued learning engagements with industry partners that involve solving significant business issues

Table 11.5 RQ3: Measurable sustainable shared value partnerships by private college and industry

Main Related Theme	Sub-theme	Result
Theme 3: For education: Development of sustainable shared value partnerships required	• Common views on sustainable shared value partnerships	• The call for measurable sustainable shared value engagements between higher education institutions and industry based on problem solving can facilitate the development of future work-ready curricula and enable continuous improvements in pedagogy and business student learning outcomes

The data analysis indicates a misalignment between the private college and industry expectations. This indicates the need to re-evaluate learning approaches and align the education framework to include the development of 21st-century skills in IR 4.0 through constructive private college and industry engagements (Nordin & Norman, 2018). The general low public confidence in local and private HEIs can be attributed to a lack of trust and limited shared values in ad-hoc collaborations (Tan, 2021).

This indicates the need for a company-wide commitment to enhancing shared value partnerships through problem-solving approaches involving collaborations with other ecosystem stakeholders. Engagements with industry stakeholders will provide business students with the learning opportunities to be better engaged and motivated to become self-directed learners.

The misalignment of priorities and objectives between the private college and industry partners will delay the establishment of sustainable shared value partnerships. The existing economic ecosystem does not yet recognise the merit of sustainable partnerships between business entities.

Modulated curricula and examination-based assessments are carried out to meet the MOHE's regulatory requirements. The current pedagogies reflect the learning outcomes based on the accredited business programme.

Again, the misalignment of priorities and objectives between the private college and industry partners appears to negatively impact the establishment of sustainable shared value partnerships. The existing economic ecosystem does not yet recognise the merit of sustainable partnerships between business entities.

Implications of findings

The findings suggest the following:

(1) Despite a soft job market, as traditional jobs are displaced, new job opportunities can be created, particularly by businesses that invest and build on digital infrastructure (Rajaendram, 2018).

(2) The current market conditions show growing demand for short courses, such as micro-credentials offered by Alibaba Global Digital Talents, that will develop future graduates to be better skilled for digital transformation (Alibaba Group, 2021).

(3) Sustainable shared value collaborations are in the initial stages of conceptualisation. Industry and academia should work together to solve workforce requirements by jointly improving the quality of the future business graduate workforce.

(4) The transformation in the local business ecosystem is being driven by digital technology. Future business graduates should be encouraged to develop agile approaches in the learning process and when building a professional presence in the future (Rajaendram, 2018).

(5) Stakeholders in education should adapt to the new normal, where transitioning of teaching and learning will enable flexibility in the learning spaces. Such flexibility includes movements from public spaces (lecture halls) to personal spaces (home) (Azman et al., 2020).

RECOMMENDATIONS TO IMPROVE EMPLOYMENT OF FUTURE BUSINESS GRADUATES

Azman et al. (2020) call on the nation of educators to develop a future-ready workforce through an open system that equips students with continuously updated knowledge, skills and attributes that contribute positively towards nation-building and global citizenship. Furthermore, higher education should include flexible learning with lifelong learning initiatives that support the 2030 Agenda for Sustainable Development. In this context, SDG Goal 4 of quality education encourages educators to offer micro-credentials and consider the accreditation of Prior Experiential Learning to keep up with changes in 21st-century skill needs towards IR 4.0. This move will also provide more opportunities to holistically address the potential rise in unemployment of future business graduates in Malaysia (MOHE, 2021). Notably, nurturing talents should start from educational institutions; however, stakeholders in the transforming ecosystem should also collaborate to ensure that business graduates are future work ready.

The business school within the private college in Malaysia should consider work-based learning transformations during the COVID-19 pandemic to encourage such shifts in the local economy by driving sustainable shared value partnerships with industry partners, as proposed in the conceptual framework in Figure 11.1. The suggested work-based learning transformation refers to Theme 4, shown earlier in Table 11.3, whereby trust issues should be addressed to enable successful future collaborations. Future initiatives should focus on gaining a better understanding of industry views to arrive at a common sustainable agenda. Foreseeably, further research will be needed to identify the enablers that support and propel institutional sustainability within the private college. The aim is to highlight the need to recognise HEIs as industry players in the digital ecosystem (MOE, 2019).

It is clear from the literature review earlier in this chapter that the growing number of graduate unemployment in Malaysia, especially among business graduates, will need to be curbed. The report from the 2018 Khazanah Research Institute survey indicates a significant concern when it reports that 35% of unemployed graduates were from the fields of social sciences, business and law (Leo, 2019). Other supporting findings include the following:

(1) The skills transformation process for business graduates has been slow because of a lack of IR 4.0 awareness, standards and skill sets (Jalal, 2017; Lee, 2017; Mohamed, 2017; Soffel, 2016).

(2) Industry and academia were not collaborating effectively to address skill mismatch (Leo, 2019; Maizatul, 2018; Mustafa, 2019).

(3) The rise in business graduates' unemployment is due to the under-utilisation of human resources that has affected the overall economic growth of the country (Che Omar & Rajoo, 2016).

(4) The 2018 School-to-Work Transition of Young Malaysians survey by Khazanah Research Institute implies that business graduates were well educated, but not enough jobs were being created in the economy to accommodate fresh graduates (Leo, 2019).

(5) The same Khazanah survey claims that employers are known to have minimal or no interaction with educational institutions and youths except during internships (Leo, 2019).

CONCLUSION

The study findings reveal that multiple factors likely contribute to the growing unemployment of business graduates in Malaysia. The reasons include the following:

(1) A lack of clarity on the 21st-century skills requirements (MOE, 2015).

(2) A lack of stakeholder confidence in the overall Malaysian education quality (Jalal, 2017; Lee, 2017; Mohamed, 2017).

(3) A collective view of Malaysian higher education being heavily regulated (Abdul Razak, 2018).

(4) Absence of expertise and incentives to encourage shared value partnerships in education (Azmi et al., 2018).

(5) General scepticism and resistance to change due to uncertainty across sectors (Katz & Kahn, 1978; Tapscott, 2018).

(6) No initiatives across sectors to improve unemployment issues of fresh graduates since 2018 (Leo, 2019).

(7) A lack of job creation in the economy, in line with the classical theory of unemployment (Keynes, 1936; Pineda, 2021).

Aligning education to industry needs requires acceptance of changes, which include mindset shifts, to enable digital transformation that prepares citizens for a successful career in the digital economy. The reconstruction of higher education and curricula may be required to fluidly align them to the constantly changing knowledge and skill needs. Considerations to this effect have been put forth in viewing education entities as an industry for private higher education (MOHE, 2019). Brick-and-mortar learning institutions must reinvent their offerings to drive digital transformation or face the reality of being phased out. Digital disruption is the new normal, and HEIs are the catalysts in reshaping higher education with endless innovation to be ready for the evolution of learning, space and technology (Azman et al., 2020).

The study in this chapter shows that stakeholders are open to building sustainable partnerships while dealing with digital disruption. The private college is also tirelessly looking into improving the quality of teaching and learning to facilitate future workforce development. Notably, trust issues should be addressed to encourage collaborations with industry stakeholders. Establishing a symbiotic relationship in the digital ecosystem is critical to achieving trustworthy and sustainable shared value partnerships as the nation transitions into IR 4.0 (Azman et al., 2020). Soon, the changing education landscape will expand stakeholder participation to include the government, public and private sector administration, the teaching and learning community, and parents.

REFERENCES

Abd Gani, N. I., Rathakrishnan, M., & Krishnasamy, H. N. (2020). A pilot test for establishing validity and reliability of qualitative interview in the blended learning English proficiency course. *Journal of Critical Reviews, 7*(5), 140–143.

Abdul Razak, D., & Zulkifli, A. R. (2018, May 21). *Education for change in a new Malaysia.* Voicing Concern. http://voicingconcern.net.my/index.php/en/2018/961-education-for-change-in-a-new-malaysia

Alibaba Group. (2021). *Culture and values.* http://www.alibabagroup.com/en/about/culture

Azman, N., Nordin, N., Crosling, G., Azman, N., & Atherton, G. (2020, December 2). *Virtual seminar on "future higher education".* Sunway Education Group. https://news.sunway.edu.my/articles/university/virtual-seminar-future-higher-education

Azmi, I. A. G., Hashim, R. C., & Yusoff, Y. M. (2018). The employability skills of Malaysian university learners. *International Journal of Modern Trends in Social Sciences, 1*(3), 1–14.

Bakar, A., Ab Wahab, N., & Rosli, R. (2015). Critical success factor of graduate employability programs. *Journal of Economic, Business and Management, 3*(8), 767–771. https://doi.org/10.7763/joebm.2015.v3.283

Battelle for Kids. (2019). *Framework for 21st century learning definitions.* P21 partnership for 21st century learning: A network of Battele for Kids. https://static.battelleforkids.org/documents/p21/P21_Framework_DefinitionsBFK.pdf

Blaschke, L. M. (2012). Heutagogy and lifelong learning: A review of heutagogical practice and self-determined learning. *The International Review of Research in Open and Distance Learning, 13*(1), 56–71. http://irrodl.org/index.php/irrodl/article/view/1076/2087

Burr, V. (2015). *Social constructionism* (3rd ed.). Routledge.

Che Omar, C. M. Z., & Rajoo, S. (2016). Unemployment among graduates in Malaysia. *International Journal of Economics, Commerce and Management United Kingdom, 4*(8), 367–374. https://ijecm.co.uk/wp-content/uploads/2016/08/4824.pdf

Chopra, I., O'Connor, J., Pancho, R., Chrzanowski, M., & Sandi-Urena, S. (2017). Reform in a general chemistry laboratory: How do learners experience change in the instructional approach? *Chemistry Education Research and Practice, 18*(1), 113–126. https://pubs.rsc.org/en/Content/Articlelanding/2017/RP/c6rp00082g#!divAbstract

Creswell, J. W., & Poth, C. N. (2018). *Qualitative inquiry and research design: Choosing among five approaches* (4th ed.). Sage.

Denzin, N. K., & Lincoln, Y. S. (2011). *The Sage handbook of qualitative research.* Sage.

Department of Statistics Malaysia. (2020). *Labour market review, second quarter 2020.*

Friedman, T. L. (2017). *Thank you for being late: An optimist's guide to thriving in the age of accelerations.* Picador.

Jalal, A. W. (2017, May 2). *Rethinking our education.* New Straits Times. https://www.nst.com.my/opinion/columnists/2017/05/235683/rethinking-our-education

Katz, D., & Kahn, R. L. (1978). *The social psychology of organizations* (2nd ed). Wiley.

Keynes, J. M. (1936). *The general theory of employment, interest, and money.* Macmillan.

Lee, C. F. (2017). Jobless rate may increase to 3.3%. *The Sun (Malaysia).* https://www.pressreader.com/malaysia/the-sun-malaysia/20170127/281621010053756

Leo, M. (2019, August 26). What you didn't know about fresh graduates unemployment in Malaysia [Infographic]. *EduAdvisor.* https://eduadvisor.my/articles/what-didnt-know-fresh-graduate-unemployment-malaysia-infographic

Maizatul, R. (2018, January 27). 2018 mandate: Embracing Industry 4.0, Higher Education 4.0: Knowledge, industry and humanity. *Higher Education Today.*

Ministry of Education (MOE). (2013). Malaysian education blueprint 2013–2025 (pre-school to postsecondary education policy). https://www.moe.gov.my/dasarmenu/pelan-pembangunan-pendidikan-2013-2025

Ministry of Education (MOE). (2015). *Malaysia education blueprint 2015–2025 (higher education).* https://www.um.edu.my/docs/um-magazine/4-executive-summary-pppm-2015-2025.pdf

Ministry of Higher Education (MOHE). (2018). *Framing Malaysia Higher Education 4.0: Future-proof talents.* https://jpt.mohe.gov.my/portal/index.php/en/publication/61-framing-malaysian-higher-education-4-0-future-proof-talent

Ministry of Higher Education (MOHE). (2018, January 24). *Developing policy in a fast changing, increasingly technology influenced world: Malaysia's experience.* https://www.mohe.gov.my/muat-turun/teks-ucapan-dan-slaid/teks-2018/258-education-world-forum-2018-malaysian-higher-education/file

Ministry of Higher Education (MOHE). (2019, December 22). *Way forward for private higher education institution: Education as an industry (2020–2025).* Issuu. https://issuu.com/sharafuddin/docs/inside_ctb_kpm_full_

Ministry of Higher Education (MOHE). (2021, March 15). Malaysian qualifications agency.

Ministry of Human Resources (MOHR). (2021). *Penjana HRDF initiative.* https://penjanahrdf.com.my

Mohamad, S. N. A. (2018, January 28). *2018 mandate: Embracing Industry 4.0.* https://snazlan.wordpress.com/2018/01/28/2018-mandate-embracing-industry-4-0

Mohamed, G. N. (2017, December 21). Evolution of the Malaysian educational system: A scenario of uncertainty and turmoil. *The Sun Daily.* https://thesun.my/archive/evolution-malaysian-educational-system--scenario-uncertainty-and-turmoil-LUarch513719

Mottain, M. (2019, September 21). Underqualified and overqualified fresh graduates. *The Star Online.* https://www.thestar.com.my/business/business-news/2019/09/21/underqualified-and-overqualified-fresh-graduates

Murugiah, T. K. (2017). Exploring the possibility of collaboration between private higher education and local industries during an economic downturn. *E-Proceedings of the 5th Global Summit on Education GSE 2017.*

Mustafa, Z. (2019, January 23). Importance of academia-industry linkages. *New Strait Times.* https://www.nst.com.my/education/2019/01/453582/importance-academia-industry-linkages

Nakagawa, K., Takata, M., Kato, K., Matsuyuki, T., & Matsuhashi, T. (2017). A university-industry collaborative entrepreneurship education program as a trading zone: The case of Osaka University. *Technology Innovation Management Review, 7*(6), 38–49. https://timreview.ca/sites/default/files/article_PDF/Nakagawa_et_al_TIMReview_June2017.pdf

Nordin, N., & Norman, H. (2018). Mapping the Fourth Industrial Revolution global transformations on 21st century education on the context of sustainable development. *Journal on Sustainable Development Education and Research, 2*(1), 1–7.

O'Connor, K. M., Lynch, K., & Owen, D. (2011). Student-community engagement and the development of graduate attributes. *Education + Training, 53*(2/3), 100–115. https://doi.org/10.1108/00400911111115654

Pineda, M. E. (2021, August 12). *Types and theories of unemployment.* Profulus. https://www.profolus.com/topics/types-and-theories-of-unemployment

Porter, M. E., & Kramer, M. R. (2011). The big idea: Creating shared value. How to reinvent capitalism—And unleash a wave of innovation and growth. *Harvard Business Review, 89*(1–2), 62–77.

Rajaendram, R. (2018, April 8). Prepare to evolve, adapt to needs. *The Star.* https://www.thestar.com.my/news/education/2018/04/08/prepare-to-evolve-adapt-to-needs/#Om5vDCFpmrtcvKo6.99

Reif, L. R. (2018). *A survival guide for the Fourth Industrial Revolution.* World Economic Forum. https://www.weforum.org/agenda/2018/01/the-fourth-industrial-revolution-a-survival-guide

Selamat, A., Tapsir, S. H., Puteh, M., Alias, R. A., & Syed Abdullah, S. N. H. (2017). Higher Education 4.0: Current status and readiness in meeting the 4th Industrial Revolution challenges [Conference presentation]. *Proceeding of the Conference on Redesigning Higher Education Towards Industry 4.0, Kuala Lumpur, Malaysia.*

Shared Value Initiative. (2019). *About shared value: Finding business opportunity in social problems.* https://www.sharedvalue.org/about-shared-value

Soffel, J. (2016, March 10). Ten 21st-century skills every student needs. *World Economic Forum.* https://www.weforum.org/agenda/2016/03/21st-century-skills-future-jobs-learners

Tan, S. M. (2021, September 9). Malaysia's jobless rate seen averaging 4.5% for 2021, as July records uptick in number of unemployed. *The Edge Malaysia.* https://theedgemalaysia.com/article/malaysias-jobless-rate-seen-averaging-45-2021-july-records-uptick-number-unemployed

Tanius, E., Johari, H., Yulia, A., Heng, C. S., & Pazim, K. H. (2018). The employability skills performance of business graduates in Malaysia: Do employers, graduates and academicians speak the same language? *Asian International Journal of Asian Social Science, 9*(1), 11–17. https://doi.org/10.18488/journal.1.2019.91.11.17

Tapscott, D. (2018). *The collaboration program.* https://dontapscott.com/consulting-services/the-collaboration-program

Thomas, J. (2021, September 21). Is structural unemployment on the horizon for Malaysia? *Free Malaysia Today.* https://www.freemalaysiatoday.com/category/nation/2021/09/21/is-structural-unemployment-on-the-horizon-for-malaysia

van Manen, M. (2014). *Phenomenology of practice: Meaning-giving methods in phenomenological research and writing.* Left Coast Press.

Chapter 12

Conclusions and Way Forward for Higher Education in the ASEAN Region

Siti Norbaya Azizan,* Glenda Crosling* & Graeme Atherton‡

INTRODUCTION

This book, *Higher Education in the ASEAN Region: Shaping the Future,* has presented varying perspectives on higher education in the region as it moves forward into the future. The views expressed in this book contribute to a cross-country understanding of some of the key factors integral to the future development of higher education in the Association of Southeast Asian Nations (ASEAN).

In Chapter 1, we note that change in higher education over time is not a new phenomenon and that the world surrounding higher education is dynamic, fluid and changing in ways that have previously been unseen. The ASEAN region is also dynamic, with higher education seen as a major way forward for the socioeconomic development of the nations within it. Such is the setting for the chapters as the authors, propelled by present circumstances, put forward their views on higher education's way forward in ASEAN.

In this final chapter, we again point to some of the recent and continuing major aspects of the external higher education environment that impact current and thus future directions. These include Industrial Revolution 4.0 (IR 4.0) which entails the following: the competitive, dynamic knowledge society and rapid increases in digitalisation in all spheres globally; the

* Sunway University, Malaysia
‡ University of West London, United Kingdom

rise of pro-democratic global movements that underpin massification and large increases in the numbers of people participating in higher education, alongside continuing calls for access and equity for those suitably qualified; internationalisation and marketisation that have seen students, academic programmes and higher education institutions (HEIs) cross national boundaries and compete for students and academic staff members worldwide; the impact of all these factors on the need for quality in higher education as reflected in curricula, teaching, learning, assessments and research-based approaches; and, significantly, the latter group of educational factors shape the attributes fostered in graduates via their studies to support positive contributions to the world.

Concurrent with these external and influencing factors, higher education activities via education, innovative research, and community and societal input feed into the socioeconomic development of their countries and thus the world. In ASEAN, with countries at different levels and stages of socioeconomic development, these factors support the development of educated populations who are able to contribute to the advancement of their countries and the region in a competitive and rapidly changing world.

Here, we draw together some key points under the five themes identified across the 10 chapters. We again point out that these themes are not exclusive, as some chapters cut across the identified themes. As will be seen in Figure 12.1, the five themes identified across the chapters are interlinked. For instance, sustainability at higher education policy and strategic levels is linked to access and equity for students from diverse backgrounds, with curriculum development underpinning such implementation. Learning, teaching and assessment approaches support and enable curriculum developments that are student-centred and research-based, contributing to the development of graduates' attributes and shaping their suitability for post-study employment. Each theme is explained briefly in the following:

(1) **Theme 1: Higher education sustainability.** The sustainability of higher education is a driver for educational change and institutional innovation (Corcoran & Wals, 2004) and is seen in the learning outcomes and processes. Discussions on sustainability in the chapters address the role

of higher education systems in organising around functions, visions or goals, approaches and practices that provide quality education for a sustainable future.

(2) **Theme 2: Access and equity.** Access and equity in higher education refer to the ways in which students are provided with equal and equitable opportunities to participate in and benefit fully from HEI provisions and policies (Great Schools Partnership, 2014). The chapters in this book discuss access and equity as two key elements that enable higher education to drive socioeconomic changes in the region and maintain the balance between quantity and quality of educational outcomes.

(3) **Theme 3: Curriculum development.** Curriculum development is a planned, purposeful, progressive and systematic process of organising pedagogical content to improve the educational system and achieve learning outcomes (Alvior, 2014). Topics on curriculum development in the chapters, in general, explore the potential to integrate into existing curricula study approaches and programmes that enhance students' learning outcomes.

(4) **Theme 4: Learning and teaching innovation.** Teaching and learning approaches refer to the relationship between what the teacher or instructor does in teaching (i.e. the teaching method) and what the student does in learning (i.e. the learning approach) (Gama, 2015). This includes a variety of processes and methods that create the intended interaction between instructors and learners. The example in the chapter under this theme is but one of many innovative approaches that respond to and foster student development in ways that suit current and future needs. The chapter is one such innovative approach for a practical intervention, addressing issues in the higher education sector.

(5) **Theme 5: Post-graduation employment.** Graduate employability, from the policy-making view, is "the development of skills and adaptable workforces in which all those capable of work are encouraged to develop the skills, knowledge, technology and adaptability to enable them to enter and remain in employment throughout their working lives" (HM Treasury, 1997, p.1, as cited in Cheng et al., 2021). In the relevant chapters, discussions on post-graduation employment go beyond the

job prospects of students. They cover the three important aspects of the graduate employment rate, institutional career support and services, and academia-industry linkages.

INTERLINKING OF THE THEMES: AN ECOSYSTEMIC APPROACH FOR THE FUTURE

The themes or components of future higher education identified via the chapters in this book are presented in Figure 12.1. These may be seen as an ecosystem of key factors for future higher education in the ASEAN region. This ecosystemic approach supports the view that higher education in the future needs to be increasingly connected, with the differing stakeholders contributing to both internal and external ecosystems of HEIs at all levels (United Nations Educational, Scientific and Cultural Organisation International Institute for Higher Education in Latin America and the Caribbean, 2021). The following section in this chapter summarises each theme and highlights key recommendations arising from each of the relevant chapters.

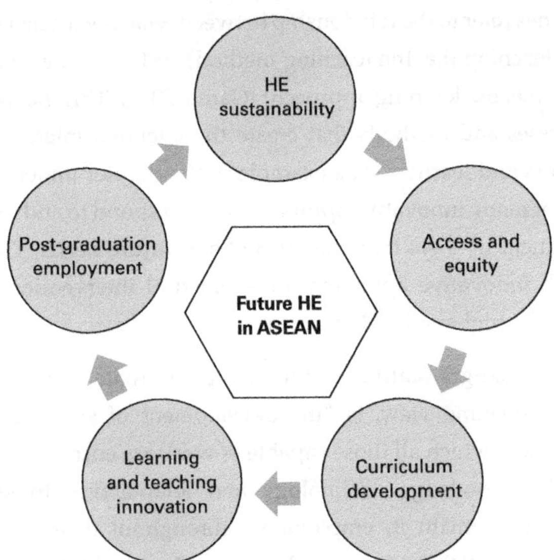

Figure 12.1 Components of future of higher education in ASEAN

Theme 1: Higher education sustainability

The first major point emerging from the chapters is the sustainability of higher education. This theme discusses higher education as a potential catalyst for sustainable development in the Southeast Asian region for the next generation. The chapters by Abdul Razak Ahmad and Morshidi Sirat, Melinda dela Peña Bandalaria and Sally Anne Param present rigorous and sound policy-level discussions about higher education sustainability, covering university leadership, governance and autonomy, internationalisation, student mobility, as well as access and participation at both national and regional levels.

Chapter 2: Malaysia's Higher Education: Getting Out of the Doldrums and Implication for ASEAN *by Abdul Razak Ahmad and Morshidi Sirat*

In the period during the Coronavirus Disease 2019 (COVID-19) pandemic, structural issues were exposed in higher education in Malaysia and other ASEAN countries. A stronger alignment of technology, economy, finance, health, social development, and environment policies is required to support a balance between post-COVID-19 recovery, growth and long-term resilience. Suggestions put forward are as follows:

(1) Develop a new governance model driven by technology, away from a closed, bureaucratic and archaic government model that will support system interdependence, inclusiveness, the power of the network, and community diversity. Such a governance model is more modern, seamless, transparent, accountable and inclusive.

(2) Develop new synergies of higher education, industrial, commercial and multinational players for long-term growth following the damaging effects of the pandemic. Alliances and collaborations across higher education and governmental and non-governmental enterprises will support a flexible mode of learning, research and governing, and thus innovation.

(3) Move internationalisation and immigration from the current major focus on international students and create off-shore campuses through collaborations and synergies. Programmes offered by Malaysian universities in international settings should also be intensified, thus transforming Malaysia from being merely a hub for higher education and international students to a knowledge and talent powerhouse.

(4) Increase digitalisation of higher education to support access for students from lower socioeconomic backgrounds. Aligned with internationalisation, such an approach will enable institutions to access global databases and research connections.

(5) Instigate cost leadership in higher education to enable private and public institutions in Malaysia to remain viable. Use online and hybrid learning to manage course fees to continue attracting international enrolment.

Chapter 3: Bridging the Higher Education Divide in Southeast Asia Through Open, Flexible and Distance eLearning (OFDeL): Now and Beyond 2030 *by Melinda dela Peña Bandalaria*

On the premise that admission to a HEI does not in itself promote equality of opportunity, students from lower socioeconomic backgrounds may need additional services to counter barriers to their study success and continuation. Barriers could include economic and financial hardship, personal, local, regional or national crises, geographic distance from campus, and physical access to campus facilities.

In the ASEAN region, in the context of the low participation in higher education studies of students from lower socioeconomic backgrounds, HEIs may consider the following, as put forward by Melinda dela Peña Bandalaria:

(1) Review and analyse data on student academic progression and graduation rate. This will identify individual or student cohorts facing barriers and necessitate the relevant services. Such services can include assistive technologies, accommodation and Internet connectivity.

(2) Instigate open, flexible and e-learning more comprehensively to reduce costs for students from lower socioeconomic backgrounds. This enables the provision of information and communication technology (ICT) to support off-campus learners, allows flexibility for students to both work and study, works against discrimination, and allows for student personal mobility.

Chapter 4: To Get Cracking: Discussing the Sustainability of Malaysia's Role as a Provider of Global Higher Education Through a Case Study of International Students *by Sally Anne Param*

Malaysia is a top destination for international students who travel to study in a country other than their home country. To maintain sustainability in this feature and retain its attractiveness as a country of study destination, Malaysia should consider the satisfaction of international students with their study experience and address arising issues. Sally Anne Param puts forward the need to do the following:

(1) Consider students' social and cultural satisfaction with their studies in Malaysia. Attention to this aspect of study experience will enhance students' overall experience.

(2) Appreciate and address the issue of international students feeling othered or excluded while studying at their institutions. Students learn from each other and, if excluded from the mainstream student group, they will be deprived of the opportunity to gain knowledge and experiences from one another, and the experience of international students in the host study environment will not be as rounded as it could be.

(3) Reshape the experience for international students to support their cross-cultural acceptance while studying. Some strategies include teachers using examples of subject issues from international students' home countries.

(4) Provide opportunities for the children of expatriates in Malaysia to study while in the country with their parents.

Theme 2: Access and equity

Another point that emerged from the book chapters concerns access and equity. Access and equity in higher education cover both inclusivity and diversity in the multifaceted aspects of educational opportunities. Two chapters in the book provide different perspectives on the theme. Stephen J Hall specifically discusses language policies and linguistic inclusivity, while Muhammad Muftahu shares a broader perspective on equity and diversity in the massified Malaysian higher education system.

Chapter 5: English Language Legacies, Policy and Practice in Malaysian Educational Systems: Reverberations in Higher Education *by Stephen J Hall*

Language development and use in Malaysian schools have a strong impact on equity and thus students' access to higher education. They also impact students' identities, which influence their educational motivation. With schools in Malaysia preparing students for participation in higher education, universities are then tasked to build future-ready university graduates. Students in Malaysia bring to their school classrooms a complex mix of languages, including Malay dialects and uncertainties about the use of English. The author points out that further complexity is produced by centralised planning in language policy and implementation, and by gaps between rural and urban planning. Suggestions by Stephen J Hall are as follows:

(1) Develop Malaysian school teachers in ways that support continuity for bilingual and multilingual mentoring and sustained, localised expertise.

(2) Support the importance of local identification with language choice. This will mean language policy and its development in Malaysia is locally driven, rather than a centrally imposed ruling.

(3) Foster inclusive developments in language policy and implementation in Malaysia by drawing on the heritage and indigenous languages of young Malaysians in schools.

Chapter 6: Attaining Equity and Diversity in the Massified System of Higher Education: A Qualitative Study of the Malaysian Context *by Muhammad Muftahu*

This chapter considers the growth in the number of students participating in higher education in Malaysia in recent times, in terms of its impact on equity and access and the diversity of attending students. While the number of students in higher education has increased, the author notes that obstacles to the participation of students from disadvantaged backgrounds remain. To support greater diversity and thus equity in higher education, some suggestions by Muhammad Muftahu include the following:

(1) Focus ministerial (that is, governmental) strategies and initiatives at institutional levels on increasing student diversity.

(2) Increase the diversity in backgrounds and geographical origins of international students in higher education in Malaysia.

(3) Review structural barriers to underprivileged higher education students by actions such as reducing the quota system, reviewing entry requirements, and increasing teaching staff members for research students.

(4) Provide functional mechanisms to address the quality of higher education in terms of the inclusion of learners from diverse backgrounds, which impacts the development of students' global mindedness.

(5) Review higher education admission of students based on prior educational achievements, consider their previous academic and career experiences, and offer fee discounts for students from disadvantaged backgrounds.

(6) Support students from disadvantaged backgrounds during their studies to foster study success.

Theme 3: Curriculum development

The third emerging theme from the preceding chapters relates to curriculum development in higher education. Under this theme, the chapters by Rafael Ibe Santos and Benedict Valentine Arulanandam et al. present two distinctive ways in which higher education curricula can be integrated (with either humanised or advanced pedagogical approaches) and how these integrations contribute to creating a more supportive and industry-relevant learning experience for higher education students.

Chapter 7: Resilient Southeast Asian Education Through Humane and Compassionate Pedagogical Framework: An Autoethnography in Online Teaching and Learning Amid COVID-19 Health Crisis *by Rafael Ibe Santos*

With changes to teaching and learning in higher education and the implementation of online learning during the pandemic, students and their families often had to study under new and possibly difficult circumstances.

In such situations, HEIs may not have perceived the human side of curricula and the challenges students face. To build a more humanistic approach that is mindful of learners' circumstances and is flexible and adaptive without compromising academic standards, Rafael Ibe Santos makes the following suggestions:

(1) Consider as crucial support strategies for students as they learn.

(2) Balance the independence integral to online learning with compassion, as seen in flexible deadlines and manageable requirements. For instance, if students have more than one assignment or test in the same week, consider rescheduling for students to manage the load. If students are required to work in groups but social distancing and lockdowns make the option difficult, look for ways to enable students to discuss under such circumstances.

(3) Provide forms of scaffolding in teaching such as encouragement and check on students' welfare and understanding of subject concepts and principles. These may be implemented through formal means such as brief surveys and informal means such as a "hands up" in class for clarification or brief discussions, in pairs, of students' understanding and sharing their responses with the class. Such approaches engage students and give the teacher some insight into students' academic progress, which can be addressed in future classes.

(4) Balance ICT training in teachers' professional development with training in compassion for students. Students' well-being while studying impacts their academic success, and it is in the interests of all that teachers are alert to students' situations. In this process of their professional development, teachers need to be aware of their responsibilities to students and the services provided at the university to support students.

Chapter 8: Rethinking Malaysian Universities' Business Models: Building Sustainable Business School Graduates *by Benedict Valentine Arulanandam, Glenda Crosling, Siti Norbaya Azizan and Graeme Atherton*

In the context where the business world increasingly uses information technology (IT) and meta-dimensional analysis in business operations, business schools in higher education need to ensure that their curricula include such knowledge and skills development for students. This will support students' post-graduation employment and the progress of businesses and the nation. To transform business schools into institutions that integrate IT and meta-dimensional analytics into the curricula, Benedict Valentine Arulanandam et al. propose the following:

(1) Invest in upgrading IT infrastructure and curriculum content to modernise the curricula. Such an investment includes resilient IT hardware and software that can avoid disruptions to students during their studies.

(2) Update and familiarise teachers and other support staff members with online materials to ensure smooth operations.

(3) Offer IT assistance for online learning. In case of difficulties, staff members and students need to be made aware of the available support and the ways to contact or access it when required. Notification of this needs to be clear across several media.

(4) Initiate professional development and training for teachers in instructional design for a more robust IT curriculum content. Teachers need to be informed about the inclusion of IT in the curricula and to view the integration as integral to developing learning outcomes rather than as mere "add-ons" or supplementary materials.

(5) Review curricula frequently to update content with IT components and ensure an adequate number of subjects related to IT are included across the years of study. Teachers must ensure that this aspect of the curricula is subject to periodic reviews, establish clear guidelines of expectations for the reviews, and follow recommendations for improvements with action plans that are evaluated at relevant times by a relevant committee.

Theme 4: Learning and teaching innovation

The ever-growing intersection between digital technologies and higher education has led to various innovations and new virtual teaching and learning environments. Even so, both opportunities and challenges have to be considered in identifying technological potentials to realise the envisaged transformation of higher education in the ASEAN region. Through the fourth theme, Nicolas Hamelin and Wendy Ong present a unique perspective with a different methodological approach and offer practical advice on the potential of emerging digital technologies in supporting the educational needs of higher education students and wider society.

Chapter 9: **Smart Education for Smart Cities: Cloud-Based EEG Solution for Mental Health and Cognitive Skills Assessment for Higher Education in the ASEAN Region *by Nicolas Hamelin and Wendy Ong***

Mental health problems, such as depression, anxiety and suicidal thoughts, are some of the alarming and prevalent health issues among higher education students today. As future workforces of ASEAN's smart cities, higher education students in the region are challenged with the need to obtain the necessary level of academic success, while maintaining their resilience in becoming highly skilled graduates for future careers. In this chapter, the authors bring forward the importance of assessing the skills and mental health status among higher education students through an innovative yet affordable solution. A cloud-based portable electroencephalogram or EEG system for early detection of mental health issues among higher education students was developed and proposed as a novel and practical solution to gauge the cognitive and emotional skills needed by students. Based on their experimental study, Nicolas Hamelin and Wendy Ong highlight the following potentials of the system:

(1) Assess the mental health of higher education students who are at great risk of developing critical psychological issues. The system also highlights the importance of establishing long-term monitoring and mental health support for students.

(2) Evaluate students' emotional intelligence and critical and creative thinking abilities by integrating the system into the curriculum components of academic programmes.

(3) Ascertain the personality and cognitive traits among society at all levels. For instance, the system can support human resource departments in their staff employment and decision-making processes.

Theme 5: Post-graduation employment

The final theme of the book concentrates on a significant topic in higher education, which is post-graduation employment. Globally, the mismatch and gap between graduate employability and workplace skills are hot issues often associated with graduate unemployment. Through this theme, the current picture of post-graduation employment in two Southeast Asian countries is presented by Razwana Begum Abdul Rahim's review of Singapore's work-study programmes (WSPs) and Thiruchelvi K Murugiah's discussion on factors of and mechanisms in addressing Malaysia's business graduate unemployment.

Chapter 10: Future-Ready Graduates: Work-Study Programme in Singapore *by Razwana Begum Abdul Rahim*

Today's job market is becoming more competitive than ever. Higher education students need to become more job-ready and well-equipped with adaptable and sustainable skills as technology advances and industries evolve. This chapter discusses the development and successful promotion of WSPs in Singapore, which have provided several useful and practical implications from which other countries can learn. Overall, the author identifies three factors leading to the country's successful WSPs: (1) effective policies and support from the government, (2) active support from employers and industrial partners, and (3) demand and support from both parents and students. Based on the reviews, Razwana Begum Abdul Rahim suggests several practices that can improve the existing work-study framework to effectively develop future-ready higher education students:

(1) Strengthen partnerships between HEIs and industrial partners. Through cooperative academia-industry collaborations, various employment issues can be addressed, such as the shortage of skilled workers and graduates' inability to apply theory into practice. At the same time, necessary support from employers is important in providing work attachments, co-creating the syllabus and course content, and assessing students' learning outcomes.

(2) Encourage HEIs to take a leading role in developing academic-related courses relevant to the job market to ensure students can gain a strong grounding in theories and knowledge applicable to their future real work environments.

(3) Consider environmental factors that may lead to disruption in the delivery of WSPs, such as economic recession and pandemic-related restrictions and measures. WSPs need to be designed and implemented in alternative

ways that are adaptive to such challenges, particularly those that assess students' learning outcomes based on their active engagement.

Chapter 11: Improving Employability of Future Business Graduates Through Sustainable Private College-Industry Partnership: A Phenomenological Study *by Thiruchelvi K Murugiah*

Unemployment issues among graduates are of great importance and urgency. In this 21st century, business study programmes involve a vastly different environment than before, where students have to acquire a wide range of knowledge and skills to thrive in the business industry. The phenomenological study reported in Chapter 11 identifies factors that lead to unemployment among Malaysian business graduates, including skill mismatch, transformation required for both business and education sectors, stakeholder gap, and the lack in academic programmes. Thiruchelvi K Murugiah highlights the following recommendations or mechanisms for institutions, policymakers and relevant stakeholders of higher education to undertake towards improving business graduates' employability in Malaysia:

(1) Restructure the business curricula to match the constantly changing skills and knowledge needed in the 21st century.

(2) Facilitate future workforce development by fostering symbiotic and sustainable relationships between educational institutions and relevant industries in the digital ecosystems.

(3) Expand and encourage inclusive participation from other stakeholders, including public and private sector administration, educators, students, parents and the community.

CONCLUSION

Higher education has a pivotal role in facilitating social and economic recovery in the ASEAN region. As radical changes take place in educational delivery globally, we therefore urge the need to develop a higher education ecosystem for the region that enables societies to prosper in the current digitalised post-pandemic era. This book provides a range of valuable theoretical and practical resources for higher education providers, practitioners and researchers who seek to explore both potential opportunities and mechanisms in addressing emerging challenges. We believe that through the five identified themes, this book has highlighted key components that contribute to building a more relevant and resilient higher education ecosystem in the ASEAN region. Such an approach assists higher education to thrive in the dynamic but challenging future.

REFERENCES

Alvior, M. G. (2014, December 13). The meaning and importance of curriculum development. *Simplyeducate.me.* https://simplyeducate.me/2014/12/13/the-meaning-and-importance-of-curriculum-development

Cheng, M., Adekola, O., Albia, J., & Cai, S. (2021). Employability in higher education: A review of key stakeholders' perspectives. *Higher Education Evaluation and Development, 16*(1), 16–31. https://doi.org/10.1108/HEED-03-2021-0025

Corcoran, P. B., & Wals, A. E. J. (Eds.). (2004). *Higher education and the challenge of sustainability: Problematics, promise, and practice.* Kluwer Academic Publishers. https://doi.org/10.1007/0-306-48515-X

Gama, V. N. (2015). *Post-graduate students' conceptions and perceptions of mathematics: A study of social science students at the Pietermaritzburg Campus, University of Kwazulu-Natal* [Master's thesis, University of KwaZulu-Natal]. https://ukzn-dspace.ukzn.ac.za/bitstream/handle/10413/14024/Gama_Vuyo_Nomzamo_2015.pdf?sequence=1&isAllowed=y.

Great Schools Partnership. (2014). *Access.* The Glossary of Educational Reform. https://www.edglossary.org/access

HM Treasury. (1997). *Gordon Brown unveils UK employment action plan.* London.

United Nations Educational, Scientific and Cultural Organisation International Institute for Higher Education in Latin America and the Caribbean. (2021). *Thinking higher and beyond perspectives on the futures of higher education to 2050.* United Nations Educational, Scientific and Cultural Organisation. https://unesdoc.unesco.org/ark:/48223/pf0000377530

INDEX

Printed and bound by CPI Group (UK) Ltd, Croydon, CR0 4YY

05/05/2026

14871579-0002